sheikh mohammad abdullah

TRAGIC HERO OF KASHMIR

OTHER LOTUS TITLES:

Adi B. Hakim, Rustom B. Bhumgara & Jal P. Bapasola	*With Cyclists Around the World*
Anil Dharker	*Icons: Men & Women Who Shaped Today's India*
Aitzaz Ahsan	*The Indus Saga: The Making of Pakistan*
Alam Srinivas	*Storms in the Sea Wind: Ambani vs Ambani*
Amir Mir	*The True Face of Jehadis: Inside Pakistan's Terror Networks*
Ashok Mitra	*The Starkness of It*
Bhawana Somayya	*Hema Malini: The Authorised Biography*
H.L.O. Garrett	*The Trial of Bahadur Shah Zafar*
Kuldip Nayar & Asif Noorani	*Tales of Two Cities*
M.J. Akbar	*India: The Siege Within*
M.J. Akbar	*Kashmir: Behind the Vale*
M.J. Akbar	*The Shade of Swords*
M.J. Akbar	*Byline*
M.J. Akbar	*Blood Brothers: A Family Saga*
Maj. Gen. Ian Cardozo	*Param Vir: Our Heroes in Battle*
Maj. Gen. Ian Cardozo	*The Sinking of INS Khukri: What Happened in 1971*
Meghnad Desai and Aitzaz Ahsan	*Divided by Democracy*
Mushirul Hasan	*India Partitioned. 2 Vols*
Mushirul Hasan	*John Company to the Republic*
Mushirul Hasan	*Knowledge, Power and Politics*
Nayantara Sahgal (ed.)	*Before Freedom: Nehru's Letters to His Sister*
Psyche Abraham	*From Kippers to Karimeen: A Life*
Sharmishta Gooptu and Boria Majumdar (eds)	*Revisiting 1857: Myth, Memory, History*
Shashi Joshi	*The Last Durbar*
Shrabani Basu	*Spy Princess: The Life of Noor Inayat Khan*
Shyam Bhatia	*Benazir Bhutto: A Political Biography*
Thomas Weber	*Gandhi, Gandhism and the Gandhians*
V. Srinivasan	*New Age Management: Philosophy from Ancient Indian Wisdom*
Vir Sanghvi	*Men of Steel: Indian Business Leaders in Candid Conversation*

FORTHCOMING TITLES:

Indian Express	*The Prize Stories*
A. Salam Qureishi	*An Indian in Silicon Valley*

sheikh mohammad abdullah

TRAGIC HERO OF KASHMIR

AJIT BHATTACHARJEA

LOTUS COLLECTION
ROLI BOOKS

Lotus Collection

First published in India, 2008
The Lotus Collection
An imprint of
Roli Books Pvt Ltd
M-75, G.K. II Market, New Delhi 110 048
Phones: ++91 (011) 2921 2271, 2921 2782
2921 0886, Fax: ++91 (011) 2921 7185
E-mail: roli@vsnl.com
Website: rolibooks.com
Also at
Varanasi, Bangalore, Kolkata, Chennai, Jaipur, & Mumbai

Cover design: Supriya Saran
Layout design: Narendra Shahi

ISBN: 978-81-7436-671-9

Typeset in Centur MT by Roli Books Pvt Ltd and
printed at Devtech Printer & Publisher, Faridabad

CONTENTS

ACKNOWLEDGEMENTS

It is scarcely possible to acknowledge my debt to all the people who have inspired the writing of this book. The most significant contributor was the subject himself, Sheikh Mohammad Abdullah. I was given opportunities to meet him early in his career as well as in the sad twilight days of his life. His determination to continue the struggle for secularism and *azaadi* in the most adverse circumstances won my admiration.

My visits to Kashmir provided glimpses of its uniquely secular history and environment. The owner of a houseboat moored on Srinagar's Jhelum bund epitomized the philosophic, tolerant Kashmiri culture, laced with cups of black tea. So did the professors of Kashmir University I met. Heir to a long tradition of learning, they are frustrated with the current plight of the state. The list of those who discussed Sheikh Abdullah and his times with me would be endless.

Some deserve special mention. Professor Mushirul Hasan, Vice-Chancellor of Delhi's Jamia Millia Islamia, has long been a friend and mentor in matters of history. In discussions on this project, his guidance and advice has been of great value. The contribution of Pran Nath Jalali was unequalled. As an alert journalist and party worker close to the Sheikh, his recollections about key personalities and their motivations provided information never published before. Fortunately, he kept a diary and retained relevant documents. From them I gleaned the name of the unknown Kashmiri hero, Gulam Mohammad Khan, and his unrecognized contribution to history.

Much of the work on this book was done in the pleasant surroundings of the India International Centre Library in New Delhi. Some of it had already been done in the library of the Institute of Advanced Study in Shimla for an earlier book, *Kashmir: The Wounded Valley*, my project as a fellow there. I must also acknowledge the timely assistance provided by the National Foundation of India. I would like to thank Sheikh Nazir Ahmad, general secretary of Jammu and Kashmir National Conference in finding, sourcing and captioning pictures used in the book. I have benefited from the rich material in the Jawaharlal Nehru Museum and Library. However, I continued to be denied permission to see the crucial correspondence between Nehru and the Sheikh in the archives. As noted elsewhere, while selections from Nehru's letters to Abdullah have been published in his *Selected Works*, the archives remain closed except to favoured scholars. For documentation relating to the history of the relationship of Jammu & Kashmir with India, researchers are obliged to consult the helpful authorities of the India Office Library in London.

The Sheikh's biography grew, and was frequently reconstructed, over the months. Members of my family cushioned moments of crisis. It could not have been completed without their support. My thanks to Mira, Suman, Namita, Aditya, and Ami, and our dog Calypso.

PREFACE

My sole hope and prayer is that Kashmir become a beacon of light in this benighted subcontinent.

– Mahatma Gandhi

Unforgettable recollections of Srinagar as an island of amity in a sea of religious bloodshed in the Indian subcontinent inspire the writing of this book. The contrast between the cordial atmosphere of Srinagar and the foetid communal fear still stalking Delhi in October 1947, from where I had flown, exceeded even the first enchanting impression of the beauty of the Valley. It provided a ray of hope that secularism could survive in India.

In the capital of India, as in much of the north of India, Muslims were under attack in reprisal for the bloody eviction of Hindus and Sikhs from the newly-born Islamic state of Pakistan. Yet in the capital of Kashmir there was no sign of religious tension: its Muslim inhabitants were helping newly-arrived elements of the Indian Army, Hindu and Sikh, to defend the city against advancing Pathan *lashkars*. The invaders came from the tribal area between Pakistan and Afghanistan, and had been armed by Pakistan. Though portrayed as fellow-Muslims intending to free Kashmiris from the oppressive rule of a Hindu maharaja, they plundered all who crossed their path ...[1]

The man whose charismatic leadership strengthened this unique delinking of nationalism from religious intolerance—an inflammable mixture still haunting India and the world—was Sheikh Abdullah. His commitment to secularism, socialism, and campaign for *azaadi* (freedom from oppression) motivated his people to rebuff the appeal of religious politics sweeping the subcontinent. The foundations of the transformation were laid by changing the name of the party he led in the struggle for popular rule against the maharaja from Muslim Conference to Kashmir National Conference, open to all communities. The historic date was 11 June 1939. The stirring manifesto of the new party was no less revolutionary. Echoing the socialist thinking of the 1930s, it promised, among other reforms, land to the tiller without compensation, a commitment that laid the foundations of the party's popularity among the vast majority of Kashmiris. Abdullah came to be known as Sher-e-Kashmir, Lion of Kashmir.

SECULARISM STRENGTHENED

Secularism was further strengthened and history made on 26 October 1947 when, with Abdullah's support, the predominantly Muslim princely state of Jammu & Kashmir joined the Indian Union rather than the adjoining Islamic state of Pakistan. In the rest of India, the accession helped Mahatma Gandhi and Prime Minister Jawaharlal Nehru to douse Hindu communal reactions to Partition. Gandhi was moved to tell a prayer meeting on 29 December 1947, two months after the state joined the Indian Union:

> It must be evident to the outsider, as it is to me, that Kashmir must be lost to the invaders, otherwise called the raiders, if Sheikh Abdullah Saheb's effort to hold together the Muslims and the minority [in the valley] fails ... My sole hope and prayer is that Kashmir become a beacon of light in this benighted subcontinent.[2]

Earlier, reacting to continuing fratricidal killings in Delhi and elsewhere, Gandhi had besought his maker on his birthday, 2 October, to take him away; he could not witness them any longer.[3] Nehru, for his part, announced that he would resign if people did not have faith in his secular leadership, but so long as he was at the helm of affairs, India would not become a Hindu state:

> I am at liberty to give up my responsibility if the people of India cease to have faith in the lead that I give. If they do not subscribe to my ideals and are not prepared to cooperate with me then I will have no choice but to resign and continue the fight for the establishment of a State where every citizen enjoys equal rights irrespective of his religion.[4]

On 2 November, a week after the first contingent of Indian troops landed in Srinagar, a revitalized prime minister broadcast to the nation:

> It would be well if this lesson was understood by the whole of India which has been poisoned by communal strife. Under the inspiration of a great leader, Sheikh Abdullah, the people of the valley, Muslim and Hindu and Sikh, were together in the defence of their common country against the invader. Our troops could have done little without this popular support and cooperation.[5]

Secularism had become an article of faith for Sheikh Mohammad Abdullah's party, the Jammu and Kashmir National Conference. They formed a volunteer militia to resist the tribal attack and provide transport and guides to the Indian soldiers. It was cruelly tested when Indian troops landed in Srinagar. Sikh soldiers had been flown there directly, still tense from patrolling shoot-at-sight, riot-crazed areas near Delhi. Soon after arrival, while guarding the airfield, they mistakenly fired at a group of National Conference militia who approached to brief them. Seven died. Those gathered to welcome the Indian troops were shocked and enraged. Less than a week had elapsed since Maharaja Hari Singh has signed the Instrument of Accession to India and Indian troops had landed in Srinagar claiming popular support. Now the tragic incident could turn popular opinion against India.

CRUCIAL SACRIFICE

Pran Nath Jalali, then a young communist political commander in the

National Conference militia, was there and maintained notes in his diary. The soldiers had buried the victims near the airport road. They had been disinterred by a pro-Pakistan group linked to the Indian Muslim League who saw an opportunity to turn popular opinion against India. The bodies were borne in procession towards the city. They were on the verge of entering the crowded area when the father of one of the victims, Gulam Mohammad Khan, intervened. Holding up the body of his son, Mohammad Ramzan Khan, he proclaimed: 'This is my sacrifice for Hindu–Muslim unity.' One of the victims happened to be a Hindu. The agitated crowd melted away. The names of the man whose magnificent gesture averted possible disaster and his son were recorded by Jalali, together with those of the victims of the tragedy.[6] After learning of this crucial but unrecorded incident, I paid my respects at the modest graves of Gulam Mohammad Khan and Mohammad Ramzan Khan in a neglected family graveyard in the heart of Srinagar.

The version of Lt Gen. L.P. (Bogey) Sen, who was commanding the troops in Srinagar at the time, confirms the serious nature of the incident but differs on the number of victims:

> On the night of November 5, an unfortunate incident occurred involving a party of National Conference volunteers. Returning to Srinagar from a patrol in the Badgam area, it approached the positions held by I Sikh after darkness had set in. It was challenged, but instead of answering the challenge they started to run. The I Sikh. sentry opened fire at the fleeing personnel, firing more at the sound than any specific target. The next morning the bodies of two men [Sen seems to have been misinformed] were found fifty yards from the I Sikh outpost. The unit could not be held to blame for the incident, as it was impossible to see the enemy in the dark and they well might have been the enemy. Where the unit did err was that the bodies having been recovered were buried in slit trenches in the unit's position, and Brigade Headquarters was not informed.
>
> The news that two of his volunteers had been killed reached Sheikh Abdullah first thing the next morning, and he asked me to meet him. I had fortunately been informed by

> Major Kak of the reason for the meeting. I arrived at Sheikh Abdullah's house to be greeted by an infuriated individual. I offered him my deepest sympathies that such an unfortunate incident should have cost two lives, but impressed on him that it was the result of a genuine mistake … He was very upset and it took time for him to accept that explanation, whereupon he climbed down. Dissident elements, however, decided to make capital out of the incident. I had no option but to move I Sikh out of its position. No sooner had I Sikh evacuated its position ... then certain locals dug up the two bodies and carried them in procession through the main roads of the city …[7]

SEEDS OF DOWNFALL

Sheikh Abdullah rose to become prime minister of the state, but also became the target of communal forces let loose by the decision to partition British India. Against this background, the bold attempt to reinforce secularism through Kashmir's example required exceptional unity of direction and purpose in New Delhi. Instead, the rise of Abdullah evoked contrary reactions. While India's first prime minister, Jawaharlal Nehru, backed him for his secular and socialist commitment, his powerful home minister, Vallabhbhai Patel, distrusted his demand for autonomy and represented forces that doubted the loyalty of Muslims to India after Partition. Some Congress leaders sided with Patel, together with Hindu communal leaders.[8] Differences on Kashmir with Nehru led Patel to offer to resign but were papered over.[9] Within the state, the last maharani, Tara Devi, took revenge for the eviction of the last maharaja of Jammu & Kashmir, Hari Singh, by fomenting Hindu reaction.

In May 1951, Abdullah delivered a historic address to the inaugural session of the Kashmir Constituent Assembly, describing the choices before the state. While regarding the option of independence as attractive, he described it as impractical and stressed the advantages of an autonomous link with India, notwithstanding the status of Muslims as a minority in the country. He rejected joining Pakistan outright. (Appendix Two) The inspirational address was prefaced by recalling the lasting impress of Kashmir's traditions of tolerance, later known as *kashmiryat.*

> After centuries, we have reached the harbour of our freedom ... Once again in the history of this State, our people have reached a peak of achievement through what I might call the classical Kashmiri genius for synthesis, born of toleration and mutual respect. Throughout the long tale of our history, the highest pinnacles of our achievement have been scaled when religious bigotry and intolerance ceased to cramp us and we have breathed the wider air of brotherhood and mutual understanding.

However, *kashmiryat* also meant resisting too close an integration with India. It was Nehru's recognition of Kashmir's desire for self-determination that had persuaded Abdullah to link its fate with India's. This was reiterated in one of Nehru's great liberal pronouncements in the Indian parliament on 7 August 1952. Speaking on the relationship between Kashmir and India in the context of proposals for plebiscite, he said:

> So while the accession was complete in law and in fact, the other fact that has nothing to do with the law remains, our pledge to the people of Kashmir—if you like to the people of the world—that this matter could be affirmed or cancelled by the people of Kashmir according to their wishes. We do not wish to win people against their will with the help of armed force; and if the people of Kashmir wish to part company with us, they may go their way and we shall go ours. We want no forced marriages, no forced unions.

Yet when Abdullah demanded the special autonomous status promised when the state acceded (Appendix One), the campaign to label him anti-national gathered strength. He had countered Muslim communalism in the Valley but was falling victim to Hindu revivalism in India. Doubts about him were voiced in the Indian parliament. Patel assigned the director of the Intelligence Bureau, B.N. Mullick, to spy on him.[10]

UN Security Council debates on Kashmir and preparations for a plebiscite in the state, revived communal tensions.

A letter from Abdullah to Nehru dated 10 July 1950, expressed the predicament in which he was placed:

> It is clear that there are powerful influences at work in India who do not see eye to eye with you regarding your ideal of making the Union a truly secular state and your Kashmir policy. Their constant endeavour is to weaken you and in order to achieve this purpose they think it necessary to bring down all those who are loyal and attached to you . . . While I can willingly go down and sacrifice myself for you, I am afraid as the guardian of 40 lacs of Kashmiris, I cannot barter away their cherished rights and privileges. I have several times stated that we acceded to India because we saw there two bright stars of hope and aspiration, namely Gandhiji and yourself, and despite our having so many affinities with Pakistan we did not join it because we thought our programme will not fit their policy. If, however, we are driven to the conclusion that we cannot build our State on our own lines, suited to our genius, what answer can I give to our people?[11]

STRIPPED OF OFFICE

Frustrated and uncertain, Abdullah spoke of self-determination and expressed concern about the advance of Hindu communalism in India. The campaign against him heightened when it became known that he had met American diplomats. It reached crescendo when Syama Prasad Mookerjee, president of the Jana Sangh, a party newly formed to foster Hindutva sentiment, died of heart failure on 23 June 1953, during a visit to Srinagar. Rumours were spread that Abdullah had become communal and was responsible. Six weeks later, framed by Mullick, in August 1953 he was stripped of the prime minister's office and detained on unproven charges of complicity with Pakistan.

Ironically, it was their concern for secularism that separated Nehru and Abdullah, after drawing them together against Pakistan's two-nation theory. Fear of forces pressing for full forcible integration with India impelled Abdullah to push for greater independence. He perceived them as driven by Hindutva parties that threatened the secular base he had shored up to divert the Muslims of the Valley from joining Pakistan. However, when his reaction was interpreted as a move to form another Pakistan, Nehru distanced himself from him, fearing that it would unleash a backlash against Muslims in the rest of India. Muslim leaders were already worried. Among those who turned against Abdullah was Congress president Abul Kalam Azad. Another leading Congress Muslim cabinet minister, Rafi Ahmed Kidwai, who had personal differences with Abdullah, supervised the coup.

International trends in the early 1950s had made Nehru ultra-sensitive to developments posing a threat to his vision of a non-aligned India capable of countering Cold War intrigues, in which Kashmir was a target. The revival of Abdullah's vision of independence, or a Sikkim or Bhutan type of limited association with India,[12] amplified the threat. Communists, who had helped draft the party's manifesto, abruptly turned against him under Moscow's orders. His meetings with US diplomats made him suspect. They outdid Hindutva spokesmen in portraying him as anti-national, and Nehru reluctantly decided to divest him of office in August 1953. His successor, Bakshi Ghulam Mohammad, ensured his prolonged detention with the aid of conspiracy charges trumped up by the Home Ministry's Intelligence Bureau.

Nehru realized that he did not have long to live when he insisted on Abdullah's release, and made the gesture of inviting him to stay at the prime minister's house. Abdullah recalled: 'Panditji expressed his deep anguish and sorrow at the past incidents. I also became very emotional and told him that I was very glad to have convinced him that I was not disloyal to him personally or to India.'[13] Nehru reiterated confidence in his secular credentials by sending him on a mission to Pakistan. Abdullah cut short his mission on 24 May 1964 to fly back to Delhi to weep at his friend's funeral pyre.

A life replete with struggle for *azaadi* ended in a compromise. In 1974, while again in detention, a tired, ageing Sheikh made a deal with

Prime Minister Indira Gandhi. Anxious to salvage glimpses of his vision for his Valley, he accepted the finality of accession and regained the limited powers of chief minister of Jammu & Kashmir (he had been prime minister earlier) in the hope of regaining some elements of the autonomy whittled away during his long years of detention. This too was however denied. He was criticized in the Valley, and some young men accepted offers of training in arms in Pakistan-held Kashmir. Yet his commitment to secularism remained undiminished. Among his last acts were to order closure of the network of fundamentalist schools run in Kashmir by the Jamaat-i-Islami funded by Arab money and ban a convention planned by its youth organization, Jamaat-i-Tulba, to be held in Srinagar in 1981.

The Lion of Kashmir died in 1982. The crowds that lined the entire route to the lakeside meadow adjoining Hazratbal Mosque where he was interred were so dense that Indira Gandhi was obliged to abandon her car and be ferried by boat to the site. His compromise however cost him dear. Today, the house he and his begum built in Saura, the village where he was born, remains unreconstructed after it was burnt by militants.

An era had ended; an era in which men with the vision of Jawaharlal Nehru and Sheikh Abdullah made history by trying to understand each other and to reconcile ethnic differences with national concerns without resorting to violence. Abdullah recalled his vital contribution with pride in his memoirs:

> One can say without fear of contradiction that the two-nation theory suffered its first severe defeat in Kashmir. Kashmir played a vital part in keeping the torch of secularism lit in India.[14]

---

1 See Major-General Akbar Khan, *Raiders in Kashmir: Story of the Kashmir War (1847–48)*, Karachi, 1970.

2 D.G. Tendulkar, *Mahatma*, vol. 8, Publications Division, Government of India, p. 222.

3 Ibid., p. 117.

4 *Selected Works of Jawaharlal Nehru,* vol. iv, pp. 107–8.

5 Jawaharlal Nehru, *Independence and After,* Publications Division, Government of India, 1949, pp. 57–8.

6 Notes maintained by Pran Nath Jalali.

7 L.P. Sen, *Slender was the Thread: Kashmir Confrontation 1947–48,* Orient Longman, New Delhi, 1969.

8 Ibid., pp. 109–14.

For the line-up in the Congress leadership ranged against Nehru, see S. Gopal, *Jawaharlal Nehru: A Biography,* vol. ii, Oxford University Press, 1979, pp. 15–16.

9 For a detailed account of the differences, including their letters to Gandhi, see *Sardar Patel's Correspondence,* vol. vi, ed. Durga Das, Navajivan Publishing House, Ahmedabad, 1971, pp. 16–31.

10 See B.N. Mullick, *My Years with Nehru: Kashmir,* Allied Publishers, New Delhi, 1971. Cited by S. Gopal, op. cit., p. 119.

11 See Sandeep Bamzai, *Bonfire of Kashmiryat: Deconstructing the Accession,* Rupa, New Delhi, 2006, pp 169–71.

12 Sheikh Mohammad Abdullah, *Flames of the Chinar,* Viking, 1993. The quotation is taken from the English translation of Abdullah's biography in Urdu by Khushwant Singh.

13 *Flames,* p. 246.

INTRODUCTION
ISLAND OF AMITY

September–October 1947 were among the worst months Delhi has known during its long turbulent history as India's capital. The separation of areas with a Muslim majority to form Pakistan out of what had been British India until Independence on 15 August 1947, provoked a mass exchange of populations in the divided province of Punjab in the northern half of the subcontinent. Hindus and Sikhs were driven out of the Islamic state of Pakistan; Muslims from the adjoining northern half of the fledgling Indian Union. Barbaric acts of killing and rape were reported from both sides of the new border.

Adjoining Punjab, Delhi could not be isolated from the thirst for revenge amongst Hindu and Sikhs refugees from Pakistan. Most of its Muslim residents were forced out of their homes to take refuge in medieval monuments protected by the army. Those unable to escape were hunted down. Notwithstanding their commitment to secularism, Mahatma Gandhi and Prime Minister Jawaharlal Nehru seemed unable to stem the tide of violence. Some of their colleagues, too, were infected by the communal virus.

The only glimmer of hope came from Kashmir, where the people, though over ninety per cent Muslims, continued to resist the two-nation theory—that Hindus and Muslims could not coexist—which was the raison d'être for the foundation of Pakistan. No communal riots marred the Valley. Kashmiris had been inspired by the politico–secular philosophy of Sheikh Mohammad Abdullah. He emerged as their leader in the early 1930s, when the princely state of Jammu & Kashmir was still under British protection. When the British withdrew, the state was free to join India or Pakistan or become independent.

On 22 October 1947, Pakistan inducted some 5000 armed Pathan tribals into the Valley to force a decision. They had reached the outskirts of Srinagar when Maharaja Hari Singh reluctantly acceded to India on 26 October to secure armed help. Reiterating his commitment to secularism, Sheikh Abdullah endorsed the accession. Workers of his National Conference party provided local security and the transport required by the first elements of the Indian Army flown in to repel the raiders.

Four days later I was offered an opportunity to fly to Srinagar. Civil aircraft had been requisitioned to fly troops and supplies to the beleaguered capital of Kashmir. Captain J.C. Kathpalia, a pilot and family friend, offered to take me, then a fledgling reporter with the *Hindustan Times,* along. The seats of his Dakota had been taken out and replaced by fuel tanks; I squeezed into the space between. After passing low over the Banihal Pass, we seemed to enter a different world. The view unfolding before us—green rice fields watered by gushing streams, rows of russet chinars and tall poplar trees, the blue expanse of the Dal Lake, the winding Jhelum river coursing through a valley encircled by high snow-covered mountain ranges—contrasted with the plain, dun-hued landscape over which we had been flying.

On landing at Srinagar's dirt airstrip we found the contrast with Delhi no less striking. The beards and baggy attire of the men unloading the Dakota aircraft lined up beside the airstrip identified them as Muslim, as were the drivers of the trucks and buses waiting to transport men and weapons to counter the tribal raiders. The airborne troops would have been immobilized without their support. By then the tribal raiders had been pushed back from their furthest advance to the outskirts of the airfield. Control of the airfield was crucial; despatching troops by land over narrow roads and the perilous Banihal Pass would have taken too long to save Srinagar and the Valley.

When we got a lift into the town, we saw no police or army checkposts. Nearer Srinagar, however, crossroads and viaducts, and the bridge over the Jhelum were guarded by the lathi-armed militia, lacking uniforms but bearing the red flag inscribed with a plough of the National Conference, the party Abdullah had pledged to secularism a decade earlier.[1] When I identified myself as a reporter with the *Hindustan Times,* we were waved on. The leader of the group on the Jhelum bridge advised me to tell people in Delhi what I was seeing. Shops were open. In Lal Chowk, the heart of the city, turbaned Sikhs and sari-clad women walked freely on the streets. We returned to Delhi reassured. My photographs of National Conference volunteers in Srinagar appeared in the newspaper.

* * *

The saving of Srinagar proved to be a turning point in the history of the subcontinent. Had it fallen, Kashmir could not have been held by India, but more important than the battle for territory was the battle in the minds of men. After the shock of the Partition killings, the prospect of newly-independent India growing into the pluralistic, secular state envisioned by Mahatma Gandhi, Jawaharlal Nehru, and the Congress party during the freedom struggle seemed slender. The forces of Hindu fundamentalism had been strengthened, but when Srinagar demonstrated that a Muslim people could fight for the secular ideal and resist the two-nation theory on which Pakistan was based, Gandhi and Nehru were revitalized. The difference between their pronouncements before and after the defence of Srinagar testified to the crucial nature of the change.

Sheikh Abdullah became the symbol and guardian of secularism. His unique achievement of transforming the Muslim Conference, a party based on appealing to the religious sentiment of the vast majority of Kashmiris, into the National Conference that reached out to all religions in the struggle for *azaadi,* was recalled. He was able partly to lessen the resentment, bred by discrimination against Muslims by the Dogra rulers, against the miniscule Hindu Pandit community. The National Conference organized the defence of Srinagar even before the Indian Army arrived; Maharaja Hari Singh and his administration had fled the capital.

The National Conference had committed itself to secularism a decade earlier. It had also adopted the wide-ranging 'Naya Kashmir' (New Kashmir) programme promising revolutionary political and socio–economic change. Jawaharlal Nehru had similar socialist views and had known Abdullah since 1938. He supported his movement against Dogra rule and was detained in June 1946 trying to enter Kashmir to defend Abdullah who was under arrest. Even after Nehru became prime minister, Hari Singh resisted his entry into his domain. However, the series of events that followed changed the course of history.

Up to 22 October 1947, Hari Singh was hoping to become independent after British rule ended by playing India and Pakistan, both neighbours of the state of Jammu & Kashmir, against each other. That day, Pakistan initiated 'Operation Gulmarg', the truck-borne invasion by Pathan tribals into Kashmir territory at Muzaffarabad.[2] The planners had been encouraged by uprisings in Poonch and other distant districts bordering Pakistan that had suffered heavily from the brutal exactions of the maharaja's forces. Disaffected elements from these areas manning the Kashmir army garrison mutinied and let the *lashkar*s across the bridge over the Jhelum river, the border with Pakistan. They were not expected to take long to reach Srinagar, 135 miles away by motorable road.

The planners of the tribal operation had calculated that Srinagar would fall in a day, integrating Kashmir with Pakistan. They had, however, miscalculated that the Muslim population of the Valley would welcome fellow-Muslims in their struggle against Dogra oppression. Kashmiris had unhappy memories of fifty years of Afghan rule just over a century earlier and had little in common with the Pathans in appearance, ethnicity, culture, even religious rituals. Besides, Abdullah's National Conference had given them a secular political ideology. Their worst fears were realized when the raiders spared none in their lust for women and loot.

The temptation to loot and rape upset the planners' timetable. The march on Srinagar had to wait until the raiders took time to loot Muzaffarabad bazar. This provided breathing space for the chief of the Kashmir state forces, Brigadier Rajinder Singh, to gather a mixed force of some 200 men in Srinagar and rush to Uri, where they blew up the bridge before he was killed and his men were forced to withdraw. That however gained two days. On 24 October, the *lashkar*s reached the power station at Mahura, fifty miles from Srinagar. When the lights went out in his palace in Srinagar, Hari Singh had no alternative other than to appeal to New Delhi for military help.

* * *

The *lashkar*s could still have reached Srinagar within hours had they not been tempted to sack the fair-sized town of Baramulla, thirty-five miles away. Here they killed, raped, and looted many of its 14,000 inhabitants, including English nuns serving the local hospital. Muslims were among their victims. A National Conference worker, Maqbool Sherwani, who had rushed back from Srinagar, was publicly crucified. His statue was later erected in the town.

Baramulla was sacked on 26 October, the day before Indian troops landed in Srinagar. Their first sortie was towards Baramulla, where they found the raiders in greater strength and better equipped than anticipated. Their commander, Lt Col. Ranjit Rai, was killed and the handful of soldiers forced to withdraw. This delaying action provided time for troops to man the defence of the airfield.

In Srinagar, news of Baramulla's fate increased popular support for the National Conference and the need for help from India. Sheikh Abdullah inspired the defence of the city after the maharaja and his entourage had left overnight for his winter palace in Jammu. From there, Hari Singh reluctantly signed the Instrument of Accession to the Union of India. Even so, he did not cede his entire authority. The agreement stipulated that the transfer of authority to the Government of India would extend only to three subjects, defence, foreign affairs, and communications; the precise items to which its jurisdiction would be limited were spelt out in a schedule.

Before flying in troops, the Indian government stated on record that the accession would be confirmed by 'a reference to the people' after peace was restored. The uncertainty created by the assurance would haunt New Delhi. The language of the reply to the maharaja's letter of accession was intended to counter the possible charge that India had used the opportunity to takeover a state with a Muslim majority that should have gone to Pakistan.[3]

As the raiders approached, Abdullah addressed public meetings in Srinagar to urge citizens to unite and resist. In his memoirs, he recalls the training and emphasizes the non-communal character of the people's militia formed hurriedly by the Jammu and Kashmir National Conference. 'Girls also joined with the Hindu, Muslim and Sikh boys,' he stated, 'and they were strictly ordered to guard the non-Muslim [Pandit] households'.[4]

Details of Baramulla's fate that emerged after the tribal raiders were pushed back increased support for the National Conference. The *New York Times* carried a despatch from its correspondent Robert Trumbull on 10 November 1947, describing the terror visited on the inhabitants of the city, irrespective of their religion:

> The city has been stripped of its wealth and young women before the tribesmen fled in terror, at midnight [on] Friday, before the advancing Indian Army. Surviving residents estimate that 3,000 of their fellow townsmen, including four Europeans and a retired British army officer, known only as Colonel Dykes, and his pregnant wife, were slain. When the raiders rushed into the town on October 26th, witnesses said one party of Masud tribesmen immediately scaled the walls of St Joseph Franciscan Hospital compound and stormed the convent hospital and the little church. Four nuns and Colonel Dykes were shot immediately . . .
>
> Murder, rape, arson, loot and the bestial murder of a local National Conference worker, Maqbool Sherwani, who had

> rallied local sentiment against the invaders, provided further evidence that they had not come to liberate their fellow-Muslims. He was crucified before being shot, to be remembered a hero.

* * *

Before Srinagar was saved, Jawaharlal Nehru had sounded increasingly defensive and isolated, as had Mahatma Gandhi. For weeks before and after Partition on 15 August every day brought reports of men, women, and children being slaughtered in the name of religion; of long columns of refugees fleeing their ancestral homes. They brought with them horrifying tales of wholesale killings, mass rape, skewered infants; concerted attacks on trains and roads even as they fled.

With revengeful refugees pouring in from Punjab, riots erupted in Delhi in September. The office of the *Hindustan Times* was located in the central shopping area of Connaught Place. One morning, we found the doors and shop-windows of all Muslim-owned shops broken. Passers-by looted the contents; police were nowhere to be seen. However, a furious Nehru arrived on the scene and chased the looters through the corridors with his lone security guard struggling to keep pace. He insisted on visiting refugee camps near Delhi, telling the inmates to avoid revenge. At one meeting, I saw his lone security guard hold him by the waist to prevent him jumping from the dais into the heckling crowd.

The prime minister suspected that the police and local administration were influenced by Hindu communal forces and had been infiltrated by members of the Hindu militant organization, the Rashtriya Swayam Sewak Sangh (RSS). Differences between him and Sardar Patel, who oversaw law and order as home minister, on handling the disturbances were widely rumoured. Patel was known to doubt the loyalty of Muslims after Partition, and it became evident that he did not share Nehru's desire to facilitate the resettlement of those who had fled their homes in Delhi but wished to return.

By 30 September, an emotional, deeply stressed Nehru could no longer contain himself. Raising his voice at a public meeting, he vowed that he would resign if the country did not support him, but that 'as long as I am at the helm of affairs, India will not become a Hindu State'. His speech in a mill area in old Delhi, open to the press, revealed the depths of his frustration:

> I am a representative of the people and am bound to vacate my office when called upon to do so by them. But I am also at liberty to give up my responsibility if the people of India cease to have faith in the lead that I give. If they do not subscribe to my ideals and are not prepared to cooperate with me then I will have no choice to resign from prime ministership and continue the fight for the establishment of a State where every citizen enjoys equal rights irrespective of his religion.[5]

A month later, the change in Jawaharlal Nehru was evident in his 2 November broadcast testifying to the lesson in secularism taught by Abdullah's leadership of the defence of Kashmir.

* * *

Gandhi preferred to remain in Calcutta than to participate in the Independence Day celebrations in Delhi. He had moved into a dilapidated building in a Muslim locality to bring peace to the city till summoned in September to do the same for Delhi. Here he found the atmosphere worse. He toured the city and its environs and began a series of public meetings calling for communal amity. When killing continued, he expressed the desire to die rather than witness such barbarism. At his prayer meeting on 13 September, referring to the family of his friend, Dr M.A. Ansari, a nationally known Delhi doctor, he said he would 'lose all interest in life if the Muslims who had produced such men could not live with perfect safety in the Union'.[6] A week later, he warned: 'Hindus, Sikhs and Muslims cannot continue to live the way they are living now. It pains me very much and I shall do everything humanly possible to remedy the situation. Let me tell you that if I cannot do what my heart desires, I shall not feel happy to remain alive.'[7]

His agony surfaced in his response to a message on his 78th

birthday on 2 October 1947. He had earlier laughingly expressed the desire to live up to 125 years to see his dreams come true:

> If I had the impertinence to openly declare my wish to live 125 years, I must have the humility, under changed circumstances, openly to shed that wish. This has not been done in a spirit of depression. The more apt term, perhaps, is helplessness. In that state, I invoke the aid of the all-embracing Power to take me away from this 'vale of tears' rather than make me a helpless witness of the butchery of man become savage, whether he dares to call himself a Musalman or Hindu or whatnot. Yet I cry "Not my will but Thine alone shall prevail". If He wants me, He will keep me here on this earth yet awhile.[8]

Gandhi, too, was revitalized by the news from Srinagar. Notwithstanding his creed of non-violence, he did not object to the despatch of Indian troops to defend Kashmir from the marauding raiders. At his prayer meeting the day after they landed there (and the death of Col. Rai), the report of his prayer meeting stated:

> He [Gandhi] would not shed a tear if the Union force was wiped out like the Spartans, bravely defending Kashmir, nor would he mind the Sheikh Saheb [Abdullah] and his Muslim, Hindu and Sikh comrades, men and women, dying at their post in defence of Kashmir. That would be a glorious example to the rest of India. Such heroic defence would infect the whole of India and we would forget that Hindus, Muslims and Sikhs were ever enemies.[9]

Gandhi used every occasion to depict Abdullah as a symbol of secularism. He contrasted the protection provided to Hindus and Sikhs in the Valley with the continuing attacks on Muslims in Jammu, where he was aware that Hindu communal groups, financed by the maharaja, now living there, were trying to embarrass Abdullah. Gandhi believed in demonstrating his beliefs. He took Abdullah with him to a celebration of Guru Nanak's birth anniversary on 28 November which was packed with Sikhs who had suffered in the riots. His words went to the heart of the matter:

> You see Sheikh Abdullah Saheb with me. I was disinclined to bring him with me, for I knew there is a great gulf between the Hindus and the Sikhs on the one side and the Muslims on the other. But the Sheikh Saheb, known as the Lion of Kashmir, although a pucca Muslim, has won the hearts of both, by making them forget that there is any difference between the three. He has not been embittered. Even though in Jammu recently the Muslims were killed by the Hindus and Sikhs, he went to Jammu and invited the evildoers to forget the past and repent the evil they had done. The Hindus and Sikhs of Jammu listened to him. I am glad, therefore, that you are receiving the two of us with cordiality.[10]

However, an embittered Hari Singh continued to foment unrest. He remained head of state, though limited to Jammu, which had a higher proportion of Hindus than the Valley of Kashmir. Most were Rajputs, traditionally loyal to the Dogra dynasty. He appointed Abdullah to the newly-created office of head of the emergency administration under pressure from Nehru but retained Mehr Chand Mahajan as his prime minister. They clashed bitterly in Jammu, the seat of the Dogra dynasty. In early November, two convoys of Muslim refugees were attacked with heavy casualties. Abdullah flew from Srinagar to calm passions.

With Hari Singh threatening his hopes that Kashmir would sustain secularism in India, Gandhi spoke out more harshly than usual. He asked him to own responsibility for the murder of Muslims and abduction of Muslim girls in Jammu for he was still the maharaja and the Dogra state troops were under his direct control. He went on to praise Abdullah for allaying passions and advised the maharaja and his prime minister to step down and allow Abdullah and the people of Kashmir to handle the situation.

Gandhi's public criticism of a Hindu maharaja on behalf of his

Muslim subjects evoked sharp responses from Hindu communal leaders and commentators. He replied even more sharply at his prayer meeting on 29 December:

> I have been lately taken to task for daring to say what I have stated about Kashmir and the Maharaja ... I have simply rendered advice which, I suppose, the lowliest can do ... It was, if accepted, designed to raise the Maharaja in his own and the world's esteem ... He is a Hindu prince, having under his sway a very large majority of Muslims. The invaders have called their invasion a holy war for the defence of the Muslims reported to be ground down under Hindu misrule. Sheikh Abdullah Saheb was called by the ruler to his task at a most critical period ...
>
> It must be evident to the outsider, as it is to me, that Kashmir must be lost to the invaders, otherwise called the raiders, if the Sheikh Abdullah Saheb's effort to hold together the Muslims and the minority fails. And it would be a mistake to think that the Union army could do it ... Is it any wonder that I have advised the ruling authority to rise to the occasion and to become like the King of England and, therefore, use his rule and his Dogra army in strict accord with the advice of Sheikh Abdullah Saheb and his emergency Cabinet? ... It is on Kashmir soil that Islam and Hinduism are being weighed now.[11]

---

1 In his *The Story of the Integration of the Indian States*, Orient Longman, New Delhi, 1985 edn, pp. 399–400, V.P. Menon recalls that on his visit on 25 October 1947, 'the road leading from the aerodrome to Srinagar was deserted. At some of the street corners 'I noticed volunteers of the National Conference with lathis who challenged passers by, but the state police were conspicuous by its absence. The Maharaja was completely unnerved.'

2 See former Maj. Gen. Akbar Khan, *Raiders in Kashmir*, Pakistan Publications Ltd, Karachi, 1970. Also V.P. Menon, op. cit., p. 410.

3 The crucial proviso was contained in a letter dated 27 October 1947 by Lord Louis Mountbatten, then governor-general of India, accepting Maharaja Hari Singh's letter of accession. It stated:

> Consistently [sic] with their policy that when the issue of accession has been the subject of dispute, the question of accession should be decided in accordance with the wishes of the people of the State, it is my Government's wish that as soon as law and order have been restored in Kashmir and her soil cleared of the raider, the question of State's accession should be settled by reference to the people. Meanwhile, in response to Your Highness's appeal for military aid, action has been taken today to send troops of the Indian Army to Kashmir to help your own forces defend your territory and to protect the lives, property and honour of your people. My government and I note with satisfaction that Your Highness has decided to invite Sheikh Abdullah to work with your Prime Minister.

4 *Selected Works of Jawaharlal Nehru*, vol. IV, pp. 107–8.

5 D.G. Tendulkar, *Mahatma*, vol. 8, p. 117.

6 *Collected Works of Mahatma Gandhi.*

7 Tendulkar, vol. 8, p. 145.

8 Ibid., pp. 168–69.

9 Ibid., p. 207.

10 Ibid., p. 222.

11 Ibid., p. 225.

ROOTS OF TOLERANCE

Kashmir ... By the power of the spirit ... yes
By the power of the sword ... never.

– Kalhana[1]

Sheikh Mohammad Abdullah had a sense of history, possibly instilled by his sufi teacher in childhood. In his memoirs he takes pride in ancient ruins discovered near Saura, the village where he was born, and notes that it was near the capital of the great fifteenth century ruler of Kashmir, Sultan Zainul-Abideen. He recalls that one of his Brahmin ancestors converted to Islam during Afghan rule.[2] In the Valley, the appellation 'Sheikh' indicates a convert rather than a noble or a prince.

Abdullah began his memoirs, *Aatish-e-Chinar* or *Flames of the Chinar,* published after his death in 1982, with three quotations recalling the long span of historical influences on Kashmiri culture and thinking. First are lines from *Rajatarangini* (River of Kings), the prodigious work of the medieval historian Kalhana chronicling the history of the rulers of the Valley long before the arrival of Islam. *Rajatarangini* traces Kashmir's history back to the reign of Gonanda I in pre-Mahabharata times. No other historical work in the subcontinent provides a connected account going that far back in time. Written in Sanskrit in the twelfth century, it describes the deeds—great and petty—of the early Hindu dynastic kings.[3] The ruins of Martand and Avantipura remain an enduring testimony to the great builders among them.

Translated into English, the passage from *Rajatarangini* cited first in Abdullah's memoirs is:

> *Kashmir ... By the power of the spirit ... yes*
> *By the power of the sword ... never.*

Rajatarangini notes the entry of Buddhism into the Valley when it became part of the empire created by the great king Ashoka (274–237 BC). The new religion was not forced upon the people by Ashoka, known for tolerance. It gradually permeated existing religious rites and philosophy, and fused with earlier Vedic beliefs. Literature and philosophy flourished in the Valley, with scholars from outside preferring its climate and verdant landscape to the hot dusty plains of north India. Among them was Nagarjuna, founder of the Madhyamika or Middle Way of Buddhism, who lived in Kashmir in the first century AD. The evolution of a religious philosophy unique to the Valley, Kashmir Shaivism, or Trikha, followed. Amongst the greatest scholars of Trikha was Abhinavagupta, author of the monumental treatise *Tantralokha.* Abhinavagupta lived in the tenth century, before Islam came to the Valley. The statue of Shankaracharya, another great scholar of Trikha, dominates Shankaracharya Hill in Srinagar. Trikha's emphasis on monism and egalitarianism is seen as easing the passage from one religion to another without the friction and bloodshed witnessed in other parts of the subcontinent.[4]

PEACEFUL TRANSITION

While the raids of Mahmud of Ghazni into western India in the early eleventh century, putting infidels to the sword, razing temples, and carrying away women and plunder, left their mark on the Hindu psyche, the contemplative orders of sufis and rishis introduced their version of Islam to Kashmir, but more by example than by force. The sufi practice of meditation had much in common with Hindu and Buddhist teaching, as did their eclectic acceptance of the universality of religions that was not accepted by orthodox Muslims.

An early sufi divine to leave a mark on the history of Kashmir was Sayyid Bulbul Shah. One of his many converts was Rinchin, a young Buddhist chieftain from Baltistan beyond the Zojila (pass), who had married the daughter of King Ramachandra and captured the throne in a palace coup in 1320. According to local legend, he wanted to embrace the renascent Hindu Shaivite cult, but the head priest ruled against his conversion because he could not be identified by caste. Impressed by the austerity of Bulbul Shah, Rinchin converted to Islam and assumed the title Sultan Sadruddin, the first of the Valley's rulers with a Muslim name.

Sheikh Abdullah's childhood tutor was a sufi, and the pervasive sufi influence in Kashmir is recognized in his memoirs. The second quotation inscribed in it is from Noor-ud-Din, a fourteenth century sufi divine whose verses still reverberate in the Valley. He was the founder of the austere, tolerant order of rishis and was popularly known as Nund Rishi. His mausoleum in Charar-i-Sharif remains a place of pilgrimage. Noor-ud-Din was adopted and inspired by a mystic revered by Hindus as Lalla Yogeshwari and by Muslims as Lalla Maji. The popular name by which she is known in the Valley is Lal Ded or mother Lalla. They were the wandering spiritual bards who carried the message of tolerance into the recesses of the Valley.

NUND RISHI AND MOTHER LALLA

The sentence inscribed in Abdullah's memoirs from Nund Rishi's teachings is simple, but perhaps indicates the far-reaching social reforms Abdullah sought to implement after assuming office:

I broke my sword and fashioned a sickle.

Another of Nund Rishi's verses stressed the essence of the sufi doctrine (in contrast to the iconoclastic fervour of Mahmud of Ghazni and his followers):

Sow thou the seed of friendship for me everywhere,
And slay not even my enemies.

Lalla taught her followers the unity of religion:

Shiva lives everywhere.
Do not divide Hindu from Muslim.
Use your sense to recognize yourself;
That is the true way to God.

And again:

Truth is not a prisoner of mosques and temples and is all-pervading;
Idol is of stone, temple is of stone;
Above and below are one;
Which of these wilt thou worship, O foolish pandit,
Cause thou the union of body and soul?

The deep-rooted cultural tradition of questioning religious dogmatism broadcast through the Valley in folksong and verse extended to protest against misuse of authority. It would provide the setting and technique for the spread of Sheikh Abdullah's message.

In his *A History of the Struggle for Freedom in Kashmir, Cultural and Political, from the Earliest Times to the Present Day* (1954), Prem Nath Bazaz, the eminent Kashmiri historian, notes:[5]

> The peaceful and rapid conversion of the large masses of the people in Kashmir to Islam, which has been the source of wonder and astonishment for many students of history, was facilitated and made possible by the spread of religious humanism taught by Lal Ded, Nund Rishi, and their followers. Islam as practised in the valley, though it surely stands on the cardinal principles taught by the Quran, has been deeply influenced by the ancient Kashmir culture: a Kashmiri Muslim shares with his Hindu compatriots many inhibitions, superstitions, idolatrous practices as well as social liberties which are unknown to Islam. Of course Islam in turn has not left Hinduism unaffected in the valley.

Earlier, the historian M.A. Stein, who translated *Rajatarangini* into

English, had drawn attention to the same virtually painless transition:

> Islam made its way into Kashmir not by forcible conquest but by gradual conversion ... The adoption of Islam by the great masses of the population, which became an accomplished fact during the latter half of the fourteenth century but which probably began towards the close of Hindu rule, did neither affect the independence of the country nor at first change, its political and cultural conditions.[6]

Sir Walter Lawrence, appointed settlement commissioner in the 1890s and renowned for trying to bring a measure of justice and order into the chaotic and rapacious practice of extorting taxes under Dogra rule, reinforced this view from his experience, as described in his *The Valley of Kashmir:*

> Generally speaking, it may be said that when one finds the Musalman shrine with its shady chinars and lofty poplars and elms, a little search will discover some old Hindu asthan. It was only natural that Musalmans, when they were converted to Islam, should cling with tenderness to the old religious places, and should adopt sacred spots already familiar to the countryside. I have shown in my chapter on Customs how certain ideas are common to the Hindus and Musalmans of Kashmir, but I attribute much of the delightful tolerance which exists between the followers of the two religions to the fact that the Kashmiri Musalmans never gave up the old Hindu religion of the country.[7]

This did not mean, however, that the Valley was always spared religious persecution. Sultan Sikandar (1389–1413) equalled Mahmud of Ghazni in his zeal to obliterate traces of Hinduism and convert its followers to Islam. Archaeologists hold him responsible for the damage inflicted on Martand and Avantipura. Hindus fled the Valley in thousands. However, seven years after his death, one of Kashmir's greatest kings, Zainul Abedin, began a fifty-year rule in which Hindus were persuaded to return, their temples rebuilt, Sanskrit studies revived. He joined their cultural festivities and even went on a pilgrimage to Amarnath. He introduced papier-mâché and revived the shawl industry for which the Valley's artisans were known in Europe and Asia. He is still revered in the Valley as Bud Shah.

One of the last indigenous rulers of Kashmir was Yusuf Shah Chak, whose queen is better known than him. Their trysts became part of romantic lore before another royal couple, Emperor Jahangir and his queen Nurjahan made the Valley's attractions famous. She was the rustic singer Zoon, also known as Habba Khatoon. One of her songs, composed when her husband was in captivity, represents Kashmir's heritage of romantic poetry:

Say friend, when will fate smile on me,
And my love come to me again? Say when?
I've waited long and patiently,
My heart is numb and idle and empty of hope.
Sweet in the ritual of love;
I would deck my love with ornament,
And in henna dye his hands;
I would anoint his body with fragrant kisses
And offer wine in golden goblets.
The lotus of love which blooms in the lake of my heart;
Say, friend, when will fate smile on me?

Betrayed into the hands of the Mughal emperor Akbar, Yusuf had been banished to Bihar and was not destined to return before his death there. His son, Yaqub Shah Chak, took over as the last ruler of an independent Kashmir before fleeing from Akbar's troops on 10 October 1586. Since then the region has been occupied and ruled by outsiders, with a history that inspires the continuing yearning for *azaadi*.

INFLUENCE OF IQBAL

The third quotation inscribed in *Flames of the Chinar* is more contemporary in origin and the author more representative of the religio–political controversies that confronted Abdullah. It is a couplet from Allama Mohammad Iqbal (1877–1938), the great Urdu poet and philosopher, whose ancestors belonged to Kashmir. The couplet explains Sheikh Abdullah's choice of the title of his autobiography. Kashmir is home to the flowering *chinar* tree that transforms the autumn landscape into splashes of red and gold:

> *Jis khaak ke zamin mein ho aatish-e-chinar*
> *Mumkin nahin ke sard ho who khaak-e-arjumand*
>
> (The dust that has in its conscience
> The fire of chinar trees
> That dust, celestial dust,
> Will never become cold.)

Abdullah came from a shawl-making family. He quotes two couplets by Iqbal expressing the agony and exploitation of Kashmiri artisans. One was in Persian:

> *Ba resham qaba Khwaja az mehnat-e-oo*
> *Naseebe-e-tanash jama-e-taar-taarey*
>
> (While you are destined to cover your body with rags,
> The Khwaja's silken robes are the fruits of your labour.)
>
> Another in Urdu:
>
> *Sarma ki hawaon me uryan hai badan uska*
> *Deta hai hunar jiska ameeron ko dushala*
>
> (In the bitter chill of winter shivers his naked body
> Whose skill wraps the rich in royal shawls.)[8]

Iqbal represented an emerging sentiment among Muslims that would impinge on Abdullah. They were in a minority in the subcontinent and, as the prospect of independence approached, found Hindus becoming politically and culturally assertive and thriving in trade and commerce.

Like Sir Syed Ahmed Khan, the founder of Aligarh Muslim University, Iqbal sought to infuse modern education and liberal ideas into a community more concerned with its past. His earliest works were coloured by Indian nationalism, but with the passage of time concern to preserve the culture of his community became uppermost.

Iqbal is remembered for composing the stirring 'Song of India', *Taranai-e-Hind.* His celebrated poem, *Saare Jahan se Achha Hindustan Hamara,* continues to be sung in Indian schools and on national occasions. They speak of the glorious land of India and the devotion due to her. Yet, without being doctrinaire, he was one of the first to promote the idea of a separate homeland for Indian Muslims, but more for cultural than religious reasons. Abdullah recalls his support for the crucial moves towards transforming communal into secular politics in Kashmir in the late 1930s.[9] This was when Abdullah persuaded his followers to change the name and constitution of their party from Muslim Conference to National Conference and invited non-Muslims to join.

Abdullah was returning to Srinagar after studying in Aligarh University when Iqbal delivered his momentous presidential address to the twenty-first session of the All India Muslim League in Allahabad on 29 December 1930. Philosophic in tone, it was a sensitive, inward-looking statement of Muslim angst. Iqbal made a case for a separate, autonomous homeland for Muslims in north-west India, where they would be free to develop their religious and cultural practices. There was no hostility to Hindus in it; rather he states, 'A community which is inspired by a feeling of ill-will towards other communities is low and ignoble. I entertain the highest respect for the customs, laws, religious and social institutions of other communities.'

At the same time, he was eloquent about the need for the fullest autonomy: 'I love the communal group which is the source of my life and behaviour; and which has formed what I am by giving me its religion, its literature, its thought, its culture, and thereby recreating its whole past, as a living operative factor, in my present consciousness.'[10]

The concluding sentences of Iqbal's address indicated his desire to modernize Islam and distance it from association with the destructive, iconoclastic raids into Sindh by Sultan Mahmud of Ghazni and his successors. Insisting that the formation of a consolidated Muslim state would be in the best interests of India and Islam, he states: 'For India it means security and peace resulting from internal balance of power; for Islam, an opportunity to rid itself of the stamp that Arabian imperialism was forced to give it, to mobilize its laws, its education, its culture, and to bring them into closer contact with its own original spirit and with the spirit of modern times.'

Iqbal's reasons for demanding a separate Muslim homeland had a social content relevant to the 1930s. Referring to Jawaharlal Nehru's socialist programme in an undated letter to Mohammad Ali Jinnah, he argued: 'The issue between social democracy and Brahmanism is not dissimilar to the one between Brahmanism and Buddhism. Whether the fate of socialism in India will be the same as the fate of Buddhism in India I cannot say. But it is clear to my mind that if Hinduism accepts social democracy it must necessarily cease to be Hinduism. For Islam the acceptance of social democracy in some suitable form and consistent with the legal principles of Islam is not a revolution but a return to the original purity of Islam.'[11]

However, events turned out differently in relation to Kashmir. Iqbal did not impress the conservative Jinnah with the virtues of social democracy. Dominated as it was by large landowners, the Muslim League was comfortable with Jinnah's support for the constitutional right of the maharajas and nawabs to rule. He showed little sympathy for their people. Socialism became a crucial point of difference with Sheikh Abdullah's views that were akin to Nehru's.

Iqbal died before Pakistan was born and before Jinnah used Islam as a political instrument to secure the state. He did not campaign specifically for a separate country for Muslims, but for a homeland with full autonomy. The bloodshed and trail of communal hostility left by the partition of the subcontinent proved to be different from the reasoned demand for cultural, social, and religious space that he proposed. Abdullah admired Iqbal and recalled in his memoirs their mutual nostalgia for Kashmir when meeting him in Lahore in 1924.

That was before Iqbal advocated separatism and Abdullah mentions the pride he took in 'being a descendant of the [Hindu] Saprus'.[12]

---

1 Kalhana, *Rajatarangini,* trans. M.A. Stein (2 vols), Archibald Constable, London, 1900; Indian ed. Motilal Banarsidas, Delhi, 1961.

2 Sheikh Abdullah, *Flames of the Chinar,* trans. from Urdu by Khushwant Singh, Viking, 1993, pp. 1–2.

3 Kalhana, *Rajataragini,* op cit.

4 See Prem Nath Bazaz, *The History of the Struggle for Freedom in Kashmir, Cultural and Political, from the Earliest Times to the Present Day,* Pamposh Publications, New Delhi, 1954. Also, P.N.K. Bamzai, *A History of Kashmir.* Metropolitan Book Co., Delhi, 1962.

5 Prem Nath Bazaz, op. cit.

6 M.A.Stein, *Rajatarangini,* vol. I, p. 130

7 Walter Lawrence, *The Valley of Kashmir,* Oxford University Press, London, 1895.

8 *Flames of the Chinar,* p. 3.

9 Ibid., p. 49.

10 Syed Sharifuddin Pirzada, *Evolution of Pakistan,* Lahore, 1963, pp. 128–29.

11 Ibid.

12 *Flames,* p. 52.

DOGRA RULE

Their fields, their crops, their streams,
Even the peasants in the vale
They sold, they sold all, alas!
How cheap was the sale.

– Mohammad Iqbal

The life and thinking of Sheikh Abdullah were shaped by two imperial forces: one recent, the other well-established. By the time he was born on 5 December 1904, the Dogra empire established by the Jammu feudatory, Raja Gulab Singh, was nearly sixty years old. Gulab Singh had gained control over the areas of Jammu & Kashmir that had been part of Ranjit Singh's Sikh empire through a classic sleight of duplicity: winning the confidence of the Sikh regime and then betraying them to the advancing British. After the collapse of the Sikh empire, the territory was sold to him by the British under the Treaty of Amritsar of 1846 for a pittance of 75 lakh rupees. In addition, he and his successors would demonstrate their fealty by paying the British Government an annual tribute of 'one horse, twelve perfect shawl goats of approved breed (six male and six female), and three pairs of Cashmere shawls'.

The raja, now elevated to maharaja, soon replenished his coffers. A contemporary English traveller, Lt Col. H.D. Torrens, wrote:

> Goolab Singh went far beyond his predecessors in the gentle acts of undue taxation and extortion. He had taxed heavily, it is

> true, but he sucked the very lifeblood of the people; they had laid violent hands on a large proportion of the fruits of the earth, the profits of the loom, and the work of men's hands, but he skinned the very flints to fill his coffers.[1]

Gulab Singh was not content with the territory purchased from the British. He was a man of unbounded energy and ambition. Rising from a common soldier, he left to his successors the largest princely state of British India, extending over the verdant Valley of Kashmir, the highest Himalayan ranges bordering Gilgit and Baltistan, and the vast stretches of Ladakh up to the Tibetan plateau. He sewed up his empire by annexing the principalities of Kishtwar, Bhimbar, Rajouri, and Poonch nearer Jammu. The diversity of the peoples he came to rule over in religion, culture, ethnic origin, language, and dialect was determined by geographic remoteness. They were easy targets for his trained army, led by intrepid generals like Zorawar Singh, whose expeditions into Tibet and Chinese Sinkiang created border uncertainties that survive.

A visiting British officer, Major Arthur Neve, painted this vivid picture of the extensive territory and variety of peoples the Dogras came to rule:

> And so Jammu became the capital of a kingdom larger than England, in fact, about equal to Great Britain, with tributary peoples speaking a dozen different languages and dialects, and at a Darbar, in the olden days, one might have seen not only the Dogra Princes and Sikh generals, with bold Rajput veterans of the many fiercely contested mountain campaigns, but those who had been subjugated, Tibetan chiefs from Leh and Zanskar, Balti rajahs from Skardu or Shigar, Dard chiefs from Astor or Gilgit, with their picturesque and truculent followers, all clad in the most diverse costumes.[2]

Money fuelled Gulab Singh's greed and achievements. After paying the British their price, a steady flow was required to maintain his armies and enforce his rule over far-flung regions. He was ruthless in securing it from his subjects and ensuring their submission. A contemporary

English traveller, G.T. Vigne, recorded that prisoners were flayed alive, their skins filled with straw and planted by the wayside for the instruction of passers-by.[3] Such barbaric methods were abandoned by his successors, but heavy taxation continued. It was required to finance the army and police a huge state with sensitive borders. The cost of maintaining the bejewelled level of luxury flaunted by maharajas had to be extracted. Continued exploitation of the people of the Valley, almost all Muslim, fuelled the rage against the Dogra dynasty that marked Abdullah's career

In 1889, under pressure from the viceroy, Maharaja Pratap Singh appointed an Indian Civil Service officer, Sir Walter Lawrence, to head a settlement commission to establish a uniform basis for payment of land revenue. This is an extract from his memoirs, *The India We Served* (1928):[4]

> When I started my work, everything was taxed. Fruit trees, birch bark, violets, hides, silk, saffron, hemp, tobacco, water-nuts and paper were treated as State monopolies and farmed out to the [Hindu] Pandits. The right to legalize marriage was farmed out, the office of grave-digger was taxed. Prostitutes were taxed and everything save air and water was brought under taxation. Meanwhile, agriculture, the only stable source of revenue languished, and the treasury was empty. The land revenue was, as a rule, extorted from villagers by violent methods. I once caught a revenue officer using a thumb-screw on an unfortunate peasant who had paid his land revenue in full, but declined to pay an equal amount as bribe to the officer.

Lawrence was impressed by, but less sympathetic to, the Pandits. Nowhere had he met, he wrote, 'a body of men so clever and courteous, but they also exploited the Muslim and resented their emancipation'.

Gulab Singh's son, Ranbir Singh, strengthened the British connection by contributing two thousand soldiers, two hundred cavalrymen, and six guns to help them retake Delhi after the great revolt of 1857. He was showered with honours by Queen Victoria and was empowered to add two guns to the regulation nineteen fired in salutes in his honour on ceremonial occasions.

Ranbir Singh strained the treasury in order to fulfil his ambition to erect as many temples in Jammu as in Varanasi on the sacred Ganga. This however did not ward off the famines, epidemics, and earthquakes that devastated the state. One-third of the population of the Valley is estimated to have died in the great famine of 1877, with dead bodies lying unburied. An anonymous memorandum to the viceroy alleged that the maharaja was drowning his Muslim subjects by the boatload; it was actually inquired into before being dismissed for lack of evidence. A disastrous earthquake in 1884 accentuated their misery.

BRITISH STRATEGY

Cordial relations with the British government did not last. The viceroy began to interfere as the state's strategic situation began to impinge on its imperial interests (interests that continued to influence developments up to its accession to the Indian Union). A British resident in Srinagar was forced on Ranbir's successor, Pratap Singh. British foreign policy required greater control and less unrest in the strategic area bordering Afghanistan, Russia, and China. The principal concern of imperial diplomacy was to counter the threat perceived from Russian penetration southwards from Central Asia, in a rivalry that became known as the 'Great Game'.

As a strategic buffer, it was necessary for Kashmir to be able to resist Russian moves. At great human cost, a road was carved out of the rocky, mountainous terrain between Srinagar and Gilgit, the strategic outpost near the northern border. The medieval practice of *begar,* or forced labour, made it possible for men to be forcibly mustered from their villages to work, and often die, clearing a road that snaked over the 13,775-foot high Burzil Pass. Not many returned.

The viceroy posted an officer, F. Henvey, in Srinagar to keep him informed of conditions in the state, buiding up a case for intervention. This is an extract from his report in 1880:

> A state which is rotten to the core within can scarcely show a bold front. A state whose soldiers are always in arrears, and

> therefore discontented, forms a sorry bulwark to the Indian Empire. A state which cannot keep its people alive would meet with difficulty in equipping and supplying a force for distant warfare in a barren country.[5]

Four years later, London concurred. Lord Kimberley, secretary of state for India, wrote: 'As to the urgent need for reforms in the administration of the State of Jammu and Kashmir, there is, unfortunately, no room for doubt ... Intervention on behalf of the Muhammedan population had been too long delayed.'[6]

Britain gradually took control of what came to be known as the Gilgit Agency. The Gilgit Scouts, commanded by British officers but part of the state army, were formed in 1913. Britain's strategic interests in the area were evident after Partition. In November 1947, after the state acceded to India, their last British officer, Major W. Brown, led his men to rebel against the maharaja and opt for Pakistan.[7]

As a strategic border area, Kashmir was a favourite haunt of intelligence agents with large secret funds at their disposal. Letters allegedly written by Pratap Singh to the czar of Russia, Britain's nightmare villain, were produced as evidence of treason. To make the case for intervention stronger, the maharaja was next charged with conspiring to actually murder the British resident in Srinagar, Trevor Plowden. His denials were rejected and he was divested of his powers in 1889. Subsequently the letters were found to be forgeries, as revealed by Calcutta's *Amrita Bazar Patrika,* in an early newspaper exposé. Pratap Singh survived these indignities and went on to demonstrate greater concern for his subjects than his predecessors. However, his orders were disregarded by corrupt court officials. He ordered construction of new roads, opened hospitals, and introduced electricity. In 1905, the viceroy, Lord Curzon, restored some of his powers.

Rather than risking a direct takeover, viceregal policy now turned to educational and cultural influences in the state. British officers and civilians were encouraged to holiday and retire in the Valley. Many families arrived to escape the heat of the plains in summer. Attracted by descriptions of the Valley's beauty in travel books, tourists followed. The

Mughal Emperor Jahangir's immortal Persian couplet was widely quoted:

Gar firdaus bar rue zamin ast
Hamin ast, hamin ast, hamin ast.

(If there be a paradise on earth
It is this, it is this, it is this.)

Accounts of the dalliances of Mughal Emperor Jahangir and his Queen, Nurjahan, in Srinagar's Mughal Gardens captured the imagination of Victorian England. Writers and poets embellished the accounts of the adventures of travellers, and Kashmir was projected as a haven of beauty and romance. In 1846, an English verse-maker, Thomas Moore, made a fortune with a novel in verse, *Lalla Rookh,* without going there. His lack of first-hand experience did not impede his romantic imagination:

If woman can make the worst wilderness dear,
Think, what a Heaven she can make of Cashmere!
So felt the magnificent son Ackbar,
When from the power and pomp and trophies of war
He flew to that Valley, forgetting them all
With the Light of the Harem, his young Nourmahal.[8]

SIGNS OF CHANGE

Life within crowded insanitary Srinagar was, however, no picnic. Engish visitors and residents preferred to live on boats on the Dal Lake and Jhelum river. Responding to the demand, local craftsmen developed the comfortable, intricately carved houseboats of various sizes for which Kashmir is famous. English and Western-style education began to spread. Srinagar's first college, later named Sri Partap College, was founded the year Abdullah was born, and it was there he was to study. A mission school was opened in Srinagar by Rev. J.S. Doxy in 1881, followed by Canon Tyndale-Biscoe whose autobiography provides a somewhat supercilious picture of the times.[9]

Prem Nath Bazaz acknowledged the change:

> The people of the valley were thus brought under the imperialism of the Dogras which itself was functioning as a vassal of the super-imperialism of the British. But though Dogra imperialism brought nothing but misery, thraldom, physical and mental deterioration in its wake, the other imperialism did not come without some blessing. By coming under the British suzerainty the valley began to have the impact of western ideas and modern civilization which finally awakened the people to demand their birthright of independence and freedom.[10]

The Muslim orthodoxy resisted schooling that departed from religious tradition, but it was welcomed by the tiny Pandit population. As a consequence, they strengthened their hold on the administration and the emerging educational system. Realizing this belatedly, leaders of the Muslim community approached the government for similar facilities but received little encouragement.[11] Even the few Muslims with educational degrees found it difficult to obtain suitable employment, as Abdullah was to discover.

A reform that had lasting consequences for the Muslim peasantry, however, after it was belatedly implemented, was the appointment of Sir Walter Lawrence's settlement commission. It was begun in 1889 and took four years to complete. The report recommended that the cultivator pay a fixed amount of thirty per cent of his gross produce, which was half or even less than the variable amounts being extracted from him. *Begar* was officially abolished. Implementation of the Lawrence report was resisted for years by recalcitrant *jagirdar*s and other officials, but it inculcated the widespread awareness of agricultural rights that would dominate Sheikh Abdullah's campaign for reforms.

---

1 H.D. Torrens, *Travels in Ladak, Tartary and Kashmir,* Otley, London, 1865.

2 Arthur Neve, *Thirty Years in Kashmir,* Edward Arnold, London, 1913.

3 Godfrey Thomas Vigne, *Travels in Kashmir, Ladak, Iskardo and the Himalayas North of Punjab* (two vols.), Henry Colburn, London, 1842.

4 Walter Lawrence, *The India We Served,* Houghton Mifflin, New York, 1928.

5 Quoted in Alder, *Roof of the World,* p. 235.

6 Quoted in Alastair Lamb, *A Disputed Legacy1846–1990,* Roxford Books, 1990, p. 13.

7 For a details of British policies in Gilgit and Ladakh, see above, pp. 17–82.

8 Thomas Moore, *Lalla Rookh,* George C. Harrap, London, 1846.

9 Oanon Tyndale-Biscoe, *Kashmir in Sunlight and Shade,* London, 1922.

10 P.N. Bazaz, *The History of Struggle for Freedom in Kashmir,* New Delhi, 1954, p. 129.

11 Ibid., p. 136.

FINDING HIS VOICE

In the State of Jammu and Kashmir, injustices of various kinds are prevalent. The Muslims, who form an overwhelming majority, are illiterate, steeped in poverty, and driven like dumb cattle. No rapport exists between the government and the people. There is no system to redress their grievances. Public opinion is not permitted. Newspapers are generally non-existent.

– Resignation letter of Sir Albion Banerji
from the office of prime minister of Jammu & Kashmir

Saura, the village where Sheikh Mohammad Abdullah was born, is close to Srinagar, now a crowded suburb. It was a centre of shawl production. His father, Sheikh Mohammad Ibrahim, was a prosperous trader in shawls. Abdullah was spared the miserable life of the weavers living in the vicinity, but family fortunes fluctuated after his father's death, and there were occasions when he was forced to help out in the stitching room. Dissensions with his stepbrothers did not contribute to a happy childhood and told on his mother, Khairunnissa. His poignant memories of her working to keep the family together, praying regularly, telling him stories of emperors and fairies that uplifted him to another world, and his grief at her death are etched in his memoirs.[1]

Though still an adolescent, Abdullah was sensitive to the gap between his family's affluence and the poverty of his neighbours. When asked to accompany officials to attach the moveable property of a Ganderbal weaver against whom court decrees had been obtained for owing money to his family, he found that all the weaver had were a few mats and kitchen utensils. 'We were living a good life thanks to these wretched workers,' he recalls in his memoirs. 'Not only had this man lost his job but thanks to us was due to lose his meagre possessions as well. I set fire to the court decrees and returned home with a heavy heart. When my brothers demanded the money, I narrated my experience. They were very angry but could not condemn my action.'[2]

There were other such cases. Exactions of corrupt officials worsened matters. Abdullah noted that the victims were Muslims and most of the lower-grade officials Pandits. He asked his mother why injustice was meted out only to Muslims in Kashmir. He received no reply, but felt destiny calling.

The pitiable plight of the weavers contrasted with the beauty of their products.[3] They earned no more than seven or eight rupees a month, of which more than half was extracted in tax. More was taken away in return for foodgrains supplied to them, leaving little. Weavers were not allowed to change their occupation, known as *shawl-baf*, lest the loss of production reduce the maharaja's revenue from their sweated labour. Conditions of work in low, crowded rooms were abysmal. Should a worker run away to Punjab or elsewhere, his wife and family were punished. It was slave labour pure and simple. A special department, Dagshali, supervised the lucrative shawl industry and regulated the labour.[4] Weavers had to report their attendance every day. Workers in the other cottage industry for which Kashmir was known, silk production, functioned under similar conditions.

Sir Francis Younghusband, British resident in Srinagar in the years of Abdullah's childhood (he had led the Younghusband Expedition to Lhasa in 1904), recalled the exploitation of the shawl trade and the extortionate level of taxation:

> The wool was taxed as it entered Kashmir; the manufacturer was taxed for every workman he employed, and at the various stages of the process according to the value of the fabric. Lastly there was an enormous duty of 85 per cent ad valorem. Butchers, bakers, carpenters, boatmen, and even prostitutes were taxed,

> and coolies who were engaged to carry loads for travellers had to give up half their earnings.[5]

Corruption and exploitation in the shawl industry provoked the first labour rising in Srinagar on 21 April 1865, which was mercilessly crushed. The weavers were required to pay five rupees in tax out of their monthly earnings of seven to eight rupees. This left barely sufficient for suvival, so they decided to march in a body to present a petition to the governor. When they refused to disperse, they were charged and pursued by soldiers. At least twenty-eight were killed and many injured. Hundreds were imprisoned, and there some died of beating, cold, and starvation.[6]

IMPRESS OF ISLAM

Religion left an early impress on Abdullah, and he grew up as a devout Muslim. Not for him, however, the narrow, orthodox version of Islam emanating from some of the schools in the subcontinent and abroad. At the age of four he was sent to the neighbourhood *maktab*, where the teacher, Akhun Mubarak Shah, belonged to the eclectic school of sufis. This childhood experience left a lasting impress on his personality. Abdullah fondly recalls Shah's gentle manner of teaching, and his wife sharing their meals with their students. As customary, students were taught to recite the Quran. Persian was taught through readings of the classics, including *Bostan* and *Gulistan*.

Early in life, Abdullah was found to have a rare talent for reciting the holy book clearly and sonorously. Often gripping the attention of all who listened, he was finding the value of his voice. Students were required to recite a paragraph of the Quran every day. Together with *namaaz* at the mosque, he recalls that, 'all through life's arduous paths they gave me sustenance and enabled me to find my way.'[7] The training presaged his ability to hypnotize crowds.

He then moved on from orthodox to regular schooling. A keen student, he walked ten miles to attend Government High School in Srinagar. After passing the Punjab University matriculation examination he joined Sri Pratap College, situated even further away in the city. He persisted though 'I left home when the morning *azaan* was being called, and returned at the time the lamps were lit'.[8] He passed the intermediate science examination 'with flying colours'.

This caused him to hope to receive the state assistance required to join a medical school; he was keen to be a doctor. Now, however, the ambitious young student came up against a barrier that was to set him on his political career. He found his name missing from the list and went on to encounter consistent discrimination against Muslims in education and government jobs. He left the state and secured admission in Islamia College in Lahore for the Bachelor of Science degree.

LEARNING IN LAHORE

It was in Lahore that Abdullah first met Allama Iqbal, whose poetry and philosophy were to influence him deeply. He also listened to Sarojini Naidu, the Indian Congress party's poet–politician, who was in town. Her 'exquisite oratory held me spellbound', he recalled. Lahore was a centre of cultural and political activity, with leaders of different viewpoints striving to be heard. Lala Lajpat Rai and Sir Sikandar Hayat Khan (chief minister of undivided Punjab from 1937 to 1942) were prominent among them.

However, it was the plight of Kashmiris forced to seek employment outside the state that moved him deeply. Their muscular bodies were exploited to carry the heavy burdens local porters could not lift; even so, they lived on the edge of penury. Many died far from their homes where no work was available. Contemptuously nicknamed 'hato', they served as beasts of burden for traders in Punjab and northern India.

Abdullah was in Lahore when two events occurred in Srinagar in 1924 reflecting the rise of public indignation against the maharaja's regime. In July, workers in the silk factory in Srinagar organized a week of demonstrations against their miserable wages and oppressive working conditions. The first major labour outbreak after the shawl workers protest in 1865, it was suppressed by the maharaja's troops with equal severity. The demonstrators were dispersed by a cavalry charge in which an unknown number were killed and wounded.

Then the British viceroy, Lord Reading, chose October, the

pleasantest time of the year, to visit Srinagar. Maharaja Pratap Singh was overjoyed. The viceroy was taken on a ceremonial river-boat procession through Srinagar, with schoolchildren organized to line the banks. However, the suppression of the silk workers protest had evoked widespread resentment. Leaders of the Muslim community signed a memorandum to be presented to the viceroy detailing their grievances. It demanded far-reaching measures to secure justice: setting up a constituent assembly with fair representation for Muslims; effective representation in the services; appointment to important posts, including governor of Kashmir; appointment of an expert to promote Muslim education, preferably a Muslim or European; protection of sacred places; proprietary rights for tenants. Distrust of the Pandit functionaries in the government was implicit.

Black flags were waved and slogans shouted as the viceregal boat procession was rowed slowly through the city. Slogans were raised seeking justice and protection against tyranny. Finally the memorandum was submitted to Lord Reading, who forwarded it to the maharaja. The regime reacted sternly. Action was taken against the signatories, all prominent citizens. Their leader, Khwaja Saduddin Shawl, was banished from the state and others removed from their posts. Some apologized.[9]

Shawl and Khwaja Noor Shah Naqshbandi found refuge with a Kashmiri family in Lahore, where Abdullah called on them. His response to the complaint that the people of Kashmir had not reacted to their banishment was typical. 'Since they did not take the people into confidence,' he noted in his memoirs, 'they should not expect anything in return from them. Both the Khwajas were annoyed. "Let us see what you will do," they said. "Let the time come," I retorted, "God willing we will show our worth".'[10]

Still in quest for higher learning, Abdullah went from Lahore to Aligarh Muslim University where he qualified for a Master of Science degree. Aligarh was the centre of the Muslim community's political and economic aspirations in the subcontinent. Separatism was a stirring issue, but this was where he first glimpsed Mahatma Gandhi. 'We watched him with great admiration,' he recalled. 'Gandhi was not a fiery orator; it was his simplicity and informality which captivated every member of the audience.'[11] Another element of his destiny was being forged.

FINDING MY VOICE

The next event to affect him was Sir Albion Banerji's resignation from the office of prime minister of Jammu & Kashmir in 1929 in protest against conditions there. A senior Bengali officer of the Government of India, he had been appointed by Maharaja Hari Singh. His public statement created a furore:

> In the State of Jammu and Kashmir, injustices of various kinds are prevalent. The Muslims, who form an overwhelming majority, are illiterate, steeped in poverty, and driven like dumb cattle. No rapport exists between the government and the people. There is no system to redress their grievances. Public opinion is not permitted. Newspapers are generally non-existent.[12]

Abdullah was provoked when some Muslims who had done well by their loyalty to the maharaja issued a counter-statement insisting that the Muslim population was leading a peaceful and prosperous life in the state. He wrote a letter to *Muslim Outlook* in Lahore describing the reality of the conditions there. When it was published, he was overjoyed: 'This was my first venture into politics which filled me with a strange rapturous feeling. I had finally found my voice.'[13]

---

1 H.D. Torrens, *Travels in Ladak, Tartary and Kashmir*, Otley, London, 1865.

2 *Flames*, pp. 4–5.

3 Ibid, pp. 10–11.

4 For centuries, Kashmir was known in Asia and Europe for the quality and designs of its exquisite shawls. The revenue they provided to the government was second only to land revenue. Exports to Europe began early in the nineteenth century. The Kashmir historian, P.N.K. Bamzai, provides a fascinating account of how it began: a blind visitor to the Valley in 1796, Sayyid Yahyah, was presented a shawl by the

governor of Kashmir, Abdullah Khan. After his return to Baghdad. Yahyah went on to Egypt and presented the shawl to the Khedive, who gifted it to Napoleon when he was in Egypt. Napoleon sent it home (presumably to Empress Josephine) and French traders were attracted to Kashmir.

5 G.H. Khan *Freedom Movement in Kashmir, 1931–40,* pp. 20–21.

6 Sir Francis Younghusband, *Kashmir,* Adam Charles Black, London, 1909, 9–179. Sir Francis led the Younghusband expedition to Lhasa in 1904.

7 Ibid., p. 79.

8 *Flames,* p. 6.

9 Ibid., p. 7.

10 Ibid., p. 17.

11 G.H. Khan, pp. 87–98.

12 *Flames,* pp. 13–15.

13 Ibid., p. 15.

14 Ibid., p. 17.

THE LION EMERGES

The year 1930 dawned. How could I have known that the nation was on the brink of an eruption? The trampled pride and hope of the people of Kashmir was like molten lava ready to flow. Nature fanned the embers which were smouldering inside me. It was left to me to take the lid off the volcano's mouth.

– Sheikh Abdullah[1]

Sheikh Abdullah returned to Srinagar in 1930 after obtaining degrees from Lahore and Aligarh, both recognized universities. He was twenty-five; an angry young man brimming with resentment against the pervasive discrimination practised by the Dogra maharajas of Jammu & Kashmir against Muslims, the majority of their subjects. The lines quoted above are from his memoirs.

Abdullah towered over the scene politically and physically. Six feet four inches in height with matching build and a voice that carried a long distance and yet was mellifluous, he attracted and dominated large gatherings. Trained from youth to recite from the holy book, the Quran, he was skilled in quoting passages that would reach out to his Muslim audiences. Some of his Pandit colleagues were unhappy; they felt the intrusion of religion into politics was against the secular commitment of the National Conference. For Abdullah, however, it was an essential means of striking a chord with mass gatherings. Unlike the use put to religious texts by the Muslim League and Hindu fundamentalist organizations, the Sheikh's references to the scriptures were not meant to propagate hostility to adherents of other religions. They were more akin to Mahatma Gandhi's use of the word *ramrajya* to communicate his vision of independent India to largely Hindu audiences.

He was easily recognizable as he led protest processions through the narrow crowded streets of Srinagar and its environs. His attire of coat and trousers, the insignia of the few Kashmiris with university education, stood out in the *pheran*-clad crowd. He was no religious tub-thumper; he dwelt on the need for change and development. His education and association with the political and intellectual leaders of the subcontinent had broadened his outlook. He differed with the orthodox leaders of the Muslim community, including the customary local religious head, the *mirwaiz,* Mohammad Yusuf Shah.

STIRRINGS OF DISCONTENT

Stirrings of discontent were unsettling the enforced calm of the maharaja's regime. Initially, however, the rise in social and political awareness did not bridge the religious divide. The Muslim and Hindu groupings that emerged represented divergent approaches and sects. They did not challenge the maharaja's authority but passed resolutions and sent memorials to him couched in respectful terms. They originated as non-political movements urging religious, social, and educational reform, with Anjuman-i-Nusrat-ul-Islam as the oldest among them. Other associations followed, such as Anjuman-i-Hamdard Islam and Young Men's Muslim Association in Jammu catalyzed by Chaudhry Ghulam Abbas, an influential leader who was to diverge from Abdullah. Hindus, especially in Jammu, were attracted by the Arya Samaj and other reformist movements. Yuvak Sabha focused on the rights of the Kashmiri Pandits; Dogra Sabha comprised loyalists to the regime.

There was more than one *mirwaiz,* a hereditary religious office, and they often pulled in different directions, though usually supportive of the regime. Sectarian differences tended to divide the community. The Ahmadiya sect (also known as Qadianis) created friction because its teachings were regarded as heretical. Their missionary zeal and commercial activities widened their influence in the Valley, arousing opposition from local religious leaders. The conflict assumed political overtones and had an impact on Abdullah's career.

Events in British India had repercussions on the state. Gandhi's Khilafat campaign for the rights of the Caliph of Turkey in the 1920s attracted Kashmiri Muslims to identify with the freedom struggle in India. Funds were collected and meetings held. The maharaja's administration, however, considered the movement as seditious, and it was weakened by the opposition of clerics loyal to the regime. In contrast to the rest of India, few non-Muslims joined the movement in the state. Had they joined, notes historian G.H. Khan, 'possibly a secular national movement in Kashmir would have emerged much earlier than it did'.[2]

The growing movement for self-rule in British India influenced the state. Students participated in Gandhi's non-cooperation movement and a *hartal* and demonstration was held in Srinagar on 6 May 1930 to protest his arrest. However, with limited literacy and access to news, Muslims were less involved than Pandits, but the latter too had reasons for resentment against the maharaja's administration. Senior positions were monopolized by non-Kashmiris from Punjab, and like the Muslims of the Valley, Pandits too were excluded from the army which was recruited from Jammu.

Maharaja Hari Singh's lavish lifestyle contrasted with the destitution of his subjects. Passive acceptance of feudal inequality was, however, being eroded by the awareness of democratic rights fostered in the subcontinent by the campaign for Indian independence. Hari Singh had sullied his reputation before he ascended the *gaddi* (throne) in 1925. An affair with a London prostitute made headlines in British scandal sheets. According to the British historian, Leonard Mosley, 'The Maharaja of Kashmir was so rich that he bought hundreds of concubines and dancing girls at 2–5,000 pounds apiece, and once paid 15,000 pounds (in blackmail) for one hour with a female crook in a London hotel bedroom.' [3]

Hari Singh's London escapade was widely reported by the British newspapers. Though originally described as 'Mr A', his identity could not be long concealed. His extravagance was confirmed by the millions spent on celebrating his coronation, and even more on festivities celebrating the birth of his son, Yuvraj Karan Singh, in 1931. The festivities began in Cannes, the French Riviera resort where the maharaja and his retinue were holidaying, and continued in Jammu and Srinagar. Karan Singh himself provides a frank, well-written record of the times in his autobiography, including glimpses of his father's arbitrary ways and fits of ill temper.[4]

THE READING ROOM PARTY

Abdullah was among the relatively few Kashmiri Muslims who were graduates but frustrated by their inability to find suitable employment. The only job he could find with his M.Sc degree was as a schoolteacher. He tried it for a few months but was drawn into the stirrings of political activity in Srinagar. As political meetings were prohibited, he and a group of young, educated, frustrated Muslim men set up what was described as a Reading Room in a private house in the Fatehkadal area of Srinagar. This imparted their meetings with an academic flavour, but they discussed political issues, read political journals, and established contacts with outside sympathizers. Mohammad Rajab was elected president and Abdullah general secretary.

The Fatehkadal Reading Room attracted the intelligent, well-educated, and frustrated cream of the Muslim community. Their concerns went beyond employment, which they found so difficult to obtain, to social and political developments. Viewing themselves as victims of an oppressive, monarchical system, they sought inspiration from what they had read of the French and more recent Russian revolutions. With its uglier aspects yet to emerge, the egalitarian thrust of the Russian revolution appeared particularly attractive. The proximity of the Soviet Asian republics to Kashmir, together with reports of the changes made in them, added to the attraction. Communism found adherents among the educated. The yearning for socio–political change turned them away from clerical orthodoxy.

Their immediate concern was to seek changes in the state civil service recruitment rules that provided scope for discrimination. One requirement was that the candidate should belong 'to a good and noble family', which was used to keep out Muslims. The first Reading Room initiative in September 1930 was to send a memorandum to the authorities complaining against the rules. The ministerial council hearing petitions, in the absence of the maharaja who was abroad, invited them to present their case. Abdullah was one of the two petitioners who appeared. He countered official speeches that the government treated Muslims well, and warned that there would be trouble if the rules were not amended. The council was not used to such bluntness and the meeting ended abruptly.

The rules remained unchanged, but Abdullah became known as an outspoken young leader and the Reading Room group as a political force. Then, within weeks, came a series of events that transformed resentment into violence, and telescoped his rise to leadership. Muslim sentiment was offended by an alleged insult to the holy Quran in Jammu's central jail. An official inquiry found the incident to be accidental, but passions were aroused when the issue was taken up by the Young Men's Muslim Association. A protest demonstration was organized in Srinagar on 8 June 1931.

This was the occasion for Abdullah to make his maiden public speech to a gathering estimated at 7000 people. He was introduced by Maulvi Yusuf Shah and spoke of the greatness and universality of the holy book that he knew so well. A resolution adopted at the meeting condemned the Hindu jail officials in Jammu. He was successful in arousing strong feelings, but he emerged as a Muslim rather than a secular leader.

When Hari Singh returned to Srinagar from abroad, retried to assuage Muslim sentiment and invited their leaders from Jammu & Kashmir to meet him. Among those nominated to represent Jammu was Chaudhri Ghulam Abbas. A public meeting was held in Srinagar to select representatives. The outcome was a committee representing a wide spectrum of views, including the influential but conservative Mirwaiz

Mohammad Yusuf Shah and Mirwaiz Ahmedullah Hamadani, but also radicals like Khwaja Ghulam Ahmad Ashai and Sheikh Abdullah.

Hopes of reconciliation were, however, dashed by an event that ignited latent popular passions. An impassioned visitor from outside the Valley got up and disrupted the tea being served in a school building after the meeting. Showering abuses on the maharaja, he insisted that the only course for Muslims was to fight his oppression with sticks and stones if they had no guns. It was a call to violence. He was arrested by the police and identified as Abdul Qadir, a non-Kashmiri servant of a visiting British army officer. Qadir's outburst and arrest sent ripples through Srinagar. When it was became known that he was to be tried in camera on 13 July, a protest meeting was organized, but people were advised by their leaders not to gather at the central jail where the case was to be heard.

MARTYRS' DAY

Ignoring this advice, a crowd estimated at between four and five thousand rushed to the jail. The governor, Raizada Trilok Chand, was pelted with stones when he ordered them to disperse. The police opened fire. Twenty-two were killed and hundreds injured. The dead were taken to Jama Masjid where they were laid out ceremoniously as martyrs. The gates were locked against the police. Meanwhile, the death of three Hindus amidst looting of Hindu shops led to communal tension.

13 July 1930 continues to be observed as Martyrs' Day, a day on which people openly clashed with authority, later described by Abdullah as having 'the same impact on our movement that the massacre at Jallianwala Bagh had on the movement for Indian independence'.[5] He was not part of the crowd that rushed to the jail, but at home where he heard about the outburst. However, seizing the opportunity to ride the gathering storm of protest, he rushed to the masjid and helped lay out the bodies of the martyrs and lock its gates against the police. Thousands joined the burial procession the following day.

The authorities reacted harshly to the unprecedented challenge. Martial law was imposed, houses were searched, and hundreds detained.

People on the streets were forced to shout *maharaja-ki-jai* (praise to the maharaja). Communal feelings were heightened because, while Muslims were picked out for punishment, Pandits were spared. Newspapers from Lahore, projecting the Muslim League line, interpreted the situation in terms of a Muslim uprising against Hindu oppression; Hindu communal papers reported the communal conflict, not the oppression.

Sheikh Abdullah was among the leaders incarcerated in the dungeons of Hari Parbat fort overlooking Srinagar, described as the Bastille of Kashmir. The town was virtually paralysed by a *hartal* until they were released three weeks later. The Congress leader, Maulana Abul Kalam Azad, on a visit to Srinagar, told the maharaja that he was being misled by his advisers and should take steps to allay Muslim grievances. He was unhappy to find the press depicting the unrest as a Hindu–Muslim conflict while in actuality it was due to the excesses of the government. His statement[6] served to counter, to a degree, the communal flavour sought to be imparted to the unrest in the Valley.

Moves were afoot to draw Kashmir into the communal politics spreading across the subcontinent. Urdu newspapers published in Lahore incited hatred not only against the maharaja but also against Hindus. The state had figured in the resolution adopted by the All India Muslim League in 1930 demanding a separate association of Muslim-majority areas in the north-west of British India. A high profile Kashmir Committee was set up in Lahore, with Iqbal prominent among its members. They decided to observe 14 August as Kashmir Day. Muslim organizations in Indian cities held meetings on that day protesting against oppression in the Valley. Iqbal is reported to have said that Muslims in India could not remain indifferent to the demands of their brethren in Kashmir, but at the same time echoed Azad in describing the agitation as of downtrodden humanity rising against autocracy, not one community against another.

A public meeting held in Srinagar on Kashmir Day attracted a large gathering. Resolutions were adopted urging action against officials who had oppressed Muslims. The efforts of a section of the leadership to bridge the communal divide were reflected in a resolution appealing to Hindus to establish communal harmony.

After the Abdul Qadir explosion, the Muslim leadership and the maharaja's administration were anxious to avoid another confrontation. The day after Kashmir Day, eleven representatives of the Muslim community waited upon Hari Singh to present a memorial of their grievances. They ranged from the conservative Mirwaiz Yusuf Shah to the fiery Abdullah. The outcome however revealed their weakness, and the schisms and divisions among them. The memorial stressed the loyalty of Muslims to the maharaja while assigning the blame for oppression to his prime minister, Raja Hari Krishen Koul. The maharaja was unmoved and the leaders were obliged to sign an accord with Koul on 26 August. The terms were humiliating: they undertook to cease political agitation, remain loyal to the maharaja, and not be influenced by external forces. They pledged to observe the laws in force in the state and even expressed their gratitude to the prime minister for his magnanimity. In return, the government agreed to release political prisoners, reinstate sacked officials, and suspend harsh police measures.

POLITICAL TACTICIAN

Abdullah's signature to the accord went against everything for which he was known to stand. When its terms were made public at a meeting in Jamia Masjid, the crowd was disappointed that the youthful Abdullah had gone along with his conservative elders. In response, he gave the government two months to fulfil its assurances, during which time he would continue to exert pressure on it. In his memoirs, he justifies the accord as 'investing us with the status of a relevant party' and allowing 'time to realign our forces'.[7] He had graduated from a crowd-puller to a political tactician. He would change tracks again to his advantage in the future, creating doubt about his willingness to place political commitment above personal advancement.

Abdullah took the opportunity of touring the Valley and criticizing the government for not living up to the accord. His criticism was regarded as a breach of the accord, and on 21 September, well before two months had elapsed, he was back in jail. The arrest restored his image. The following day thousands assembled at Jamia Masjid to protest his arrest. Police and army units surrounded the mosque to prevent them from taking out a procession. When stones were thrown, they opened fire leading to the death of four and injuries to about thirty. Curfew was imposed, but demonstrations broke out and another ten persons were killed in police firing. Unrest widened, occasionally violent, and the army and police were accorded special powers to repress it under a dictatorial state order, Ordinance 19-L.

This did not prevent thousands, brandishing crude weapons, from coming out on to the streets. On 24 September the police did not dare to leave their barracks. The uprising spread to Anantnag and Shopian. The regime responded with harsher measures, deploying Dogra Rajput troops. People were whipped in public near Lal Chowk, the central market square. The degree to which the military misused their powers, and the bribery involved, was noted later by an English officer, L. Middleton, who was deputed to inquire into the disturbances. The historian Prem Nath Bazaz, in his *Inside Kashmir,*[8] provides a vivid contemporary account of the repression:

> It was easy for the police to report anyone as a turbulent man, get him summarily tried and convicted. Public flogging was the punishment awarded. People were mortally afraid of this barbarous method of dealing out justice. They paid handsome amounts to escape this torture and insult … One hundred respectable and grown-up men were sentenced to flogging … From all accounts, official and non-official, it can easily be gathered that there was no law in the town [Shopian]. A large number of people left the place or went into hiding … While the villagers were thus engaged, the chivalrous Rajput soldiers would go about the town, enter their houses, loot them and abuse their womenfolk. Several cases of rape were reported to Middleton …

Although the agitation was fired by a sense of injustice and discrimination against Muslims, efforts were made to reach out to the

Pandits. Posters appeared in Srinagar stating that Muslims had no quarrel with Hindus but had declared jehad against the maharaja's government. The communities were linked by the strong cultural and historical ties of *kashmiryat,* and the preference given to Dogras and non-Kashmiris in superior appointments and their continuing exclusion from the army. At the grassroot level, Hindu peasants and workers were no better off than Muslims.

Now it was the maharaja's turn to step back. Advice from New Delhi, relayed through the resident, suggested he take steps to pacify his subjects. Continued unrest in Kashmir was a threat to imperial strategy. Unrest and oppression in the Valley was also becoming an issue in adjoining areas of British India. The maharaja announced a general amnesty for all political prisoners on 5 October, his birthday, accompanied by a proclamation expressing sorrow at the loss of lives and inviting the Muslims to list their grievances and demands. The language of the proclamation, however, betrayed the unchanged mentality of the princely order. It noted that:

> Parents have at times to use force in bringing refractory children to order. But the parent has not the heart to continue to punish the child after it has ceased to be disobedient. What applies to the parents in their dealing with the children applies to the rulers of the Indian states in dealing with their people ... The law has been vindicated and the impression that it could be defied with impunity no longer exists ...

Accordingly, the emergency measures were withdrawn and amnesty ordered, but here, too, with the proviso that the maharaja was 'relying on the loyalty and devotion of my Muslim subjects to my Throne and Person ... The distinction between Muslim and Hindu subjects was overt.

Discussion and drafting of a memorial in response to the maharaja's invitation exposed differences amongst the Muslim leadership. Two groups that had been providing volunteers and financial support to the unrest from outside the state were the Qadianis and

Majlis-e-Ahrar, a peasant organization in northern India. They exploited the rivalry between Abdullah and Mirwaiz Yusuf Shah. Abdullah was initially closer to the Qadianis, but distanced himself from them when termed a Qadiani, virtually a term of abuse for orthodox Muslims. The gulf between Abdullah and the *mirwaiz,* however, became too wide to be bridged, with their followers being identified as *sher* (lion) after him or *bakra* (goat) after the beards of the orthodox supporters of the *mirwaiz.*

Most of the demands in the memorial were secular and democratic in nature, among them the establishment of a legislature and provision of other democratic rights. Some reflected specific Muslim demands for entry into the army, for more schools, and reservation of seats in professional and technical institutions. The demands were supported by Muslim organizations in India.

GLANCY COMMISSION

New Delhi felt that more was needed to allay the Muslim unrest that threatened the stability of the state, its lifeline to Gilgit, and beyond to Central Asia. It proposed the appointment of an officer of the Government of India to inquire into complaints of discrimination. Hari Singh was reluctant, arguing that such an appointment would undermine his rule.[9] New Delhi however insisted, and in November 1931 agreed to appoint a commission headed by Sir Bertrand J. Glancy, a senior officer of the Foreign and Political Department of the Government of India, whose services were loaned to the state government. It had two Muslim and two Hindu members, one of whom was the historian Prem Nath Bazaz.

The commission attempted to allay Muslim grievances. It recommended that religious places in possession of the government should be restored and better educational facilities provided. One recommendation went to the heart of the primary grievance of educated Muslims: that qualifications should not be pitched unnecessarily high so that they could compete, and that measures be taken to prevent the interests of any community being neglected.

This upset the Pandit community which felt that their near

monopoly of mid-level government jobs was threatened. They argued that efficiency alone should be the criterion and boycotted the commission, demanding that its Hindu members withdraw. Bazaz refused, and the Pandits went on to organize their Roti agitation, complaining that the recommendations would deprive them of their livelihood. In Jammu, protestors became rowdy when taking out a funeral procession to inter the Glancy report; three were killed and fifty injured when the police opened fire.

A Constitutional Reforms Commission was also set up in response to the demand for responsible government. It recommended a legislative assembly representing all parts of the state, including the far-flung areas of Ladakh and Gilgit, with separate seats for Hindus, Muslims, and Sikhs. Out of a total membership of sixty, thirty-three would be elected, the rest nominated. However, a franchise committee subsequently altered the system to provide for a nominated majority. Provoked, Sheikh Abdullah issued a statement:

> The people of this country did not spill their blood for such a mock show. Sir B.J. Glancy though not agreeing with the legitimate aspirations of the Muslims had recommended an elected majority in the proposed assembly in unambiguous terms. It was not business of the Franchise Committee to turn down this recommendation. What hopes can the people of this country have in this kind of assembly where the dead weight of the official and nominated majority will always be ready to crush the popular vote.

As expected, the franchise committee's version came into force and the first general election under it was held in September 1934. The Assembly was composed of seventy-five members. Thirty-three were elected: twenty-one Muslims, ten Hindus, and two Sikhs. As many as forty-two were nominated. The maharaja retained overriding powers. The results demonstrated the popularity of the Muslim Conference, headed by Abdullah over the Azad Party Muslim Conference set up his rival Mirwaiz Yusuf Shah, which failed to win a single seat. The Muslim

Conference had been founded in the Valley as a reaction to Hindu communal associations that had been founded earlier and which identified themselves with the hated Dogra dynasty.

---

1 *Flames*, p. 10.

2 Ibid., pp. 86–87.

3 Leonard Mosley, *The Last Days of the British Raj*, Weidenfeld & Nicholson, London, 1964.

4 Karan Singh, *Heir Apparent*, Oxford University Press, New Delhi, 1982.

5 *Flames*, p. 22.

6 *Aljamiat*, Delhi, 13 August 1931, quoted by G.H. Khan.

7 *Flames*, pp. 25–26.

8 Prem Nath Bazaz, *Inside Kashmir*, Kashmir Publishing Co., Srinagar, 1941, pp. 146–156.

9 G.H. Khan, p. 188.

THE SECULAR PROCESS

We have repeatedly declared that the Kashmir movement is not communal; it is a platform to address the grievances of every section of people. We shall always be prepared to help our compatriots, Hindus and Sikhs. No progress is possible unless we learn to live in amity. For that, mutual respect for each other's legitimate rights is an important pre-condition. I repeat, the Kashmir movement is not a communal movement.

– Sheikh Abdullah[1]

Sheikh Abdullah's meteoric rise to leadership within two years of his return to the Valley was fuelled by igniting the long pent-up feelings that Muslims were exploited and discriminated against by the ruling Dogra dynasty. He found a ready audience by reciting selected passages from the holy Quran that articulated their desire for a better life. Repeated incarceration in the maharaja's jails enhanced his standing. With Muslims comprising ninety-six per cent of the population of the Valley and seventy of Jammu province, the future trajectory of his career seemed assured. This was the time that Muslim separatism was on the rise in the subcontinent, with Kashmir specifically included in the group of north western areas marked for separation.

Yet Abdullah rejected the separatist role. Instead, he committed his party and people to a secular movement for representative government with a radical socio–economic reform agenda; a commitment that went against the communal tide sweeping much of India. The quotations he selected from the Quran highlighted its social teachings; they were not used to propagate suspicion and dislike of Hinduism, as the Muslim League was doing in British India. This was a unique transformation, changing the course of history and, as described earlier, reinforcing secularism in India when it was under severe attack by Hindu religious organizations after Partition.

The cultural ground for secular protest was laid by the folksongs and popular verse of the people's poet, Ghulam Mohammad Mahjoor, and his compatriots. Abdullah's imposing presence and resonant voice provided an iconic leader. As he moved through the countryside, he gained a reverential following amongst villagers. Folksongs and verses expressing the hope that the Sher-e-Kashmir would transform conditions in the state began resonating in the Valley. Holidaying in Pahalgam in his youth, Inder Kumar Gujral, former prime minister of India, recalls his surprise at seeing a crowd of villagers surrounding a tall man and gathering the dust off his feet. He was informed the man was the Kashmiri leader Sheikh Mohammad Abdullah.[2]

Bilqees Taseer, was about the same age when she met Abdullah in Kashmir in 1937. A talented writer, educated in Cambridge, she was one of the liberal, educated Muslims who worked for India's freedom. In Lahore she married the noted poet, M.D. Taseer, before Partition and stayed on in Pakistan; one of the group of intellectuals who gathered around her brother-in-law, the poet Faiz Ahmed Faiz. Her recollections of the rising young Abdullah recall the era:

> Sheikh Abdullah coming to the forefront at the time when conditions were ripe for revolt and tutored by those people working with him quickly acquired from the beginning the skill of captivating his audiences, who were then mostly the simple, uneducated, underprivileged masses, who had been enslaved for decades, and conveying to them his message. Sheikh Abdullah was deeply religious, but a subtle politician. The masses were too downtrodden, too ignorant to be awakened by mere politics.

> They followed him as a religious leader who, in the early days, lived among them as one of them. Mixing politics with religion as he did was resented by some of his critics, but he nevertheless used this method. When he first came on the scene mass meetings, processions, demonstrations were still either forbidden or frowned upon, but by speaking to his people in congregations of thousands, after first having recited in his melodious voice a passage from the Holy Koran and then quoting some of the simple, relevant lines of Iqbal he was able to arouse them to action.
>
> Like Mahatma Gandhi, Sheikh Abdullah had within him a sense of history. To see the rapport which he had with huge gatherings of people, most of them illiterate and poorly dressed, was an overwhelming experience. The rapport was a two-way experience. He reached the masses, but they gave him back what bolstered his confidence and his determination to continue his struggle for their uplift. Their affection for him, their gathering in tens of thousands to see and hear and if possible touch him, were spontaneous. They felt that something new was happening in their drab lives, that he really cared for them, understood their problems and was determined to do something about them. The zeal in his eyes and dedication in his face was what made him supreme in the eyes of his fellow Kashmiris. They came not only to see him but also to bring him offerings of money and the heavy silver jewellery of their women.[3]

Abdullah's technique of introducing a secular note into a discourse on Islamic practices is recalled by Pran Nath Jalali, a young Pandit communist leader who was close to him in the early days. At Abdullah's request, Jalali, who had a powerful voice, would begin the meetings by singing a popular Kashmiri song. 'Then Sheikh Abdullah would come and start the proceedings by reciting the Quran,' Jalali recalls:

> He had a very good voice. There would be pin-drop silence and everybody listened with reverence. The listeners were craftsmen, and he would always address a meeting on Friday because

> craftsmen would come after listening to their *waiz* [preacher], who would say something whose exact meaning would be known only to the *mullah*.
>
> But Sheikh Abdullah would tell them about the real Islam. He would start with what the Prophet did, how he fought oppressors ... He would say it is this egalitarian approach I want to build in Kashmir. I want people around me who are capable of making sacrifices and who do not differentiate between man and man. For us Hindu is as human as Muslim. The real difference is not between one religion and another; it is between the oppressor and the oppressed ... Muslim landlords exploit Muslim tenants as much as Hindu landlords exploit Hindu tenants.[4]

AKBAR JAHAN

Political campaigning, fired by the urge to change society, dominated Abdullah's waking hours. He nonethless found time to get married in October 1933. It was an unusual marriage. The bride was Akbar Jahan, daughter of Michael Harry Nedou, son of a prosperous Austrian hotelier who owned the chain of Nedou's hotels in Srinagar, Lahore, and Poona. Harry Nedou had fallen in love with a Gujar milkmaid and converted to Islam to marry her. The romantic Nedou blood seemed to have coursed in the veins of their daughter.

After schooling in a convent, she met a guest at her father's hotel, who was no other than Colonel T.E. Lawrence, famous as 'Lawrence of Arabia' for his exploits in Arabia and Mesopotamia during the First World War. He was in Lahore, apparently incognito, after an espionage mission for British Military Intelligence in Afghanistan.[5] She was fresh out of school, an attractive blend of Kashmiri and Swiss blood. A brief flirtation led to marriage at her father's insistence. Lawrence was, however, recalled to London when his cover was blown and his espionage activities disclosed in the press. Before he left, Harry Nedou insisted on divorce. Four years later, Akbar Jahan married Sheikh Abdullah. Lawrence's biography confirms that he was in India from 1926 to 1928 and was called back hurriedly to London. Tariq Ali suggests that disguised as Karam Shah, an Arab, Lawrence was involved in the toppling of King Amanullah of Afghanistan.

Akbar Jahan's previous brief marriage to an Englishman proved no obstacle to her remarriage, and she provided the firm support that Abdullah required. She retained her dynamism and proved a strong influence on her husband's career. She was to bear five children and, with her husband engrossed in politics in the early years, gave them the parental care and affection they needed. Farooq, the eldest, recalls his father as a stern taskmaster who beat him for his mischievous escapades.[6] It was an advantageous alliance. Her affluent background helped because Abdullah had no regular income. In the early years the couple stayed in part of her father's estate behind Nedou's Hotel. She was able to take the children to Lahore with her parents to escape the bitter winter cold in the Valley.

In his memoirs, Abdullah pays tribute to Akbar Jahan's contribution to the family and the circumstances that compelled her to enter political life. He quotes a couplet from the renowned nineteenth century Urdu poet Mirza Ghalib to signify the degree of confusion in his life into which she introduced a measure of order. The couplet is:

> *Rau mein hai raksh-e-umr kahan dekhiye thamey*
> *Nai haath baag parhai na paa hai rakaab mein*
>
> (Fast speeds the steed of life
> Neither is my foot in the stirrup nor my hand at the reins.)

In this state of disorder, he recalls:

> Patiently, facing all the trials, she was my source of strength and inspiration. In my absence, she ran the house single-handedly and never complained. It was her untiring effort that resulted in my children completing their education notwithstanding my continued absence from the domestic scene.[7]

When freed of her domestic chores, Akbar Jahan developed the personality latent in her. She raised funds for educational institutions and for the National Conference, and deputized for her husband when he was in jail. She was regarded as being even more committed to securing Kashmir's autonomy than her husband. Known in the Valley as 'Madr-i-Meharban' (kind mother), she was to be accused by the Intelligence Bureau of having links with Pakistan in the final conspiracy case filed against her husband and his associates.

The disorder recalled by Abdullah was confined to family affairs. The essentials of his political philosophy emerged early and were sharpened by the response he evoked. The first political party he organized reached out to the religion of the vast majority of Kashmiris with the name of All India Jammu and Kashmir Muslim Conference. That was in 1932, two years after his return to Srinagar to set up the Reading Room group. His distinctive approach, however, was made clear in his presidential address in October in which he said:

> We have repeatedly declared that the Kashmir movement is not communal; it is a platform to address the grievances of every section of people. We shall always be prepared to help our compatriots, Hindus and Sikhs. No progress is possible unless we learn to live in amity. For that, mutual respect for each other's legitimate rights is an important pre-condition. I repeat, the Kashmir movement is not a communal movement.[8]

His views echoed the common sufi heritage going back to the popular mystics Lal Ded and Sheikh Nuruddin, founder of the austere rishi order, in the fourteenth century. He also emphasized the need for social change. The address itself reflected the fusion of religious and ethnic nationality in the Valley. Hindu organizations, particularly the Dogra Sabha which was identified the Dogra dynasty and with Jammu culture, generated negative reactions in the predominantly Muslim Valley. The founding of the Dogra Sabha in 1904, which happened to be the year Sheikh Abdullah was born, led to the founding of the Muslim Conference. The reaction was, therefore, more cultural and nationalistic than religious. The Muslims of Kashmir were not united by religion; they were split into rival antagonistic groups.[9]

ORTHODOX OPPOSITION

Some of Abdullah's colleagues refused to go along with his secular approach and broke away. They felt he was swimming against the tide in seeking to divert a popular upsurge rooted in a deep-seated sense of religious discrimination against Muslims into a secular movement. The fount of oppression was seen as a Hindu ruler; the principal beneficiaries of discrimination were the better-educated members of the miniscule but well-established Pandit community. They feared that Abdullah was being unduly influenced by the Congress party leaders in British India.

The conservative members of the community were, however, themselves split. The Ahmadiyas, Ahrars, and other supporting groups outside the Valley had divergent objectives. Mirwaiz Yusuf Shah organized a breakaway Kashmir Azad Muslim Conference and traded charges of corruption with Abdullah. Another religious leader, Mirwaiz Hamadani, criticized his fellow *mirwaiz.* Their attacks on each other became so inflammatory that the local administration imposed a ban on political speeches in Srinagar.

Abdullah was not alone in demanding change; he represented the impatience of the educated younger generation with the religious leaders, unwillingness to question orthodox customs and beliefs. Other groups were also giving social reform and ethnic kinship priority over religious affiliation. The Young Men's Muslim Association, for instance, went further than the Muslim Conference in clarifying the secular character of their organization. In a resolution adopted as early as 1932, it stated that the movement is 'not against any particular individual or community. It is a movement for the emancipation of the oppressed.' It went on to declare: 'This movement is not and can never be against the non-Muslims ... What we want is to snatch our rights from the oppressors.'[10]

That very year saw a number of meetings between Muslim and Hindu leaders in Srinagar to resolve conflicts and join in achieving socio–economic goals. Funds were collected for the repair of damaged properties of both communities. Two potentially inflammatory disputes over ownership of religious sites were defused by referring them to a conciliation board.

Non-communal labour unions were also beginning to emerge, including the popular Carpet Weavers' Association and Tonga Drivers' Association. The Kashmir Motor Drivers' Association was destined to play a conspicuous role. They joined together to form the Mazdoor Sabha in 1937. Addressing one of the largest demonstrations in Srinagar on 4 October 1937, Abdullah reiterated the theme that both Hindu and Muslim workers were prey to capitalists. It was necessary to form a united front of workers and peasants.[11]

A Kashmir Students Federation was formed that very year. It elected a Hindu, Kashi Nath Bamzai, as president, and a Muslim, Mohammad Sultan Wani, as general secretary. A Kashmir Students Uplift Association was established at the same time. Again their names signified their different religions. Its president was Pandit Durga Prasad Dhar (who later became an adviser to Prime Minister Indira Gandhi) and general secretary, Khwaja Hussan-ud-Din.[12]

Thus far, political activity had been directed principally towards attracting urban and educated Kashmiris. In 1937, Abdullah decided to widen his movement to rural areas and sponsored a Kisan Sabha in October. Among the leading participants was the popular Sikh peasant leader from Jammu, Sardar Budh Singh. He became a close associate of Abdullah and played an important role in establishing his secular image.

However, the principal challenge faced by Abdullah was to win over leaders of the powerful Hindu Pandit community. As a tiny minority that had survived and done well in the administration by supporting the Dogra dynasty, the community tended to resist Muslim demands for equality and representative government. Nonetheless, the educated youth among them were becoming aware of movements for representative government and social justice in the world, particularly in British India. and realized that many Hindus, especially in rural areas, were no less oppressed than Muslims.

BAZAZ AND 'HAMDARD'

Pandit leaders remained reluctant to cooperate with Abdullah, but their criticism was blunted when a well-known and articulate personality among them publicly endorsed his secular stand. This proved to be crucial. Prem Nath Bazaz, who had been a member of the Glancy Commission, had the stature of a historian known for his independent views and willingness to incur the criticism of his own community. In 1933 he organized a public reception on behalf of Hindus and Muslims after Abdullah's release from a stint in prison. Most Pandit politicians remained unhappy, but there was a perceptible change in the political environment and Abdullah was heartened by the response.

The relationship between Abdullah and Bazaz symbolized the spirit of the 1930s. A distinctive mark of their collaboration emerged on 1 August 1935 with the publication of *Hamdard,* a political weekly in Urdu, under their joint signatures. The journal continued to propagate communal unity, social equality, and resistance to oppression even though it was eventually closed and fined by the authorities.

Bazaz was a political activist with strong leftist views as well as a noted academic. In 1936 he attracted Hindu and Muslim students to join the Kashmir Youth League committed to opposing 'discrimination on ground of religion or creed'. While he tried to convince the Pandits, Abdullah's address to the new organization indicated the effort he was making to win over the Muslim majority to secular politics. He said:

> Thank God we are now coming out of the mire of communalism and treading the right path. Muslims should particularly associate themselves with the youth movement. They are in a majority and have a great responsibility which they have to shoulder when a responsible government is established in the State, and for that they have to win the confidence of minorities ...

Bazaz was in touch with Indian leaders, including Gandhi, and it was he who paved the way for their association with Abdullah. Bazaz knew the Mahatma well enough to seek a message for the journal. Gandhi's reply was characteristic: 'Let the baby be born, then ask me to bless her.'[13]

Abdullah had earlier decided that the time was ripe to establish the popularity of the Muslim Conference by participating in the state's first general election in 1934, though the newly-formed legislature had limited powers and merely an advisory role. The party did well in the contest for seats reserved for Muslims while its principal rival, the Azad Conference of Mirwaiz Yusuf Shah, did not win a single Muslim seat. The Muslim Conference maintained its strength in the snap 1937 elections and confirmed its growing popularity by winning 19 of the 20 Muslim seats in 1938. However, to protest against the limited suffrage and powers of the Assembly, it continued to struggle in the streets for fully responsible government.

Although seats were allotted on a religious basis, members representing Muslim and Hindu constituencies found themselves on occasion joining together against the government. On one occasion, sparked by the resignation of Sardar Budh Singh, all Muslim and all but one Hindu member walked out, making it necessary to hold mid-term elections in 1937.[14]

NEHRU REACHES OUT

In the 1930s, educated Kashmiris were influenced by what they read and heard of communism as a tool for radical social change. This helped to counter the grip of traditional religion-based parties. Their studies on the distinction between religion and nation, between church and state in Europe provoked new thinking, as did discussions of the socio–economic changes wrought by the Soviet revolution. This group included a few Pandits, known for their intellectual prowess, but most were Muslims smarting under a sense of discrimination. Influential among them was the leftist Ghulam Mohammad Sadiq, who was to become a future chief minister. Also influential, but more for managerial than intellectual skills, was Bakshi Ghulam Mohammad, whose capacity for party management and intrigue would enable him to take over Sheikh Abdullah's office.

The process of secularization was encouraged by the support given by the Congress party in British India to movements for responsible government in the princely states. It set up the All India States Peoples Conference (AISPC) to link with popular movements in the states opposed by most of their rulers. The confrontation between rulers and ruled intensified after Jawaharlal Nehru declared that the Congress movement for freedom included the freedom of the people of the princely states at the Karachi session of the AISPC in 1935. In contrast, the conservative, landlord-dominated All India Muslim League showed no interest in social reform and representative government in the princely states. It dealt with the rulers. The League had it eyes on Hyderabad, the richest and second largest princely state in the subcontinent, and did not want to weaken the Muslim *nizam*, most of whose subjects were Hindu.

Though the situation in Jammu & Kashmir was the obverse, with a Hindu maharaja ruling over a majority of Muslim subjects, the Congress reached out to the people at the cost of antagonizing the ruler. Not all Congress leaders were supportive, but the party found it hard to exclude princely India from the struggle for responsible government in British India. The principal critic of the princes was Jawaharlal Nehru. The Hindu Mahasabha, claiming to represent Hindu nationalism, on the other hand, opposed any move to curtail the maharaja's authority. As early as 1931, it adopted a resolution condemning the 'fiery propaganda carried on against the Maharaja of Kashmir ...'.

In 1936, Mohammad Ali Jinnah paid a brief visit to Kashmir. The concept of Partition was still vague and theoretical, and the Muslim League was engaged in fighting elections in the United Provinces (later Uttar Pradesh) in which electoral agreements with the Congress were attempted. At the time, he had not shed his nationalist origins, and in a speech in Srinagar described himself as 'a great lover of Hindu–Muslim unity', and advised the Muslim majority in the state to win the confidence of minorities.[15] Abdullah records Jinnah's visit in his memoirs. Praising his political sagacity and legal acumen, he noted approvingly his advice to respect the sentiments of non-Muslims. There was no hint of the sharp differences that were to develop.[16]

A very different relationship was forged in January 1938 when Abdullah met Jawaharlal Nehru for the first time, though they had been in indirect touch through Prem Nath Bazaz. It was a relationship that would mould the future of the subcontinent when they joined hands to secure the accession of Jammu & Kashmir to India. This was still far in the future. For Abdullah, and the world at large, the year 1938 was memorable for the achievement of the the goal of transforming religious into secular politics, symbolized by renaming the Kashmir Muslim Conference as the Kashmir National Conference.

---

1 *Flames,* p. 35.

2 Conversation with Inder Kumar Gujral, New Delhi, 8 February 2007.

3 C. Bilqees Taseer, *The Kashmir of Sheikh Abdullah,* Messrs Ferozsons Pvt. Ltd, Lahore, 1986; and Gulshan Books, Srinagar, pp. 17–18.

4 Pran Nath Jalali, Oral History Project of the Nehru Memorial Museum & Library.

5 Tariq Ali, *The Clash of Fundamentalisms,* Rupa, Delhi, 2002, pp. 229–30. Lawrence's self-glorificatory account of his exploits in *The Seven Pillars of Wisdom,* first published privately in London in 1926, made him famous and was the subject of the film *Lawrence of Arabia.*

6 Aditya Sinha, *Farooq Adbullah, Kashmir's Prodigal Son,* UBSPD, 1996, pp. 15–19.

7 *Flames,* p. 43.

8 *Flames,* p. 35.

9 See Gul Mohd Wani, *Kashmir Politics: Problems and Prospects,* Ashish Publishing House, New Delhi, 1993, for a detailed account of the emergence of religious politics in Jammu & Kashmir.

10 *Aina Weekly,* Srinagar, quoted by Khan, p. 306.

11 Khan, p. 340–41.

12 Ibid., pp. 331–34.

13 Nagin Bazaz, *Ahead of His Times: Prem Nath Bazaz, His Life and Time,* Sterling Publications, New Delhi, 2006.

14 Bazaz, pp. 190–94.

15 G.H. Khan, pp. 344–46.

16 *Flames,* p. 59.

SECULAR PARTNERSHIP

I am quite clear therefore that the Kashmiri Pandits must revise their present policy and must in future develop political and other contacts with the advanced groups in the country. They should give up their narrow communal outlook and think of their own welfare in terms of the welfare of Kashmir as a whole, that is to say the great majority of the people of Kashmir.

– Jawaharlal Nehru[1]

Sixteen years in age and a vast difference in political and cultural backgrounds separated Sheikh Abdullah and Jawaharlal Nehru when they met in 1938. Nearing fifty, Nehru had an affluent Westernized upbringing, schooling in Harrow and Cambridge. He found ready entry into the leadership ranks of the Indian National Congress, of which he first became president in 1930. He was widely travelled, his patrician bearing and intellectual prowess impressing audiences everywhere. However, as occasionally happens, he turned rebel against his élitist past. Beginning his political career by joining peasant movements against the exactions of zamindars in the United Provinces, he went on to associate himself with radical left-wing causes at home and abroad.

When Sheikh Abdullah was setting up his Reading Room party, Nehru was already Congress president. Abdullah's political interests focused on Kashmir, whereas the Congress canvas was the entire subcontinent. It was a period of social and political unrest and rivalry accentuated by negotiations leading upto and following adoption of the Government of India Act of 1935 by the British parliament. Sectarian fears and political ambitions were aroused by general elections and bargaining for subsequent ministerial office in the provinces. The Muslim League separatist movement led by Mohammad Ali Jinnah gathered strength, as did Hindu communal parties.

Abdullah and Nehru had little in common in appearance and articulation though they came from the same Kashmiri Brahmin stock. Nehru described himself as an atheist to reinforce his secular credentials. The Sheikh was a devout Muslim who used religious references to support his egalitarian and non-communal philosophy. He towered over his guest on the dais at public meetings, though deferential in manner towards him. Notwithstanding his delicate appearance, Nehru spoke in Urdu with equal passion on exploitation and autocracy. He was heard with attention; to his listeners he represented trends in India and the world at large that affected their future. They were proud to claim him as a Kashmiri.

Nehru and Abdullah came together at a critical phase of their careers. With secularism under siege, Nehru sorely needed the support of an acknowledged secular Muslim leader with a mass Muslim following to counter the thesis propagated by the Muslim League and the Hindu Mahasabha that Muslims and Hindus belonged to different nationalities. Abdullah fitted the bill, but it was not a one-way street. Abdullah needed evidence that although the great majority of Congress members were Hindus, the party was committed to secularism. Nehru's commitment was unquestionable, but other Congress leaders developed second thoughts after Partition. That Nehru organized Congress support for representative government in Jammu & Kashmir although the ruler was a Hindu was appreciated in the Valley. It helped the emergence of the National Conference and its campaign for responsible government. Nehru and Abdullah strengthened each other in the struggle against communal politics.

SHARED COMMITMENT

Equally binding was their shared commitment to socialism. Abdullah did not have the benefit of Nehru's extensive leftist associations, but the oppressive conditions in Kashmir—worse under Dogra rule than in British India—called for a revolutionary approach. He conferred with noted leftist academics and communist sympathizers who contributed to the radical tone of Muslim, and later National Conference manifestos.

The Government of India Act of 1935 had a wide-ranging impact on Indian politics when it was adopted by the British parliament. It envisaged a federal structure for the country and paved the way for elections to provincial governments. It aroused political expectations in the princely states as well as in British India. The Congress Working Committee's resolution on the issue bore Nehru's stamp:

> The Indian National Congress recognizes that the people of the Indian States have an inherent right to Swaraj no less than the people of British India. It has accordingly declared itself in favour of establishment of representative responsible government in the States and has in that behalf not only appealed to the Princes to establish such responsible government in their States and to guarantee fundamental rights of citizenship, like freedom of person, speech, association, of the press, to their people but has also pledged to the States' people its sympathy and support in their legitimate and peaceful struggle for the attainment of full responsible government.

This evoked a prompt response in Kashmir. A public meeting was organized in Srinagar to celebrate the fiftieth anniversary of the Indian National Congress in December 1935. The liberal cleric, Maulana Mohammad Syed Masoodi, who would play a prominent role in the National Conference, moved a resolution assuring the Congress president of Kashmiri support in the fight for freedom.[2]

Prem Nath Bazaz played an important role in bringing Nehru and Abdullah together. In 1933, he wrote to Nehru praising Abdullah's secular stance. He was also in touch with Gandhi and wrote to both in

1934 to counter press reports that the 1931 uprising in Srinagar was anti-Hindu and Abdullah was communal. In his biography of his father, *Ahead of His Times*, Bazaz's son quotes the historian Hori Lal Saxena, as making the point that following this correspondence, Nehru began to take a keen interest in the political affairs of Kashmir. Earlier, he had nurtured only a romantic, ancestral interest in it.[3] His first visit to Kashmir in 1916 had nothing to do with politics. It was a mixture of high altitude trekking and shikar. He shot a bear, but the trip was made memorable by his falling into a crevasse, from which he was pulled out by a rope; a narrow providential escape.[4]

In 1936, Abdullah joined Bazaz in inviting Nehru to visit Kashmir. 'It is not necessary for you to invite me to my homeland,' was the nostalgic reply, 'for the desire to go there is always present within me.' However, expressing his current concerns, he wrote, 'the fate of Kashmir is bound up with that of the rest of India. If India is freed, Kashmir will participate in that freedom.'

ROLE OF THE PANDITS

Bazaz had dwelt on the crucial issues facing the Pandits in a letter also sent to Gandhi. They were 'between the devil and the deep sea', treated as a 'subject race' by the Dogra rulers but threatened by the rise of Muslim political consciousness in the Valley:

> Kashmiri Pandits therefore never liked Dogra autocracy and were crying for [a] democratic form of government. But communal agitation of Muslim leaders has terrified them. It has so unnerved them that, to my dismay, many of them have become greater communalists than Muslims now ... Hindus here, like the Anglo-Indians in British India, have in season and out of season sided with the Government to suppress Muslims ... Should we adopt a national programme and give up communalism altogether. If so, won't we be risking our culture, life and property in the hands of pan-Islamists?

Nehru's reply was unequivocal and was significant in influencing Pandit attitudes towards the emerging National Conference. Referring to the 1931 disturbances in which Pandits had suffered, he wrote:

> I can well understand that this experience as well as the feeling that they are surrounded by a hostile majority, should have terrified many of them into a kind of alliance with the State Government. But while I understand this, I deplore it, for this is both bad principle and bad policy ... No special weightage or protection on behalf of the State can possibly protect them against a huge hostile majority ... The Kashmiri Pandits are small in numbers but they are far better educated and are highly intelligent. In any progressive movement or radical reforms they are bound to play an important part by virtue of their education and intelligence.
>
> I am quite clear therefore that the Kashmiri Pandits must revise their present policy and must in future develop political and other contacts with the advanced groups in the country. They should give up their narrow communal outlook and think of their own welfare in terms of the welfare of Kashmir as a whole, that is to say the great majority of the people of Kashmir.[5]

The Pandit response is documented by Jia Lal Kilam, spokesman and leader of the community, in his *History of the Kashmiri Pandits*. Like Bazaz, he pointed out that it was the Pandits who first demanded democratization of the administration, but were put off by Muslim communalism. However, when presiding over the first Pandit Conference, he recalls that 'Mr Abdullah [who was present] was so much impressed with the nationalist sentiments found therein that he picked up a garland and jumped on the rostrum and garlanded the present writer'. The seeds of nationalism were once again sown, but it took time for them to germinate.[6]

FIRST MEETING

Although they had glimpsed each other earlier, the first occasion that Abdullah exchanged views with Nehru was in January 1938. The meeting was unplanned but paved the way for the momentous developments that were to follow. Nehru had asked Mian Iftikharuddin, president of the Punjab Provincial Congress Committee, to meet him at Lahore railway station while he was en route by train to Peshawar to meet Khan Abdul Ghaffar Khan, the Frontier Gandhi, also known as Badshah Khan. Iftikharuddin took Abdullah and Bakshi Ghulam Mohammad, who happened to be with him, along. They were engrossed in conversation when the train started. Bakshi alighted at the next station, but Nehru invited Abdullah to accompany him to the Frontier Province, an opportunity he promptly accepted.[7]

On the tour, he was introduced to the Frontier Gandhi, the other Muslim leader of the subcontinent who had been able to infuse his Muslim Red Shirt followers with a secular philosophy. Although unplanned, the meeting strengthened Abdullah's efforts to secularize the Muslim Conference. Nehru also stressed the need to finally open its doors to non-Muslims. Abdullah, in turn, invited Nehru and Badshah Khan to visit the Valley. On returning to Srinagar, he told his followers that there was no alternative to replacing the Muslim Conference with a national organization. Some criticism of the Nehru–Abdullah meeting came from Mirwaiz Yusuf Shah's Azad Muslim Conference.[8]

The stage was set for Abdullah and the Congress to move closer. He was in jail when the All India States Peoples' Conference met in Ludhiana in February, but in his presidential address Nehru condemned his incarceration and demanded his release. A resolution was adopted expressing 'solidarity with the people of Jammu and Kashmir in their struggle for responsible government'.

On his release from jail, Abdullah's importance was recognized by an invitation to preside over the All India States People's Conference session in March in Tripura. The entire Congress leadership was there. In his presidential address, he assured his audience that the people of Kashmir would end the politics of communalism and would 'rest only after having owned the ideals and basic principles of the Indian National

Congress'. The Congress struggle for freedom was inseparable from that of the people of the princely states.[9]

Then in May 1939, Nehru and Badshah Khan visited Kashmir in response to Abdullah's invitation. Nehru addressed a series of meetings supporting the demand for responsible government and urging the need for a non-communal approach to politics. He insisted that he had come to Kashmir not as a tourist but as a son of the soil.[10] The historic transformation of the Muslim into the National Conference took place the following month.

In an extended interview, published as the *Testament of Sheikh Abdullah*, the Sheikh recalled Nehru's influence on him:

> He [Nehru] suggested opening the Kashmir Muslim Conference to non-Muslims as well. When I expressed doubt about it, he explained that by opening the membership to all, any campaign against the ruler would gain more strength. Each time we met thereafter our friendship grew stronger but it was the first meeting that I remember most vividly.

Abdullah's affection for Nehru apparently survived the harrowing experience of his ejection from office in 1953 and release from prolonged imprisonment. The *Testament* appeared in 1964.[11]

1 Prem Nath Bazaz, *Kashmir in Crucible*, Pamposh Publications, New Delhi, pp. 171–83.

2 G. H. Khan, op. cit., pp. 346–47.

3 Nagin Bazaz, op cit., p. 52.

4 Sarvepalli Gopal, *Jawaharlal Nehru: A Biography;* vol. I, Oxford University Press, Bombay, p. 32.

5 Prem Nath Bazaz, *Kashmir in Crucible*, Pamposh Publications, New Delhi, pp. 171–83.

6 Jia Lal Kilam, *A History of the Kashmiri Pandits*, pp. 298–301.

7 M.J. Akbar, *Kashmir Behind the Vale*, Viking, London, p. 79.

8 G.H. Khan, op. cit., pp. 347–48.

9 G.H. Khan, op. cit., pp. 367–68.

10 *Flames,* p. 51.

11 Sheikh Mohammad Abdullah, *Testament of Sheikh Abdullah, with a monograph by Y.D. Gundevia* (former foreign secretary), Palit & Palit, Dehra Dun.

DREAM COME TRUE

This day will be written in golden letters in the history of Jammu and Kashmir.

– Mohammad Sadiq, future chief minister

'A Dream Come True,' is the heading of the chapter in Sheikh Abdullah's memoirs recalling the adoption of the resolution changing the name of the party he had formed and led for seven years, the Kashmir Muslim Conference, to National Conference. The final vote came after midnight on the night of 11–12 June 1939, indicating the protracted discussion on the issue. Although eventually passed by 173 votes to three, the outcome was not without hiccups. The debate went through all the stages and democratic procedures required to ensure that the final resolution could be seen to reflect the views of a majority of the members.

The manner in which critics were gradually won over and the discussions orchestrated with other political developments were testimony to Abdullah's skill and tactical leadership. Excerpts from his speeches and statements in the crucial months before his dream came true indicate a carefully measured advance towards his target. He did not monopolize the rostrum; other leaders presided over key sessions.

The process of secularization began, as noted in a previous chapter, with Abdullah's address to the inaugural session of the Muslim

Conference in October 1932, that it was not designed to be a communal body but to express popular grievances. The first move to reshape it on secular lines was taken in March 1933 when a subcommittee was formed to suggest ways of uniting Hindus and Muslims. Not much came of it, but the publication of *Hamdard* in 1935 and Prem Nath Bazaz's efforts brought the issue to the forefront. The influence of the secular ideology of the Congress party in India was represented by the invitation to the Congress leader, Dr Saifuddin Kitchlew, to inaugurate the journal.

At its earliest sessions, the Muslim Conference focused on the objective of achieving responsible government. In 1934, it proposed that a constitution be drafted for this purpose to be submitted to the maharaja for his approval. Hindus were invited to join the movement, but few responded. Interestingly, Chaudhry Ghulam Abbas, the Jammu leader who later broke away, assured them that the struggle to achieve the rights of Muslims had not been initiated to deprive Hindus of their legitimate rights. Reduction in taxes would benefit both. 'Let us therefore,' he concluded, 'join hands and struggle for the emancipation of our country. I hope that, for the good of the country, the Hindu leaders will consider my appeal with courage and sincerity.'[1]

However, *Daily Martand*, the organ of the Hindu Yuvak Sabha, was not convinced. It described the Muslim Conference as an 'organization of communalist Muslims ... established with the idea of crushing Hindus'. Its members were advised to quit the Conference and establish a truly national body.[2] However, response to the appeal of the Muslim Conference to observe a Responsible Government Day on 8 May 1936 was different. According to Bazaz, 'at many places, notably Srinagar, Poonch and Jammu, presidents of the public meetings held in this connection, as also the principal speakers, were either Hindus or Sikhs'.[3]

OBSTACLES OVERCOME

The move to change the name of the Muslim Conference gathered force but obstacles remained. Moving a resolution for this purpose at a meeting of the Working Committee in Jammu in January 1938,

Maulana Syed Masoodi endorsed the objective no less enthusiastically than Abdullah:

> The people of Jammu and Kashmir State are in favour of the establishment of an organization that will lead them, irrespective of religion, creed, race and colour, on the path of progress and prosperity ... Now the time has approached when the biggest and State-wide organization of the Muslim Conference should call upon its non-Muslim countrymen to join its fold so that the aim of unity between the two communities is achieved. This will illumine us as a nation.

The resolution could not, however, be passed because last-ditch critics insisted that under the party constitution such a major change could only be made at the annual session of the Conference, with at least a two-thirds majority of members present and voting.

Abdullah added his presidential weight to the move at the annual session of the Muslim Conference in Jammu on 26 March. He amplified the case for attracting Hindus and Sikhs to join the organization, emphasizing the common conditions of the peasantry:

> Like us the large majority of Hindus and Sikhs in the State have immensely suffered at the hands of irresponsible government. They are also steeped in deep ignorance, have to pay large taxes and are in debt and starving. Establishment of responsible government is as much a necessity for them as for us ... The main problem therefore now before us is to organize joint action and a united front ... This will require rechristening of our organization as a non-communal political body ... Firstly, we must end communalism by ceasing to think in terms of Muslims and non-Muslims when discussing our political problems. Secondly, there must be universal suffrage on the basis of joint electorates.[4]

Most members supported him but some objected. Abdul Majid Qureshi feared that the more aware and educationally advanced Pandits would takeover and exploit the organization. He accused Hindus and Sikhs of opposing Muslim interests. Some others took the same line. Abdullah intervened, suggesting that public opinion be sought. The decisive majority he sought still seemed beyond his grasp.

However, events in the remaining months of 1938 accelerated the process. His meeting with Nehru at the start of the year, and involvement in the States Peoples Conference, influenced the final outcome. Abdullah's leadership was strengthened by the overwhelming victory won by the Muslim Conference in the Assembly elections in April. Mirwaiz Yusuf Shah's Azad Muslim Conference had been decisively defeated. In a statement to the press, Abdullah said:

> Now that we have succeeded in gathering together all Muslims under one banner, we are more worried than before about the minorities' problem. The problem still awaits solution and it should be decided by some peaceful means. The prevailing circumstances and the need of the time demand that we must change the basic constitution of our organization in such a way as to accommodate all freedom fighters in the wider range of our movement so that all of us are enabled to wage a joint struggle for the achievement of our freedom ... Being in the majority, it is our sacred duty as Muslims that we should continue our efforts to win the confidence of the minorities.

On 28 June Abdullah went on to place a resolution before the Working Committee. The text read:

> Whereas in the opinion of the Working Committee the time has now come when all the progressive forces in the country should be rallied under one banner to fight for the achievement of responsible government, the Working Committee recommends to the General Council that in the forthcoming session of the Conference that name and the constitution of the organization be so altered and amended that all such people who desire to participate in this political struggle may easily become members of the Conference irrespective of their caste, creed and religion.

The resolution was adopted by fourteen votes to four. Among the dissenters were Chaudhary Ghulam Abbas, who kept changing his stand, and Abdul Majid Qureishi. They reiterated the view that it was premature for the committee to recommend changing the constitution.

NATIONAL DEMAND

Political activity was not limited to discussions in the Muslim Conference. On 29 August, representatives of other communities signed a joint manifesto called the National Demand to achieve responsible government and social reform. 'Our movement has a gigantic urge behind it,' it began. 'It is the urge of hunger and starvation which propels it onwards in the most adverse circumstances.' The only remedy for the miserable plight of the people was a basic change in the system of government. The list of twelve prominent signatories was headed by Abdullah. It included the familiar names of M.M. Sayeed, G.M. Sadiq, Mian Ahmed Yar, Mirza Afzal Beg, Pandit Kashyap Bandhu, Sardar Budh Singh, Pandit Jia Lal Kilam, Bakshi Ghulam Mohammad, Sham Lal Saraf, Shamboo Nath Peshin, and Prem Nath Bazaz.[5]

The National Demand was praised by Nehru but sparked strong criticism from Muslim and Hindu conservatives in the state. Eighteen non-Muslim MLAs issued a statement that it did not reflect their will. To accept the demand without guaranteed protection for the minorities, they felt, was equal to accepting purely Muslim rule. At the other extreme, Mirwaiz Yusuf Shah and other Muslim leaders critical of Abdullah suggested that a branch of the Muslim League be opened in Kashmir to counter such pro-Congress activities.

The imminent change in the name and membership of the Muslim Conference, coupled with Abdullah's close relations with the Congress, provoked Jinnah to react. In an address at Aligarh University, he said:

> I can say with certainty that he [Abdullah] is in the wrong. Having got himself ensnared by the Congress, which is thoroughly a Hindu organization, he has put the ship of his

> community in a whirlpool. I understand that he is doing this out of ignorance and some misunderstanding.

A group of students expressed the same view in Srinagar and distributed pamphlets and posters warning Muslims against what was described as the turncoat attitude of Abdullah and his colleagues. Others insisted that the continuance of the Muslim Conference was essential to safeguard Muslim interests, which would be ignored under responsible government.

Abdullah responded by contrasting the Congress policy of supporting the people's movement against princely autocracy with the Muslim League's policy of non-interference. Quoting Jinnah's statement that the Hindu majority in British India should win the confidence of the minority to achieve independence, he asked why was it then wrong for him to try win over the Hindu and Sikh minority in Kashmir.[6]

The maharaja's government too was shaken by the prospect of Muslims winning over a section of the Hindus, especially the intellectuals, on whose loyalty it depended. It responded with a wave of repression during which Abdullah, Abbas, and Bazaz were jailed. As recalled by Bazaz, 'Although among those put behind the prison bars were such respected people as municipal commissioners, lawyers, journalists, doctors, leading businessmen and college students, yet the Government called them goondas'.[7] They were released in February 1939. Jia Lal Kilam confirmed that a hundred Pandits were among the thousand jailed, including himself, Kashyap Bandhu, Shyam Lal Saraf, Janki Nath Zutshi, and other Pandit leaders.[8]

When the General Council of the Muslim Conference met on 29 April 1939 to consider the amendment changing the name, the meeting was disrupted by a group of students. It, however, reassembled the following day and decided to hold a special session of the Conference for the passage of the amendment. Three days later the council met again to hear the views of provincial members. A heated discussion followed, with several members opposing the change on the ground that Muslims were backward and would lose out, but it was decided to go ahead.

HISTORIC SESSION

Processions in Srinagar, decorated with arches named after Congress and Kashmiri leaders, heralded the historic special session finally held at Pathar Masjid on 10 and 11 June 1939. Abdullah read out a message of greetings from Jawaharlal Nehru, but left the principal speeches to others. Ghulam Mohammad Sadiq presided, and non-Muslim leaders were invited to participate. Sadiq rose to the occasion. 'This day will be written in golden letters in the history of Jammu and Kashmir,' he declared. Placing it in the context of developments in the subcontinent, he said politics in the state would influence developments in other princely states. Recalling Quranic precedents, Maulana Masoodi pointed out that Islam permitted Muslims to enter into alliances with non-Muslims.

Among the leaders who, surprisingly, supported the amendment was Chaudhary Ghulam Abbas. The movement was in its infancy in 1931, he said, and now it was time to mature. It was necessary for all communities to be on a common platform to put an end to the unresponsive character of the state government. He advised delegates not to be misled by slogans of Islam in danger raised by reactionaries. Another prominent leader, Mirza Afzal Beg, reiterated the point that in Kashmir it was the duty of the Muslims to gain the confidence of minorities.

Though outnumbered, the opponents were not silenced. Chaudhury Hamidullah Khan summed up their arguments: non-Muslims, who formed just twenty per cent of the population but held ninety per cent of the government jobs, were unlikely to cooperate. He insisted that whatever had been gained by Muslims so far had been due to the efforts of the Muslim Conference. The National Conference would not be able to work for Muslims.

Eventually, the National Conference resolution was passed well after midnight, and Abdullah could claim an overwhelming victory. The long-debated motion to change the name of the Jammu and Kashmir Muslim Conference was adopted by a massive majority of one hundred and seventy-five votes to three. The party flag—a plough inscribed over a red background—symbolized the effort to portray itself as a movement committed to revolutionizing the appalling condition of the peasantry, the bulk of the people of the state.

The move away from religious associations had a cascading impact. Mir Qasim recalls Abdullah successfully advising students in the early 1940s to wind up the Muslim Bloc in Sri Pratap College in Srinagar. Mir Qasim was a student there and Abdullah a former student. Some thirty-five years later he would relinquish the office of chief minister of the state to enable Abdullah to take over. The impact was not limited to Kashmir. Mir Qasim went on, like Abdullah, to study at Aligarh University where Kashmiri students in the Jammu and Kashmir Muslim Students Union had rejected the attempt of a Pandit student to join. A campaign led to changing the name to Jammu and Kashmir Aligarh Students Union, with membership open to all.[9]

---

1 Prem Nath Bazaz, *Kashmir in Crucible,* Pamposh Publications, New Delhi, pp. 171–83.

2 Khan, pp. 324–25.

3 Prem Nath Bazaz, *Inside Kashmir,* Kashmir Publishing Co., Srinagar, 1941, pp. 191–92.

4 Ibid., p. 68.

5 Ibid., pp. 348–52.

6 Khan, pp. 370–74.

7 Bazaz, pp. 197–98.

8 Jia Lal Kilam, *A History of Kashmiri Pandits,* pp. 300–01.

9 Mir Qasim, *My Life and Times,* Allied Publishers, New Delhi, 1992, pp. 14, 19.

NAYA KASHMIR

When I, after careful consideration, suggested that the Mussalmans should organize themselves under one flag and on one platform, not only was my advice not acceptable to Sheikh Abdullah but, as is his habit, which has become second nature to him, he indulged in all sort of language of a most offensive and vituperative character in attacking me.

– Mohammad Ali Jinnah[1]

The first annual session of the National Conference was held in Baramulla from 27–29 September 1940. Sardar Budh Singh was elected president, but the enthusiasm evoked by the birth of the National Conference three months earlier was flagging. Expectations had been aroused amongst both the Muslim and Pandit communities; critics in them insisted that nothing had changed. Educated Muslims who had hoped that they would have access to more government jobs found no sign of improvement.

Meanwhile, the Second World War had broken out earlier in September. It had far-reaching consequences, altering the political landscape of the subcontinent and reshaping the future of Jammu & Kashmir. When the viceroy, Lord Linlithgow, announced India's participation in the war without consulting the Congress or other parties, the Congress resolved not to cooperate in the war effort. Congress ministries in the provinces resigned. This came after repeated efforts by Jawaharlal Nehru and other leaders to convince the viceroy that they shared British repugnance for Hitler and Nazism, but could only participate in a war for freedom if India's freedom was included in the Allied war aims. Linlithgow, however, a large man, was adamant, provoking Nehru's acid comment on him, as 'heavy of body and slow of mind, solid as a rock with almost a rock's lack of awareness'.[2] The Cripps Mission sent by the British Government in 1942 to discuss India's future failed partly due to differences between him and the viceroy.

The Muslim League, however, cooperated fully with the government and the viceroy responded. It was afforded facilities and encouragement while restrictions were placed on the Congress. Assembling in Lahore in March 1940, it adopted the resolution on Pakistan that eventually led to the partition of British India. As noted earlier, the concept of a separate, autonomous homeland for Muslims, including Kashmir, had been proposed by Mohammad Iqbal in 1930, but not in a way that conflicted with Hindu sentiment. The target was autonomy rather than independence. The name Pakistan was conceived by Rahmat Ali, then a student in Cambridge, in 1933. Now, with the advantages gained by the war and the possibility of independence under discussion, it was refined into a specific demand bearing the stamp of Mohammad Ali Jinnah's legal and political expertise:

> Resolved that it is the considered view of this session of the All-India Muslim League that no constitutional plan would be workable in this country or acceptable to the Muslims unless it is designed on the following principle, viz., that geographically contiguous units are demarcated into regions which should be so constituted with such territorial adjustments as may be necessary, that the areas in which the Muslims are numerically in a majority, as in the north-western and eastern zones of India, should be grouped to constitute "independent States" in which the constituents shall be autonomous and sovereign.

Kashmir was part of the north-western zone and constituted the 'K' in Pakistan. The 'P' for Punjab became a base for operations in Jammu & Kashmir.

A charge against Abdullah that gained some support in the newly-formed National Conference was that he was getting too close to the Congress. The accepted party line was to take a middle course between it and the Muslim League. In March 1940 he had attended the Ramgarh session of the Congress, though it was followed by a visit to the League's Lahore session. A prominent personality who resigned from the National Conference on the charge that it was too cosy with the Congress was the Jammu leader, Ghulam Abbas. He went on to reconstitute the Muslim Conference in Jammu and form 'Azad Kashmir' in areas taken over by Pakistan in 1948.

The influx of Hindus and Sikhs into the Conference worried a section of the Muslims that the dominance they enjoyed in the Muslim Conference would be lost. Besides, a gesture made by Abdullah to Hindus on the sensitive issue of language and script increased their concern. He sponsored a resolution at the Mirpur session of the National Conference Working Committee urging inclusion of Hindustani as one of the compulsory subjects for the Kashmir civil service examination, with 'facility to be given to the candidates to use either Persian or Devanagari scripts, as they like'. It was a departure from the existing official language of the state which was Urdu in the Persian script.

'A MUSLIM FIRST'

Under concerted attack, Abdullah felt it advisable to revive his base and re-establish his Muslim credentials. He began to take particular interest in Islamic projects, including the renovation of the famous Hazratbal Mosque and in the Islamic Endowments Committee that maintained the many mosques and shrines in the Valley. Reiterating his Muslim beliefs, he uttered a phrase that embarrassed some of his Pandit colleagues. This was to the effect that Islam was the sun and other religions stars. The liberal Pandit leaders, Jia Lal Kilam and Kashyap Bandhu, were offended and offered to resign but Abdullah was not apologetic. Questioned at a Conference Working Committee meeting in April 1940, he is reported to have insisted that he was a 'Muslim first and Muslim last'.[3]

This was interpreted as a reversal of his anti-communal stand by his critics in Kashmir and beyond. In reality it was no more than a statement by a devout Muslim of the superiority of the creed in which he believed. In his memoirs, Abdullah recalls that some notable Pandits 'having protested against several practices followed at our meetings', sent in their resignations. 'They presented their objections to my religious orientation before Pandit Nehru who rejected it with the contempt it deserved ... On my part, I had to face the Muslim opposition ... In Jammu, the leaders of the National Conference were vacillating.'

Abdullah's predicament, which was to continue, was effectively expressed: 'We were being pulverized, caught in the obscurantist grinding mill-stones of the Hindus and the Muslims.'[4]

Nehru's ten-day tour in May repaired some of the damage, but at the cost of offending the more conservative Pandit leaders. He reiterated his advice that they should not expect special privileges but make common cause with the Muslim majority. This offset the charge that the Congress favoured Hindus, but Ghulam Abbas and the hard core members of the Muslim Conference were not impressed. They were receptive to the emerging Muslim League line on achieving Pakistan.

Developments in the subcontinent also began to favour the League. With the British government refusing to consider its demand for Indian independence as a war aim and that a national government be set up in India to fight it, the Congress was now preparing for a non-violent confrontation. The viceroy was adamant. In a message to Lord Zetland, the secretary of state for India in London, he is quoted as stating: 'I am not too keen to start talking about a period after which British rule would have ceased in India. I suspect that is very remote and I feel the least we say about it in all probability is the better.'[5]

However, the entry of Japan into the war and the rapid advance of its forces into Southeast Asia raised second thoughts. The Cripps Mission was sent by London to negotiate with Indian leaders, but to no avail. The entire Congress leadership was detained after the adoption of the Quit India resolution on 9 August 1942. They were consequently unable to counter the League's propaganda to which the British allowed free play.

Abdullah was also accused by his critics of being too close to the communists. His radical views on social change meshed with theirs and some of their leading intellectuals, notably B.P.L. and Freda Bedi, stayed in Srinagar and helped draft his programmes. Their influence was reflected in the language of the resolution adopted by the National Conference after Germany attacked the Soviet Union in 1941. It spoke in familiar terms of the need for 'global defeat of fascist and oppressive powers', that made it 'imperative that the people of Kashmir should help to defeat the world's fascist powers'. However, when the government suppressed the Quit India movement, the Conference did not follow the diktat of the Communist Party of India to continue to support the government. Its Working Committee condemned 'the reign of terror and repression which the Government of India have launched by declaring the Indian National Congress illegal, by the arrest of leaders, and by shooting down unarmed people'.

JINNAH IN SRINAGAR

In 1944, the Japanese threat to India receded and speculation revived about the future of the subcontinent after the war. The Congress leaders were still in detention while the Muslim League campaign for Pakistan was in high gear. Abdullah thought it advisable to consult Jinnah, and met him in Delhi together with his lieutenant, Bakshi Ghulam Mohammad. He had hoped that Jinnah would bridge the differences between him and Ghulam Abbas, who had revived the Muslim Conference.[6] Jinnah arrived in Srinagar on 10 May and stayed for two months. The visit began with an enthusiastic reception at Banihal Pass and the League supremo spent much of the time recuperating from the heat of north India. The amity did not however last. Soon Jinnah was asking all Muslims to unite under the Muslim Conference to which Abdullah replied that the 'ills of this land can be remedied only by carrying Hindus, Muslims and Sikhs together'. The exchange became abusive, with Jinnah calling the National Conference a band of gangsters and Abdullah warning him not to interfere in state politics.

In a farewell statement, Jinnah maintained:

> When I, after careful consideration, suggested that the Mussalmans should organize themselves under one flag and on one platform, not only was my advice not acceptable to Sheikh Abdullah but, as is his habit, which has become second nature to him, he indulged in all sort of language of a most offensive and vituperative character in attacking me.[7]

Abdullah issued a statement on 24 June charging Jinnah with violating the spirit in which he was received in Kashmir. His defence of the National Conference is worth reproducing:

> As for the National Conference, we certainly owe no apologies to Mr Jinnah. Starting the Muslim Conference as a sectional organization in 1932, we passed on to higher stage of political evolution in 1939. Thus we passed Mr Jinnah's milestone over five years ago. Viewing the position from an all-India perspective, we find that Mr Jinnah has repeatedly declared that he does not extend his plans of Pakistan to the Indian States. Thus his conception of Islamic sovereignty halts at the customs barrier which divides our State from British India. Yet when it comes to giving advice, Mr Jinnah trespasses his own boundaries.

The bond between Nehru and Abdullah revived after the Congress leaders were freed from detention in June 1945, having been detained since August 1942. The Second World War was virtually won; Japan was atom-bombed into surrender on 15 August. However, Britain too had been economically devastated by five years of war and could no longer police its empire, notwithstanding Winston Churchill's fulminations. Talks on the transfer of power began in Simla. With Jinnah implacably committed to the two-nation theory to justify Pakistan, the role of Abdullah was crucial to counter his thesis that it had the acceptance of all the Muslims in the subcontinent.

Therefore, two months after they were freed, Nehru, accompanied by Maulana Abul Kalam Azad (then Congress president) attended the annual session of the National Conference in Srinagar. With them was the Frontier Gandhi and well-known Muslim leaders, including Mian Iftikharuddin (who drifted to Pakistan), Asaf Ali, and Samad Khan Achakzai. The presence of an array of prominent Muslim leaders of the subcontinent strengthened Abdullah's hand. He organized the traditional boat procession for them through Srinagar, with decorated boats rowed by oarsmen in bright liveries and additional boats carrying folk musicians trailing behind them. At one place on the river, followers of Mirwaiz Yusuf Shah, Abdullah's principal opponent in the Valley, threw stones and hurled abuses, but were prevented from disturbing the river procession by National Conference cadres.

Abdullah was rewarded by the praise he received. Badshah Khan described him as a 'gift of God' and Azad said that 'nature has bestowed on this country an able and great leader in Sheikh Abdullah'. Nehru declared, to cheers, that Kashmir was in his blood and stamped on his head and heart. He went on to again advise the Pandits to join the National Conference in large numbers and thus influence its decisions; otherwise no safeguards or weightage could protect them.

LAND TO THE TILLER

Apart from Azad, who was ill, all the leaders were present at the Sopore session of the National Conference in September 1944. There, Abdullah unfolded the comprehensive 'Naya [New] Kashmir' manifesto, diverting attention away from religious politicking to social change. Drafted mostly by the leftist intellectuals in the party and advisers, it bore the stamp of the most liberal political philosophy of the 1930s. It even included the objective of equal rights for women, unique in any Muslim society. Radical in content, it stopped short of advocating a revolution against the maharaja, to whom the document was submitted.

The most revolutionary and popular pledge was abolition of landlordism and distribution of land to the tiller. Even Nehru had been unable to persuade the Congress to go this far. The reform was to be carried out, though it provided a handle against Abdullah because most of the landlords were Hindu and tenants Muslim. It also aroused concern among Congress conservatives, Sardar Patel prominent among them, who feared it could serve as a model. Naya Kashmir also promised free universal education, which was implemented when the National Conference came to power; the right to work; equality of opportunity and popular democratic institutions at all levels.

The language of the manifesto was reminiscent of the idealistic declarations of social change in any country, and was almost Nehruvian in tone. It was intended:

> ... to perfect our union in the fullest equality and self-determination, to raise ourselves and our children forever from the abyss of oppression and poverty, degradation and superstition, from medieval darkness and ignorance, into the sunlit valleys of plenty, ruled by freedom, science and honest toil ...

The provision for women's rights could scarcely be improved upon today:

> Women citizens shall be accorded equal rights with men in all fields of national life: economic, cultural, political, and in the state services. These rights shall be realized by affording women the right to work in every employment upon equal terms and for equal wages with men. Women shall be ensured rest, social insurance and education equally with men. The law shall give special protection to the interests of mother and child.

After Sopore, Abdullah rewarded Nehru with an excursion to the mountains, Nehru's first holiday after his long incarceration, reminiscent of his first visit to his homeland in 1912.

---

1 Bazaz, *History of the Struggle for Freedom in Kashmir*, Pamposh Publications, New Delhi, 1967, p. 212.

2 Jawaharlal Nehru, *Discovery of India,* Calcutta, 1946, p. 437.

3 Nagin Bazaz, op. cit., pp. 68–69.

4 *Flames,* pp. 50–51.

5 Cited by Sarvepalli Gopal, *Jawaharlal Nehru: A Biography,* vol. I, Oxford University Press, Bombay, p. 263.

6 *Flames,* pp. 59–60.

7 Bazaz, *History of the Struggle for Freedom in Kashmir,* Pamposh Publications, New Delhi, 1967, p. 212.

DISENCHANTMENT WITH THE CONGRESS

We saw the fires burning in the Punjab and heard every day of the killings. The plan for partition offered a way out and we took it . . . We expected that partition would be temporary, that Pakistan was bound to come back to us.

– Jawaharlal Nehru

The Sopore session of the National Conference in September 1945 was held after the British government's plans to transfer power to Indian hands were announced by King George VI. He would no longer be emperor of India. The king announced that 'his Government are determined to do their utmost to promote in conjunction with the leaders of Indian opinion the early realization of full self-government for India'. This was followed on 21 August by the announcement that elections would be held in India that winter. Soon after, the then viceroy, Field Marshal Lord Archibald Wavell, stated that he would hold discussions with the elected representatives on the formation of a constitution-making body. Discussions would also be held with representatives of the Indian states on how best they could participate in the constitution-making body; they would henceforth no longer enjoy the protection of the paramount power. The largest among them was Jammu & Kashmir.

A distinct difference soon surfaced between Muslim League

confidence that Pakistan would be achieved and Congress vacillation on the issue. Partition was no longer being opposed in principle. In September itself, the Congress Working Committee had prepared the ground for retreat by adopting a resolution reiterating unity as an ideal, but with the significant proviso that unity did not imply 'compelling the people of any territorial unit to remain in an Indian Union against their declared and established will'. As historian R.C. Majumdar observed, 'The impending elections served, in a sense, to clear the political sky in India. The Muslims outside the Muslim League could clearly feel which way the wind was blowing and flocked to the standard of the League.'[1]

SYMPATHY FOR PAKISTAN

Abdullah was only too conscious of these trends. Notwithstanding the public display of amity with the Congress leaders at Sopore, he did not wish to give the impression that he was a camp follower, drawing attention to the Congress failure to attract Muslims. Addressing the 'esteemed Maulana Sahib' (Azad was Congress president), he said:

> We would like to know why it is that despite the sacrifices made by the Congress, the greatness of its leaders, and undeniable urge for freedom among Muslims, so few of them are with the Congress. We strongly urge the need for a changed attitude. It is your responsibility to assess the modus operandi of the Muslim League and other Muslim organizations. Its just demands must be conceded.[2]

He had earlier regretted the failure of the Congress to reach agreement with the League on forming a coalition government after the 1937 elections in the United Provinces, a failure to which some historians trace the beginnings of Jinnah's insistence on Partition.[3] In his memoirs, Abdullah admits to 'a subconscious sympathy for the slogan "Pakistan" because it was a Muslim reaction against Hindu communalism. However, I realized that it was perhaps only an emotional response, and likely to harm Muslim interests more than a reasonable one would. I regarded the demand for Pakistan an escapist device.' Lest he be misunderstood, he goes on add that at the Mirpur session of the

National Conference, he made a point of stating in his presidential address that 'India is our homeland and it shall always remain so'.[4] His doubts about the Congress were however soon vindicated.

The results of the elections held in British India at the end of the year confirmed the League's optimism. Except in the North-West Frontier Province, it won the majority of the seats reserved for Muslims in the provinces and all the seats in the Central Legislature. It claimed to speak for the majority of Muslims in British India, though in fact the electorate was limited to the upper-income thirty per cent of the population. Contributing to the Congress failure was lacklustre campaigning. Nehru's biographer notes, 'leaders at every level were tired, unenthusiastic and pulling in contrary directions. Jawaharlal did a little campaigning but nothing like his effort of ten years before.'[5]

The mood of the Congress leadership in the crucial period leading up to Partition was later expressed by Nehru himself in an interview with the British author, Leonard Mosley. He is reported as admitting:

> The truth is that we were tired men, and we were getting on in years too. Few of us could stand the prospect of going to prison again—and if we stood out for a united India as we wished it, prison obviously awaited us. We saw the fires burning in the Punjab and heard every day of the killings. The plan for partition offered a way out and we took it ... We expected that partition would be temporary, that Pakistan was bound to come back to us.[6]

In actuality the killings multiplied after Partition. Nehru's unrealistic assumption that Pakistan would return to the fold proved self-delusory. Gandhi alone remained firmly opposed to Partition.

Abdullah shared the disenchantment of Muslim leaders who had stood by the Congress. The seniormost was Maulana Azad who later blamed Nehru, and more strongly Vallabhbhai Patel, for conceding to Partition. The views expressed by Azad in his autobiography, *India Wins Freedom*, about their approach to the last round of negotiations that led to Partition are relevant in interpreting their differing subsequent approaches to the Kashmir issue:

> I found that Patel was so much in favour of partition that he was hardly prepared to listen to any other point of view. For over two hours I argued with him ... Partition would not solve the communal problem but make it a permanent feature of the country. Jinnah had raised the slogan of two nations. To accept partition was to accept that slogan ... I was surprised and pained when Patel in reply said that whether we liked it or not, there were two nations in India. He was not convinced that Muslims and Hindus could be united into one nation ...
>
> I now turned to Jawaharlal. He did not speak of partition in the way that Patel did. In fact, he admitted that partition was by nature wrong. He had however lost all hopes of joint action ... It was clear that in spite of his repugnance to the idea of partition, he was coming to the conclusion day by day that there was no alternative.[7]

Abdullah's views about the treatment of Khan Abdul Ghaffar (Badshah) Khan, the Frontier Gandhi, who had performed the near-miracle of transforming gun-bearing Pathan tribesmen into his non-violent Khudai Khidmatgar followers, is revealing. Under Badshah Khan's leadership the Muslim North-West Frontier Province had supported the Congress and elected Azad to the central legislature. However, after the Congress leaders bowed to Partition, the tide turned and the Muslim League won a plebiscite, with the Khudai Khidmatgars abstaining. Abdullah notes: 'Badshah Khan felt betrayed, hence he presented his demand for including an independent Pakhtoonistan (along with Pakistan and India) in the proposed plebiscite. He felt he could offer no moral justification for his people to join India.'

The reference to an independent Pakhtoonistan echoed Abdullah's own hopes for Kashmir, though he knew that he had no option but to depend on Nehru and Gandhi. In a further passage he seems to project his own frustrations through Badshah Khan:

> Despite the increasing odds against him, Khan Abdul Ghaffar Khan continued to oppose the two-nation theory. He claimed that more than the League, the leadership of the Congress was responsible for the partition of the country and the creation of Pakistan. He believed that the Congress aimed to create an essentially Hindu State and did not relish the idea of many Muslims joining the Congress. The Congress leaders had pointed accusing fingers at the Muslim leadership as the harbingers of partition; they failed to see that the Congress was also partly responsible.[8]

With a touch of irony, he added: 'The first anti-partition front opened in Kashmir, which had a majority of Muslims. In fact it was they who single-handedly confronted the Pakistani expansionists before any armed reinforcements arrived from the Centre.'

Abdullah shared the disappointment of Azad and Abdul Ghaffar Khan with the easy acceptance of Partition by the Congress leaders, but he was placed differently. As residents of British India, they were subject to decisions negotiated between the viceroy and the Congress and Muslim League leaders. He was the resident of a princely state that was not bound by these decisions.

The 1945, election results had thrown up a significant aspect of the upper-class Muslim response to the League's propaganda in British India, from which lessons could be drawn in Jammu & Kashmir, though the state did not participate in them. Muslims in provinces in which they were in a minority, like the United Provinces, tended to vote for the League. However, where they were in a majority, as in the Punjab and NWFP, they did not. This suggested that Muslims were uneasy in areas in which they were in a minority, but were less attracted to the League's two-nation theory where they were in a majority.

This strengthened Abdullah's conviction that the two-nation theory could be countered by emphasizing Kashmir's separate *kashmiryat* identity as Muslims were in an overwhelming majority. That was the basis for the popularity of the National Conference. The situation could, however, change should there be apprehensions of Hindu domination from within or outside the state. Much would depend on the powers enjoyed by the Centre after independence. The arrival in India of the three-man British Cabinet Mission, in March 1946, indicated that time was running out.

Hari Singh had done his utmost to demonstrate his loyalty to the British crown during the Second World War. His state contributed heavily in men and arms to the war effort. State troops saw action in the Middle East and Italy. Awarded in return with the honorary rank of major general, he toured the war front in Europe. He was accorded a popular reception on his return to Srinagar in July 1944, in which the National Conference participated. The appointment of N. Gopalaswami Ayyangar, a talented, soft-spoken civil servant from Madras, as prime minister had suggested a renewed effort to take steps towards popular rule. He involved National Conference workers in arrangements for the distribution of essential commodities that had become scarce in wartime. The same approach was attempted by his successor, Sir Benegal N. Rao.

In October, after his return from the front in full uniform, the maharaja announced the appointment of two MLAs, a Muslim from Kashmir and a Hindu from Jammu, as ministers in an experiment in dyarchy. One of them was Mirza Afzal Beg, Abdullah's closest aide and an expert in constitutional law, then leader of the National Conference Assembly Party. The other was a little-known Ganga Ram.

Beg's initial response was enthusiastic. Speaking in the Assembly, he said: 'When we see that in spite of being able to put off any progress till some time in the future [in wartime], His Highness has come forward and conferred reforms on the people of the State, we feel sure of the intention which underlies the Command and of the unerring instinct for constitutional government that His Highness the Maharaja Bahadur possesses.'[9] This air of amity however soon evaporated. Ganga Ram was given the important portfolios of home and education; Beg got public works, for which he found there were inadequate funds and was unresponsive to his concerns. Friction increased, and in March 1946 Beg resigned.

Beg's resignation was the occasion for a switch in National Conference tactics. The underlying reason was the prospect of British withdrawal. Under dyarchy, the maharaja would continue to enjoy final authority in deciding the future of the state. Abdullah described the system of dyarchy as farcical and warned that this state of affairs would not be permitted to last.[10] Preparations for confrontation on a large scale began.

---

1 R.C. Mazumdar, *History of the Freedom Movement in India,* vol. III, Firma KLM Ltd, Calcutta, 1963, pp. 617–18.

2 *Flames,* p. 65.

3 Gopal, op. cit., pp. 226–28.

4 *Flames,* pp. 56–57.

5 Gopal, op. cit., p. 305.

6 Leonard, Mosley, *The Last Days of the British Raj,* Weidenfeld & Nicholson, London, 1962.

7 Maulana Abul Kalam, Azad, *India Wins Freedom,* Orient Longman, New Delhi, 1959, pp. 184–88.

8 Sonia Gandhi (ed.), *Two Alone: Two Together: Letters between Indira Gandhi and Jawaharlal Nehru (1940–64),* Hodder & Stoughton, London, 1992, pp. 532–34.

9 Cited by Dina Nath Raina in *Unhappy Kashmir: The Inside Story,* Reliance Publishing House, New Delhi, 1990, p. 29.

10 Cited in *Kashmir on Trial: State versus Sheikh Abdullah,* Lion Press, Lahore, 1946, pp. 4–6.

A lonely secularist: Sheikh Mohammad Abdullah

A formidable support: Jawaharlal Nehru on his first visit after accession of Jammu & Kashmir to India in 1947

Secular partnership: Jawaharlal Nehru addressing public at Lal Chowk in Srinagar

Bakshi Ghulam Mohammad being administered oath of office as deputy prime minister of Jammu & Kashmir by the Sadar-i-Riyasat Karan Singh while Sheikh Abdullah witnesses the oath ceremony

Lady Mountbatten being received by Sheikh Abdullah in 1947

Sheikh Abdullah addressing security forces in 1975

Sheikh Abdullah presents a momento to General K.M. Cariappa, Army Chief, as Bakshi Ghulam Mohammad, deputy prime minister of Jammu & Kashmir, witnesses the ceremony

After the revival of Jammu and Kashmir National Conference, the party held a convention at Jammu; its president, Sheikh Mohammad Abdullah, being taken out in a procession in Jammu's famous Raghu Nath Bazar 1975

Sheikh Abdullah attempted to maintain the secular sentiment in the valley by taking frequent tours

Dr Radhakrishnan the president of India takes the guard of honour

Below: The president of India, Dr Rajendra Prasad at a reception being hosted by prime minister Sheikh Abdullah at the famous Shalimar Gardens

Dr Radhakrishnan was given a boat reception on his visit to Jammu & Kashmir

8422
WG

Facing page (top): Sheikh Abdullah being shown round the Chittaranjan Railway Engine factory in West Bengal by Pandit Jawaharlal Nehru

Facing page (below): Sheikh Abdullah with Begum Abdullah at the factory; also seen in the picture are Girdari Lal Dogra and Balraj Puri

End of an Era: Sheikh Abdullah pays his last respect to Jawaharlal Nehru.

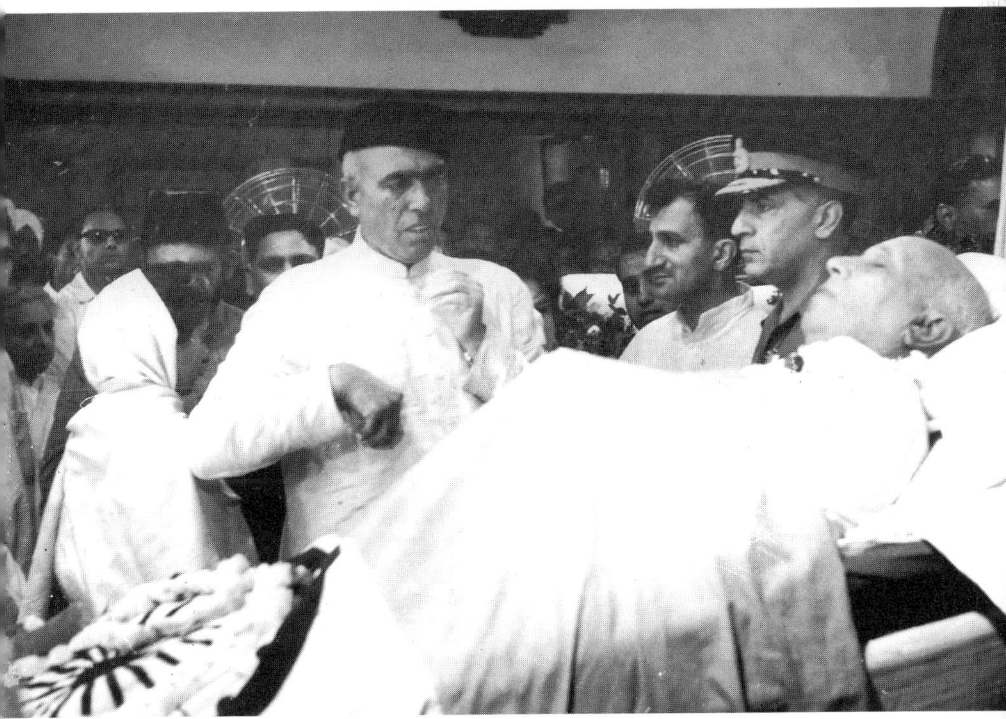

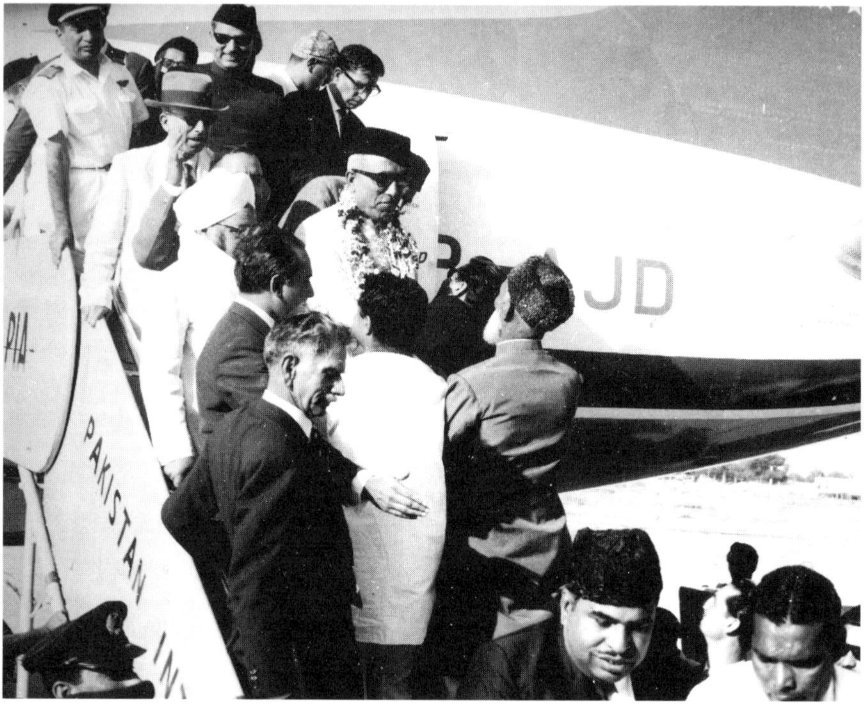

PIA
PAKISTAN IN
JD
LEB 5204

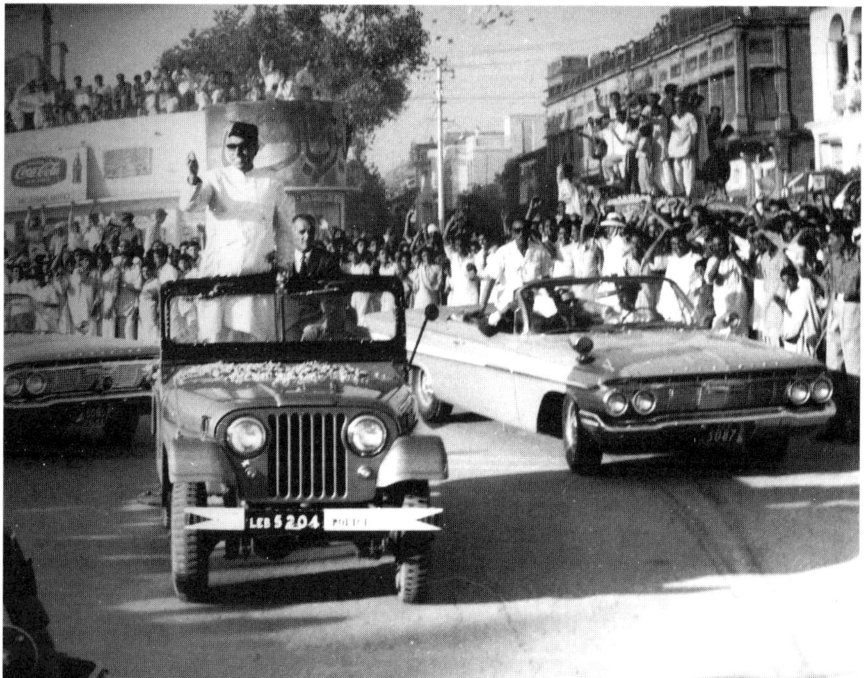

Sheikh Abdullah calls on the president of Pakistan, Mohammad Ayub Khan, at President's House; also seen in the picture is Mirza Mohammad Afzal Beg

Facing page (top): Sheikh Abdullah being welcomed by Zulfikar Ali Bhutto, foreign minister of Pakistan, and Khan Habibulla Khan, home minister of Pakistan, at Chaklala Airport, Rawalpindi, on 24 May 1964; also seen in the picture is Moulana Mohammad Yousuf Shah

Facing page (below): A grand reception: Sheikh Abdullah's procession passes through the main streets of Rawalpindi.

Sheikh Abdullah with Prime Minister Morarji Desai at a reception hosted at Kashmir House in New Delhi

Sheikh Abdullah with External Affairs Minister Atal Bihari Vajpayee

Chaudhary Charan Singh being received by Sheikh Abdullah at a reception

Sheikh Abdullah with Indira Gandhi

Sheikh Abdullah with his family at 3 Kotla Lane, Delhi, where he was detained in 1969

Sheikh Abdullah with music director Naushad and actress Nargis Dutt during his visit to Bombay

Sheikh Abdullah along with his family members on a visit to Goa

Tomb of Sher-e-Kashmir Sheikh Mohammad Abdullah, on the banks of Nagin Lake, Srinagar

(Pictures Courtesy: Sheikh Nazir Ahmad, General Secretary, Jammu and Kashmir National Conference)

QUIT KASHMIR

Naturally my Government had to take action and took it, with the result that Abdullah and a number of his little friends were arrested. At the time of his arrest, Abdullah was apparently on his way to see his Guru Jawaharlal and so Jawaharlal's personal vanity was greatly injured by the fact that his Lieutenant was arrested when on his way to take sanctuary with him. Being what he is, Jawaharlal has completely gone off the deep end.

– Maharaja Hari Singh in a letter to Victor Rosenthal

Sheikh Abdullah's aversion to the Dogra dynasty could not be contained when the British Cabinet Mission's negotiations on Indian independence raised the prospect of Maharaja Hari Singh determining the future of the state. He was in Lahore when he learnt that the mission had gone to Kashmir for a break from the summer heat in Delhi, and promptly sent a lengthy telegram addressed to Sir Stafford Cripps. Its essence was that Kashmir had been bought by the Dogras for a mere 75 lakh rupees in 1846, a hundred years earlier. The dynasty had no right to rule the state; its future should be decided by the people. Here are the extracts:

> Today the people of Kashmir cannot be pacified with only a representative system of governance. They want freedom. Total freedom from the autocratic Maharaja ... We challenge the political and moral status of this sale deed, this instrument of

> subjugation, handed by the East India Company to a bunch of Dogras ...
>
> This is a historic moment. The future of the Indian people is being determined, while the Cabinet Mission is working out a constitutional framework of the country. The right of accession is a contentious issue between the three parties, the people, the rulers and the federation. We Kashmiris have to put it in its historical perspective. A sale deed does not have the status of a treaty. Therefore after the British rule, Kashmir has the right to become independent. We Kashmiris want to inscribe our own destiny and we want the Cabinet Mission to reaffirm the correctness of our stand ...
>
> Ours in also a unique polity. We have a tradition of communal harmony and joint struggle. Consequently all communities and classes are supporting this joint national demand.

Abdullah followed this with public speeches declaring that the end of the British regime would mean an end to the rulers. He appealed to people to contribute one rupee each towards a collection of 75 lakhs so that they could buy back Kashmir's independence.[1] The slogan 'Quit Kashmir' was coined. However, in contrast to British India, where the British were asked to quit in 1942, here the target was the maharaja. Loyalists objected that Hari Singh could not be asked to abandon his own homeland, but Abdullah was convinced that it was time to demonstrate the power of the people.

Nehru wanted Abdullah to come to Delhi to brief him, but he was arrested on the way on 20 May 1946, and detained in Srinagar's Badami Bagh cantonment. Widespread demonstrations and arrests followed. The police opened fire and twenty deaths were officially admitted. National Conference leaders were arrested. Bakshi Ghulam Mohammad and G.M. Sadiq escaped to Lahore.

PRIME MINISTER KAK

The prime minister of the state, Ram Chandra Kak, told the press: 'We shall be ruthlessly firm and we make no apology about it.' A sharp, authoritarian bureaucrat, Pandit Kak had risen from the ranks and had the advantage of having married an Englishwoman who had been Yuvraj Karan Singh's governess. His role was controversial. Hari Singh presumably appointed him because he favoured independence for the state and balanced pressures from India by maintaining amicable relations with the leaders of the Muslim League. He was, however, identified with repression and was summarily removed from office on the eve of the creation of Pakistan.

Bakshi made his way to Delhi. After listening to him, Nehru reacted with a statement infused with the passion and sentiment he felt for Kashmir. Entitled 'Srinagar: Almost a City of the Dead', he vowed to stand by Abdullah:

> Everyone who knows Kashmir knows also the position of Sheikh Mohammad Abdullah there. He is the Sher-e-Kashmir, beloved of the remotest valleys of Kashmir. Numerous legends and popular songs have grown around his personality ... Does anyone think we were going to desert him or his comrades in Kashmir because the Kashmir State authorities have a few guns at their disposal? We shall stand by the people of Kashmir and their leaders in this heavy trial they are going through.

Nehru had reported for Lucknow's *National Herald* and developed a colourful reportorial style. His account of the situation in Kashmir was graphically written, but seems to have been drawn from the exaggerated accounts received from Bakshi, as longer excerpts show. His article, written without verification, reflected the impulsiveness he was apt to display on issues about which he felt strongly:

> The whole valley was handed over to military administration. The police, being Kashmiris, were withdrawn. A reign of terrorism and frightfulness then began, Kashmir has been practically cut off from the outside world since then. My information is that far more people than officially admitted have been killed. A much larger number who were wounded were sent to jails instead of hospitals.

> Srinagar is almost a city of the dead where movement is difficult and large numbers of people are practically interned in their own houses, apart from the many hundreds who have been put in prison. Clashes occur daily and even women have been shot down. But what is worse is the deliberate attempt, reminiscent of the martial law days in Punjab in 1919, to humiliate human beings. I understand that people are made to crawl in some of the streets, that sometimes they are made to take off their turbans to clean the streets and pavements, that they are made to shout at the point of the bayonet 'Maharaj ki jai'. Dead bodies are not being handed over to relatives for burial according to religious rites, but are soaked in petrol and burnt. The mosques, including the inner shrines have been occupied by the military. A wall of the Jama Masjid of Srinagar has been knocked down to make a passage for military lorries. A dangerous feature of the situation is the deliberate attempt to foment communal trouble.

Later, Nehru admitted that reports of dead bodies being burnt and the breaking of the Jama Masjid wall were exaggerated, but repeated the principal details in a letter to the viceroy, Lord Wavell, indirectly urging intervention. He wrote:

> So far as I can gather the State authorities are bent on breaking and crushing the spirit of the people and are using the army as if they were occupying recently conquered enemy territory ... If I went my first business would be to see some of my friends and colleagues in prison, notably Sheikh Mohammad Abdulla ... The problem of Kashmir has been causing me a lot of trouble and anxiety for I do not wish to do anything that might worsen an already bad situation. I have decided therefore to mention this to you, to find out how far the Political Department [of the viceroy's government] is involved in it. Obviously the Resident in Kashmir cannot be a neutral observer.

NEHRU'S ARREST

When he heard that Abdullah's trial would begin on 21 June, Nehru impetuously announced that he would defend him personally. Though decades had passed since he had received his legal degree from the Inner Temple in London, he was a qualified lawyer. He persisted even though denied permission to enter the state. Advancing by road from Rawalpindi, he was confronted by an armed police detachment at the state border at Kohala. After an angry five-hour confrontation, he was arrested and taken to the dak bungalow at Domel.

The arrest made headlines, with Nehru reported to having received a bayonet wound. Serious as it was, he treated the episode as high adventure and wrote to his daughter, Indira:

> ... we must offer thanks to the Kashmir Govt. for the astonishing folly with which it conducts it affairs. It tried to stop me at Kohala. It did not succeed. I spent five hours there getting more and more bored. Then we sallied out and faced the Kashmir police and pushed forward. I felt in my element as I always do when there is a question of forcing a barricade ... What an odd mixture is my life. There is talk of a Provisional Government and at the same time I am functioning as a lawbreaker!

His senior colleagues in the Congress had not welcomed his entering Kashmir. Negotiations with the viceroy for transfer of power were at an advanced stage and Nehru was expected to lead the interim government to be set up in August. He was however unfazed. In a second letter assuring Indira that he was unhurt, he wrote:

> I imagine I have managed to upset many an applecart. Well, what am I to do about it? If the Kashmir Govt. wants to behave with crass stupidity and discourtesy things will happen. I offered them an opportunity to adopt a correct course gracefully and without loss of dignity. They were too conceited to accept my suggestion which was merely to allow me to go to Srinagar for a day or two. I expressed my desire to meet the Maharaja. But no, they took a different course and now they will have to face the consequences.[2]

The Congress president, Maulana Azad, now stepped in. He arranged to phone Nehru at the dak bungalow where he had been detained and told him he should return to Delhi as soon as possible. It was not proper for him to insist on entering Kashmir at this stage. He would take up the Kashmir issue himself and work for the release of Abdullah. Nehru turned back. He was permitted to spend four days in Srinagar the following month, but with little effect on Abdullah's trial.

FROM HARI TO VICTOR

Hari Singh was in no mood to meet Nehru. He expressed his feelings in a letter to his close friend and confidante, Victor Rosenthal, a suave white Russian émigré who had attached himself to his court, but was then residing in Rangoon. The letter provides a rare glimpse into the inner thoughts of the maharaja, his reluctant admission of the seriousness of the situation, and his contempt for Nehru and Abdullah. A photocopy of the letter appears in *Kashmir on Trial*, a record of Abdullah's trial with an introduction by Nehru.[3] Hari Singh's letter to 'Dear Victor' is dated I June 1946. It reads:

> You have, no doubt, read in the papers about the trouble in Kashmir but it is not a thousandth part of what interested parties make it appear to be in the Press. The trouble started with the local demagogue, Abdullah, who is frankly communist and anti-State, suddenly discovering that he could not with impunity carry out his policy of disrupting the Government from within through the agency of his friend who had been appointed Minister [Afzal Beg] while simultaneously battering the Government from outside by making inflammatory speeches and levelling baseless accusations. Naturally my Government had to take action and took it, with the result that Abdullah and a number of his little friends were arrested. At the time of his arrest, Abdullah was apparently on his way to see his Guru Jawaharlal and so Jawaharlal's personal vanity was greatly injured by the fact that his Lieutenant was arrested when on his way to take sanctuary with him. Being what he is, Jawaharlal has completely gone off the deep end.

> Except for a day or two after Abdullah's arrest life here has been normal and everybody goes about his business. In one quarter of the town between the 3rd and the 4th bridges, a mosque has been converted into a political stage and two or three thousand people including women collect there daily ostensibly for prayers but in reality to keep the show of agitation alive by making inflammatory speeches and using objectionable slogans. We are keeping our cool up well and nobody interested in us need feel any anxiety. The movement was, of course, very dangerous but we have weathered the storm. In fact our main headache now is hostile and baseless criticism from Jawaharlal, but even his ranting must have a limit. In any case we are prepared for anything he may say or do—and we think he knows it—in fact in the end he may feel that discretion is the better part of valour and shut up, anyway we will fight and fight to the end. This is a test case for all the States.

The importance the Congress accorded the trial was demonstrated by sending two leading lawyers, Asaf Ali and Diwan Chaman Lal, to Srinagar for the defence. A local defence committee, headed by the eminent Pandit lawyer–politician Jia Lal Kilam, was set up. After a three-month trial, widely reported in India, Abdullah was sentenced to three years' imprisonment.

In his introduction to *Kashmir on Trial,* Nehru linked the Kashmir struggle with the ferment in other princely states and reiterated praise for Abdullah as 'the living and outstanding symbol of the urge of the Kashmir people for their freedom'. In the ultimate analysis, his trial was actually 'of the State authorities who had tried to stem the flowing river of the great popular movement'.

He added, significantly for the future, that the story of the struggle would continue 'till it reaches the logical end that can only be the establishment of freedom in Kashmir within the larger framework of a free and independent India'.[4] The introduction was dated 24 September 1946, after he had taken over as head of the interim national government, the office to which he had alluded in his letter to Indira while under detention by Hari Singh. It, however, took another year for

Nehru to become prime minister of independent India and secure Abdullah's release.

---

1 *Flames,* p. 79.

2 Sonia Gandhi (ed.), *Two Alone: Two Together: Letters Between Indira Gandhi and Jawaharlal Nehru (1940–64),* Hodder & Stoughton, London, 1992, pp. 523–34.

3 *State versus Sheikh Abdullah: Kashmir on Trial,* Lion Press, Lahore, 1947.

4 Ibid., Introduction.

THE LAST MAHARAJA

Recent events have shown that those who are likely to assume the reins of government in India in future are not disposed to show consideration for the security of the State and are prone to interfere and coerce even in regard to purely internal affairs on the flimsiest grounds. Not only that, agitators inside the State are encouraged if not invited to create trouble.

– Kashmir Prime Minister
Ram Chandra Kak to the viceroy

As the ruler of the largest princely state in the subcontinent, Lieutenant General His Highness Inder Mahandar Rejrajeshwer Mahadhiraj Sir Hari Singh, Jammu & Kashmir, Naresh Tatha Tibbet adi Deshadhipathi was fully conscious of his exalted position. He could lay claim to over 80,000 square miles of territory. Kashmir had an undefined border with the Tibet region of China and the Chinese province of Sinkiang; in Afghanistan, with only the narrow Wakhan tract separating it from the Soviet Union. Jammu was the seat of the hundred-year-old Dogra dynasty, with their summer capital in Srinagar. The prospect of independence after British withdrawal was tempting.

Hari Singh inherited the state in 1926. He implemented limited measures of democratic reform but continued to wield authoritarian powers and enjoy the luxurious life he had inherited. He had built himself a new palace in Srinagar, located on a ridge overlooking the Dal Lake, with an enchanting view extending to the Shalimar Gardens laid by Mughal Emperor Jahangir in the seventeenth century.

In his autobiography, Yuvraj Karan Singh, Hari Singh's son, provides fascinating insights into the atmosphere of the maharaja's court. Apart from Victor Rosenthal, he mentions Swami Sant Dev, of whom Hari Singh became a devout follower, and who in 1946 was staying at the select Chashmashahi guesthouse adjoining the palace. According to Karan Singh, the swami played upon his father's feudal ambitions, 'planting in my father's mind visions of an extended kingdom sweeping down to Lahore itself, where our ancestor Maharaja Gulab Singh and his brothers Raja Dhyan Singh and Raja Suchet Singh had played such a crucial role a century earlier'.[2]

The first official indication of Hari Singh's ambitions emerged in a statement on 15 July 1946, in which he declared his approach to the plan then being discussed of an independent united India with its constituents, including the princely states, being linked by a loose federal relationship: ' We look forward to taking our due place in the new constitutional structure of India ... But our concern for the progress of India does not imply acceptance by us of dictation in our internal affairs.' This was an obvious signal that he would not accept domination by New Delhi—a precursor of things to come.

Obviously referring to Nehru's arrest the previous month, the announcement justified denial of access to his state: 'If we are convinced that such access in any case will lead inevitably to strife, disorder and consequent bloodshed amongst my people ...'[3] He was blunter about his refusal to accept outside interference in a letter written directly to Nehru four days earlier:

> The reason why my Government felt it their duty to prevent you from proceeding to Srinagar was that they were convinced, in view of the controversial nature of what you had stated in the Press, in public and in your communications to me, that your coming at that juncture would be certain to result in danger to the public peace.[4]

CLOSER TO PATEL

Hari Singh got on better with Sardar Patel who did not share Nehru's socialistic and anti-monarchical zeal. Nor did he share Nehru's concern to assure Muslims that they would have a place in a secular India despite the pressures for Partition. This was reflected in Kak's warm invitation to Patel on 25 August: 'When you are in a position to fix a date for your visit to Kashmir will you kindly send me a wire? We must insist on having you as a guest of the State or of my wife and myself.'[5]

Kak hoped to exploit these differences but eventually overplayed his hand. He did not realize that Patel, more than Nehru, would ensure that there was no diminution in New Delhi's authority after independence. Patel had become invaluable to the Congress over the years as a firm and effective administrator, and he would soon display these skills in dealing with the princely order. He accepted Nehru's instructions even when he did not agree, until that is they became too sharp over Kashmir to be papered over, but that was in the future. At this time he relayed to Kak, Nehru's and the Congress party's desire that Abdullah be released and steps be taken to improve relations between ruler and ruled.

Kak did not take kindly to the suggestion that the relations were less than perfect, indicating resentment at outside interference. 'If, however, our affairs still give the [Congress] Working Committee cause for concern even in the press of India's so much more urgent needs,' he replied in a letter on 12 September, 'I owe it to you to make it clear that the policy of this Government is clear-cut as regards this matter and that we have not sought, nor would we accept, the arbitration of any third party.'

Expressing his determination to protect the independence of the maharaja's regime, Kak rejected the thesis that the interim government, set up in advance of Indian independence, would inherit British authority. His impassioned response to Patel provided an unmistakeable signal of the state's future policy:

> The analogy you draw between the British Government and the Interim Government on one side and this Government on the other is misleading. This Government is fundamentally of this country. Its history is our history, its hills and valley were

> traversed and occupied by our forebears countless centuries ago. The Government is indigenous and broad-based and its members are not drawn from any single section, class or community. It contains a substantial popular element. From the Ruler downwards we have the advantage of generations of local associations and knowledge behind us.

Kak had gone too far. An angry Patel implicitly rejected the notion of complete independence in a letter dated 28 September:

> I tried to arrive at a friendly and honourable understanding of the Kashmir question. I had no other interest in coming to Kashmir at present. I felt that I could render a service to H.H. the Maharaja Sahib and you by placing my services at your disposal. But your reply betrayed a cold, official touch-me-not attitude.... The State can lose nothing by allowing daylight to shine on the doings of Kashmir. No State can regard itself as outside the purview of India or regard Indians outside its boundary as strangers or foreigners.[6]

KAK'S APPEAL TO THE VICEROY

Now Kak turned to the crown representative (the viceroy's title in dealing with the princes). Enclosing his message on 14 November, the British resident in Kashmir, Lt Col. Webb, added his own note, 'I am seriously inclined to think that the Maharaja and Kak are seriously considering the possibility of Kashmir not joining the Union if it is formed'. Kak's message sought assurances in the event of the state remaining outside the Indian Union:

> Recent events have ... shown that those who are likely to assume the reins of government in India in future are not disposed to show consideration for the security of the State and are prone to interfere and coerce even in regard to purely internal affairs on the flimsiest grounds. Not only that, agitators inside the State are encouraged if not invited to create trouble.
>
> The State does not naturally feel happy about the future and unless satisfactory assurances are forthcoming that

> interference in its internal affairs in any shape or form will in future not be made, may even decide to decline the Indian Union, should it materialize.
>
> If such a contingency does arise, what would the nature of this State's relations with the Crown be? Would necessary wherewithal be supplied to maintain the integrity of the State for such time as it may be able to stand on its own feet?[7]

No such assurance was however available. Two weeks later, Webb was authorized to repeat to Kak the line taken by the British Cabinet Mission. In effect, this was to hope that the states would come into the new constitution and that the Cabinet Mission could not deal with a hypothetical question. He was asked to make two points: '(1) that Kashmir is economically so dependent on India [Pakistan had yet to be created] that it cannot afford to alienate India; and (2) that Kashmir is strategically of such importance to India as a whole that India cannot afford to alienate a Kashmir in which Ruler and subject are united.'[8] The hint was obvious, but months were to pass before Kak was sacked.

The pace of events accelerated sharply when the self-assured, aristocratic Lord Louis Mountbatten, cousin of King George, replaced Archibald Wavell as viceroy on 20 February 1947. His mission was to pull out of India as rapidly as possible, whatever the risk. With relentless, single-minded pressure, the new and last viceroy was able to bring round the vacillating Congress leaders to accept Partition and announced it on 3 June. He went on to speed the process of transfer of power by changing the target date from June 1948 to 15 August 1947. To ensure that the message got across, he had official calendars printed with tear-off sheets for the seventy-three days remaining

Modelled on the surprise secret landings on which he had specialized in the British navy during the war, Mountbatten's shock tactics took the Indian leadership, as well as the princes, by surprise. They went along because they had no alternative plan and were rushed into acceptance though the toll of communal killings began to rise ominously as the prospect of Partition neared.

Mountbatten had no ready plans for Kashmir. As a princely state, it was not treated on the same basis as British India. The confrontation between Hari Singh and the National Conference was mounting. Abdullah went on hunger-strike with other political detenus in jail on 28 February to demand better treatment. Nehru showed his concern by sending a telegram to Begum Abdullah expressing his distress and reaffirming 'Kashmir people's cause our own and we can never forget them ... Hope to visit Kashmir myself later.' He, however, advised abandonment of the hunger-strike at this juncture.[9]

At the Gwalior session of the Congress in April, Nehru championed the re-election of Abdullah as president of the All India States People's Conference though he was still imprisoned. He used the occasion to exert pressure on Hari Singh as well as to reiterate Abdullah's links with India by drawing attention to the 'fierce repression' continuing in Kashmir . 'For ten months now this conflict has continued,' he said, 'and Sheikh Abdullah has become the symbol of freedom not only for the people of Kashmir but also for the people of other States.'[10]

MOUNTBATTEN VISIT

After announcing the 3 June plan, Mountbatten flew to Srinagar on 18 June and stayed for five days. The future of Jammu & Kashmir was becoming the most complex issue in the subcontinent. With British India being divided on the basis of religion, Jinnah had a claim on the Muslim-majority state. The claim was strengthened by the close economic and transport links the state had with neighbouring areas of would-be Pakistan. However, the princes were free to decide their future and their states were not bound by the two-nation theory. The greatest obtacle in Jinnah's path was the commitment of Sheikh Mohammad Abdullah and his National Conference to a secular polity. Their popularity was at the heart of India's claim, as Nehru repeatedly emphasized.

The maharaja laid on a sumptuous ceremonial reception for the viceroy but avoided an interview with him. Karan Singh recalls his father's delaying tactics:

> I suspect that in his heart my father still did not believe that the British would actually leave ... A typical feudal reaction to a difficult situation is to avoid facing it, and my father was particularly prone to resort to this. Instead of taking advantage of Mountbatten's visit and discuss the whole situation meaningfully and trying to arrive at a rational decision, he first sent the Viceroy on a prolonged fishing trip to Thricker (where Mountbatten shocked our staff by sunbathing in the nude) and then—having fixed a meeting just before his departure—got out of it on the plea that he had suddenly developed a severe attack of colic ... Thus the last real chance of working out a viable political settlement was lost.[11]

Mountbatten did however have a session with Kak. According to the official viceregal account, his advice was that the state join either India or Pakistan, but it would find itself in difficulties if it joined neither. Some sentences are prescient, though undiplomatically worded. The report was meant for private record and reference:

> H.E. [Mountbatten] pointed out that Pandit Nehru felt very strongly about Kashmir, and it would be very difficult for him (H.E.) to do anything to protect Kashmir after 15th August, when Pandit Nehru would become Prime Minister of Hindu India, and H.E., even if he remained, would become only a constitutional Governor-General. The only protection for Kashmir was to join one or other Constituent Assemblies.[12]

Before Mountbatten went to Srinagar, Nehru sent him a note emphasizing the need for Abdullah to be freed and for him to form a government replacing Kak. As the National Conference stood for joining India's Constituent Assembly that should be the obvious course for the state. The viceroy did not follow this brief or secure Abdullah's release, but noted in his report to London that Gandhi and Nehru had become 'pathological' on the subject of the princely states.[13] Nehru, on the other hand, wrote acidly to Mountbatten: 'Your visit to Kashmir from my particular point of view was not a success and things continue as before.' Although the viceroy had advised him against visiting Kashmir, he had decided to go on 4 August.[14]

The following day, Mountbatten turned to Gandhi, suggesting that he visit Kashmir in Nehru's place , 'for I really do not know how the future Prime Minister can be spared from Delhi with only 18 days left for him to take over power.' On 28 July Nehru gave vent to his exasperation with Mountbatten and insisted, rather petulantly, 'I shall go ahead with my plans. As between being in Kashmir when my people need me there and being Prime Minister, I prefer the former.'[15]

Sardar Patel had urged Hari Singh, as a sincere friend and well-wisher, to join the Indian Union. He was not a personal critic and his approach differed from that of Gandhi and Nehru. On 29 July, Mountbatten called a meeting with Gandhi, Nehru, and Patel, and suggested that it would be preferable for Gandhi to go to Kashmir at this juncture than a Congress leader. Then, according to the viceroy's report on the meeting:

> Sardar Patel gave it as his view that neither of them should go, but in view of Pandit Nehru's great mental distress if his mission in Kashmir were to remain unfulfilled, he agreed that one of them must go. He very bluntly remarked, "It is a choice between two evils and I consider that Gandhi's visit would be a lesser evil."[16]

In a subsequent report to London, he added a story (obviously emanating from Patel) that when Patel saw Nehru before the meeting, Nehru broke down and wept, explaining that Kashmir meant more to him at the moment than anything else.[17] Patel was justifying his view that Nehru was over-emotional.

GANDHI INTERVENES

Eventually Gandhi went. Mountbatten had assured Kak that he would make no public speeches but his prayer meetings attracted crowds. He was unable to see Abdullah who was in jail, but he met Begum Abdullah whom he invited to read from the Quran at his prayer meetings. In a note he informed Nehru and Patel that he had told Kak how unpopular he was and Kak had offered to resign. He also met the maharaja and maharani.

On his way back from Srinagar on 6 August, Gandhi commiserated with Hindu and Sikh refugees from the pre-Partition riots at Wah camp near Rawalpindi. It was crowded with angry Hindus and Sikhs forced to flee their homes in an area that would soon be Pakistan. For Gandhi, however, it was an occasion to emphasize the ties between Hindus and Muslims in Kashmir and Abdullah's role in bringing them closer. He said:

> The State had a predominantly Muslim population. But he saw that Sheikh Sahib had fired the Kashmiris with local patriotism ... They had one language, culture and, so far as he could see, they were one people. He could not distinguish readily between a Kashmiri Hindu and a Kashmiri Mussalman ... Common sense dictated that the will of the Kashmiris should decide the future of Jammu and Kashmir ...[18]

The Wah camp refugees formed a miniscule part of the millions who would seek to cross the new border between India and Pakistan to escape communal killings. Both new governments had their hands full. Gandhi stayed in Calcutta, away from the festivities in New Delhi on 15 August. However, rival claims to Kashmir soon aroused national sentiment on both sides, and military preparations followed.

A letter from Nehru to Patel on 27 September showed awareness of the approaching danger. He asked him to exert his influence on Hari Singh to defuse the impending crisis by releasing Abdullah and acceding to India. The letter anticipated events a month later:

> The Muslim League in the Punjab and the NWFP are making preparations to enter Kashmir in large numbers. The approach of winter is going to cut off Kashmir from the rest of India ... Therefore it is important that something should be done before winter conditions set in ... I understand that the Pakistan strategy is to infiltrate into Kashmir now and to take some big

> action as soon as Kashmir is isolated because of the coming winter ...
>
> It becomes important, therefore, that the Maharaja should make friends with the National Conference so that there could be this popular support against Pakistan. Indeed, it seems to be that there is no other course open to the Maharaja but this: to release Sheikh Abdullah and the National Conference leaders, to make a friendly approach to them ... and then to declare adhesion to the Indian Union ... Abdullah is very anxious to keep out of Pakistan and relies upon us a great deal for advice. At the same time he cannot carry his people with him unless he has something definite to place before them ...[19]

Patel did not approve of Nehru's projection of Abdullah, but saw no alternative and conveyed his message. Also, now as minister for home affairs, he initiated steps to defend Kashmir against the threat foreseen by the prime minister. One part of the message seemed to get through: Abdullah was released on 29 September; Hari Singh continued to dither over accession until forced a month later by the accuracy of Nehru's anticipation about infiltration from Pakistan.

---

1 Mosley, op. cit., p. 60.

2 Karan Singh, *Heir Apparent: An Autobiography*, Oxford University Press, Delhi, 1982, p. 38.

3 Enclosed in a letter to Sardar Patel from Kashmir Prime Minister Ram Chandra Kak dt. 25 Aug. 1946. *Sardar Patel's Correspondence*, vol. I, pp. 13–15.

4 Ibid., p. 7.

5 Ibid., pp. 12–13.

6 Ibid., pp. 100–1.

7 *The Transfer of Power 1942–47* documents, vol. ix, doc. 37, pp. 71–72; HMG, London, 1983.

8 Alan Campell-Johnson, *Mission With*, Robert Hale, London, 1951, pp. 555–56.

9 *Selected Works of Jawaharlal Nehru*, vol II, Oxford Univesity Press, New Delhi, 1984, p. 263.

10 Ibid., p.

11 Karan Singh, *Heir Apparent: An Autobiography*, Oxford University Press, Delhi, 1982.

12 *Transfer of Power*, vol. xi, doc. 319, pp. 555–56.

13 Ibid., doc. 386, pp. 717–19.

14 Ibid., xii, doc. 249, p. 368.

15 Pyarelal, *Mahatma Gandhi; The Last Phase, vol. II*, Navajivan Trust, Ahmedabad, 1958, p. 363.

16 *Transfer of Power* XII, doc. 269, pp. 397–9.

17 Ibid., XII, doc. 302, pp. 449–50.

18 *Collected Works of Mahatma Gandhi*, vol. 89, pp. 5–6. From *Harijan*, 24 Aug. 1947.

19 Patel, op. cit., p. 57.

BRIEF INDEPENDENCE

In spite of what has happened in the past I assure Your Highness that myself and my party have never harboured any sentiment of disloyalty towards Your Highness's person, throne or dynasty. The development of this beautiful State and the betterment of its people is our common aim and interest and I assure Your Highness the fullest and loyal support of myself and my organization....

– Sheikh Abdullah to Maharaja Hari Singh

Sheikh Abdullah faced a political situation that had been transformed completely out of recognition when he emerged from jail on 20 September 1947. Kashmir's hopes of securing independence were under threat. He had been incarcerated for sixteen months after launching the Quit Kashmir movement. A boat procession on the Jhelum was organized to celebrate his release. However, a marked change was revealed in a letter subsequently disclosed from the maharaja's files by his son, Karan Singh. Thakur Nachint Ram, private secretary to the maharaja, met him in jail just before he was freed.

Under pressure, Hari Singh had turned to his friend, Sardar Patel, for help and appointed Mehr Chand Mahajan (who later became chief justice of the Supreme Court of India) as his new prime minister. Mahajan was a High Court judge in East Punjab and had been the Hindu representative on the Boundary Commission advising on the partition of Punjab. He was a protégé of Patel and had been initially approached by Maharani Tara Devi, who was known to exercise a regressive influence over her husband.

Patel personally cleared the administrative hurdles in the way of a serving Indian judge accepting service in another country (which Jammu & Kashmir then was). Hari Singh asked Mahajan to 'convince the persons concerned' in New Delhi that he would require time to associate the people with the government after accession. Nehru, however, 'wanted an immediate change in the internal administration of the State and he felt somewhat annoyed when I conveyed to him the Maharaja's views. Pandit Nehru also asked me to see that Sheikh Abdullah was set free.'

According to Mahajan, who had been invited to Srinagar to discuss the terms of his appointment, Hari Singh consulted him on negotiations for Abdullah's release. He was told that the maharaja's advisers wanted a letter of apology and a letter pledging loyalty. Abdullah was in poor health and said to be 'half willing to give a qualified and guarded undertaking as would not affect his leadership later on'.[1]

OBSEQUIOUS LETTER

In contrast to previous pronouncements, Abdullah's letter from jail was fulsome and obsequious. Perhaps he thought he could work with Hari Singh to make their dream of independence a reality in the changed circumstances. While in jail, he and his colleagues became increasingly concerned about the uncertainty of the future of the state and their inability to do anything in captivity. Expectations of Pakistani moves to take it over were mounting; unless he was free there would be no popular resistance.

Abdullah did not go along with Nehru's suggestion that the maharaja accede promptly to India. He wanted the decision to be taken by an elected government in the state, not by the maharaja. He also wanted the option of independence to be retained; a dream he shared with Hari Singh. Circumstances were drawing them closer notwithstanding a history of deep-rooted suspicion and antagonism.

Abdullah's letter noted that he had been heartened by the sacking of his inveterate enemy, Ram Chandra Kak, as the maharaja's prime minister. Written the day prior to his release in the traditional style of a subject approaching the maharaja, it read:

> May it please Your Highness,
>
> It is after one and a half year's incarceration that—as long wished—I had an opportunity of having detailed talks with Thakur Nachint Singh Ji. What unfortunate things happened during this period in the State I need not mention. But this is now realized by every well-wisher of the State that many of the regrettable happenings in the past have mainly been due to the misunderstandings which appear now to have deliberately been created by interested people in order to achieve their own ends. R.B. Ramchandra Kak, the ex-Prime Minister, through his mischievous methods and masterly manouverings brought these misunderstandings to a climax and succeeded in his attempt, though temporarily, to a certain extent. He painted me and my organization in darkest colours and everything we did or attempted to do to bring Your Highness and your people closer; base and selfish motives were attributed to me. But God be thanked that these enemies of our Highness and the State stand exposed today.
>
> In spite of what has happened in the past I assure Your Highness that myself and my party have never harboured any sentiment of disloyalty towards Your Highness's person, throne or dynasty. The development of this beautiful State and the betterment of its people is our common aim and interest and I assure Your Highness the fullest and loyal support of myself and my organization. Not only this but I assure Your Highness that any party, within or without the State, which may attempt to create any impediments in our effort to gain our goal, will be treated as an enemy and will be treated as such.
>
> In order to achieve common aim set forth above, mutual trust and confidence must be the mainstay. Without this it would not be possible to face successfully the great difficulties that beset our State on all sides at present.

> Before I close this letter I beg to assure Your Highness once again of my steadfast loyalty and pray that God under Your Highness's aegis bring such an era of Peace, Prosperity and Good Government that it may be second to none and be an ideal for others to copy.
>
> Your Highness's most obedient subject,
> S.M. Abdullah[2]

***

HARI SINGH FOR NEUTRALITY

Jammu & Kashmir was independent after British paramountcy and protection was withdrawn from the princely states on 15 August 1947. Vigorous at fifty-two, and now absolute ruler of the largest princely state in the subcontinent, Hari Singh's reluctance to accede either to India or Pakistan was understandable. He was concerned about the tensions either choice would generate with communal passions mounting in both countries. He felt it necessary to instruct his new deputy prime minister, R.L. Batra, to relay his approach to the press in New Delhi as late as 12 October:

> Despite constant rumours, we have no intention of joining either India or Pakistan, and the Maharaja and his government have decided that no decision will be made until there is peace on the plains. The only thing that will change this decision is if one side or other decides to use force against us ... The Maharaja has told me that his ambition is to make Kashmir the Switzerland of the East—a State that is completely neutral.[3]

Abdullah also regarded Switzerland as a model, and after his release it seemed that he and the maharaja might work together to achieve an independent, neutral status for Jammu & Kashmir. However, Abdullah's insistence that the final decision on the future of the state should be taken by an elected government, not the maharaja, kept them apart. His address to a Srinagar rally on 2 October, Gandhi's birthday, reflected the altered scenario:

> For more than a year I was separated from the people and from the rapidly changing conditions in my country. When I went into prison, I took a last look at undivided India. Today it has been broken into two fragments. We the people of Kashmir must see to it that our long-cherished dream is fulfilled; the dream of freedom, welfare and progress. No decision, however, is possible while we are slaves. It is, therefore, imperative to set up, without delay, a representative government which chalks out a plan to safeguard the rights and interests of the people of the State. "Freedom before accession" should become our resounding slogan.

Abdullah's address to another public meeting was notable for leaving the choice open between three, not two, options. He recalled his friendship with Nehru and respect for Gandhi, and recognized the support afforded by the Congress but insisted that the question would be decided after getting 'rid of Dogra domination'. Then the people would be free to choose between India, Pakistan, and independence. If then the people decided to accede to Pakistan, 'I will be the first one to sign my name'. He, however, added that he would never support the two-nation theory that had breathed poison into the atmosphere.[4]

However, the speed with which events moved left no time for Abdullah's and Hari Singh's plans to fructify. The first indication that the state would be dragged into a India–Pakistan conflict came in Jammu. Unlike the mountain-girt valley, Jammu was exposed to the Partition riots in adjoining Punjab. Refugees from adjoining areas, mostly Hindu, felt safer in the home of the Hindu Dogra dynasty. Clashes occurred with Jammu's Muslims, who were then in a majority in the province, especially in the area adjoining Pakistan. The maharaja's police and administration supported the refugees and their local supporters, and a reverse flow of Muslims began into Pakistan. Poonch district, known for its martial traditions and home to hundreds of Muslim war veterans, was already in a state of near-revolt. It had a history of unrest against Dogra oppression. Now it was next to Pakistan, and that fanned the flames. The revolt was harshly quelled, but trans-border raids into Jammu were stepped up in September and October.

Meanwhile, Pakistan was tightening the economic screws on Kashmir by holding up essential supplies on the road and rail links passing through its territory notwithstanding the signature of a Standstill Agreement to maintain services. The only surface access that the state had from Indian territory was the dirt road connecting Pathankot with Jammu; from there the road over the Banihal Pass to Srinagar was a greater obstacle. Shortages soon developed and prices rose sharply. Fruit exports, the Valley's major source of revenue, rotted on the ground.

CONTINGENCY PLANS

These developments pushed Hari Singh into making contingency plans for help while officially maintaining neutrality. Split into small groups guarding the borders of his huge state, his army could quell local uprisings, as in Poonch, but was too small to repel an organized attack. On 13 September, the state government approached the Government of India for the loan of an Indian Army officer to replace an Englishman, Major General Scott, as commander-in-chief of his army. At this stage, New Delhi deputed only the aptly named Lt Col. Kashmir Singh Katoch for the post; in fact he functioned only as military adviser and took time to assume his post. The next move was to appoint Mahajan as his prime minister on 2 October. Patel assured the maharaja:

> I am expediting as much as possible the linking up of the State with the Indian Dominion by means of telegraph, telephones, wireless and roads. We fully realize the need for despatch and urgency and I can assure you we shall do our best.[5]

A letter from Batra to Patel reveals an additional dimension to the preparations. In addition to referring to an indent of military equipment, it said that after Mahajan had met Patel, he had 'conveyed the hope that it would be possible for the Indian Dominion to concentrate some military force at Madhopore [on the Punjab–Jammu border] or at any equally near and convenient centre for rendering this State succour in case it is needed'.[6]

On 7 October Patel urged the defence minister, Baldev Singh, to expedite supply of arms and ammunition to Kashmir by air if necessary, adding, after receiving Nehru's letter: 'There is not time to lose if the reports which we hear of similar preparations for intervention on the part of the Pakistan Government are correct.'[7]

Pakistan portrayed the uprising in Poonch in terms of a legitimate revolt against the maharaja's misrule, with Pathan tribals entering to help, similar to the line it would take to justify infiltration into the Valley. An official note to the Kashmir government on 12 October was a veiled warning. It alleged that armed bands, including state troops, were attacking Muslim villages in Poonch. The Pakistan army obtained a large number of recruits from Poonch. Their feelings were rising 'and the situation is fraught with danger'.

Mahajan's response as prime minister three days later was no less portentous. Unless infiltration ceased, his government, 'much against its wishes, will have no option but to ask for friendly assistance to withstand aggressive and unfriendly actions of the Pakistan people along our border'. This warning was reinforced three days later with a detailed note describing the problems faced by the state due to the virtual blockade imposed by Pakistan; attacks on Kashmiri nationals on the Kohala border; armed infiltration into Poonch; and propaganda against the maharaja's government in the Pakistani media. If this request to end these provocations was not heeded, 'the government would fully hope that you would agree that it would be justified in asking for friendly assistance and oppose trespass on its fundamental rights'.

The visit of an emissary, Major A.S.B. Shah, sent by Jinnah (now governor-general of Pakistan) to Srinagar increased the friction. When Mahajan turned down his demand to meet Jinnah in Lahore, he records that 'my refusal to decide the question of accession immediately might result in serious consequences. When he said that, I blurted out that a threat of that kind would throw the State into the lap of India.'[8]

The Pakistan government responded with a counter-threat. It took a most serious view of the suppression of Muslims in Kashmir and the reference to joining India and warned: 'If this policy is not changed and the preparations and the measures that you are now taking in implementing this policy are not stopped, the gravest consequences will follow for which you alone will be held responsible.'

Finally, on 20 October , when the tribal *lashkars* let in by Pakistan were moving to attack the Valley, Jinnah sent a telegram to Hari Singh reiterating previous charges and suggested, 'the real aim of your government's policy is to seek an opportunity to join the Indian Dominion through a *coup d'ètat* by securing the intervention and assistance of that Dominion'. He contrasted the favourable treatment accorded to Abdullah's National Conference with the continued detention of Ghulam Abbas and the leaders of the Muslim Conference.[9]

This recognized the role of the National Conference in strengthening opposition to Pakistan at this critical juncture. However, Abdullah's campaign for representative government was creating tensions. The crisis induced Patel to revise his attitude to fit Nehru's. He wrote to Mahajan on 21 October:

> I myself feel that the position which Sheikh Abdullah takes up is understandable and reasonable. In the mounting demands for the introduction of responsible government in the States, such as you have witnessed in Travancore and Mysore, it is impossible for you to isolate yourself. It is obvious that in your dealings with the external dangers and internal commotion with which you are faced, mere brute force is not enough. We, on our part, have pledged to give you the maximum support and we will do so. But I am afraid, without some measure of popular backing, particularly from the community which represents such an overwhelming majority in Kashmir, it would be difficult to make such support go to the farthest limits that is necessary if we are to crush the disruptive forces that are being raised and organized. Nor do I think it would be possible for you to maintain for long the exclusive or the predominant monopoly of any community in your security services.

Patel's advice was meant to be conveyed to the maharaja, but other events intervened: the tribal raiders entered Kashmir and attacked Muzaffarabad on 22 October. Mahajan's reply showed signs of panic, and he complained that the help India had promised had not arrived.[10]

The maharaja now turned to his fellow princes for help. The maharaja of Patiala responded and despatched a battalion of infantry and a battery of mountain artillery in early October. Patiala forces had not been integrated into the Indian Army, and therefore the ruler did not require New Delhi's permission to send them out of the state. When Indian troops landed in Srinagar on 27 October, they found Patiala gunners encamped there.[11] The Patiala detachment was, however, inadequate to withstand a far larger invasion than anticipated.

SHATTERED DREAM

Official Indian help arrived on 27 October when Hari Singh was obliged to sign the Instrument of Accession to India. Pakistan advanced a number of reasons to describe the accession as fraudulent. One supported by the UK was that the maharaja was not entitled to sign away the state at a time when parts of it were engulfed by rebellion.[12] Doubts were raised about the date on which the Instrument was signed: whether before or after the arrival of Indian troops. Scholars have not found access to the original document.

Nevertheless, Hari Singh's dream of independence was now rudely shattered. V.P. Menon, secretary in Patel's Ministry of States, provides a graphic description of the last hours of the maharaja's independence. The scene was set in Hari Singh's palace in Jammu, to where he and his entourage had fled from Srinagar:

> On arrival at the palace, I found it in a state of utter turmoil with valuable articles strewn all over the place. The Maharaja was asleep; he had left Srinagar the previous evening and had been driving all night. I woke him up and told him what had taken place at the Defence Committee meeting [where it was decided that military forces could not be sent to Kashmir until

> it acceded to India]. He was ready to accede at once. He then composed a letter to the Governor-General [Mountbatten] that it was his intention to set up an interim government at once and ask Sheikh Abdullah to carry the responsibilities in this emergency with Mahajan, his Prime Minister.
>
> Just as I was leaving, he told me that before he went to sleep, he had left instructions with his ADC that if I came back from Delhi he was not to be disturbed as it would mean the Government of India had decided to come to his rescue and he should therefore be allowed to sleep in peace; but if I failed to return, it meant everything was lost and, in that case, his ADC was to shoot him in his sleep.[13]

Hari Singh's letter to Mountbatten did not hide his reluctance to abandon the option of independence until forced by the tribal invasion. 'I wanted to take time to decide to which Dominion I should accede [and] whether it is not in the best interest of both Dominions and my State to stand independent,' he wrote. 'With the conditions obtaining at present in my State and the great emergency of the situation as it exists, I have no option but to ask for help from the Indian Dominion. Naturally they cannot send the help asked for without my State acceding to the Dominion of India. I have accordingly decided to do so and I attach the Instrument of Accession by your government.'[14]

The last maharaja of Jammu & Kashmir never returned to the luxurious palace he had laid out overlooking the Dal Lake in Srinagar. It is now a luxury hotel.

---

1 Mehr Chand Mahajan, *Looking Back: An Autobiography*, Asia Publising House, New Delhi, 1963, p 125–27.

2 Karan Singh, op. cit., pp. 81–82.

3 *Hindustan Times*, New Delhi, 14 October 1947.

4 *Flames*, p. 86.

5 Ibid., pp. 40–43.

6 Ibid., p. 48.

7 Ibid., p. 57.

8 Mehr Chand Mahajan, op. cit., pp. 141–42.

9 P.L. Lakhanpal, *Essential Documents and Notes on Kashmir Dispute*, pp. 50–54.

10 Patel, op. cit., pp. 61–73.

11 Alastair Lamb, *Kashmir, a Disputed Legacy*, 184–1990, Roxford Books, London, p. 131.

12 Op. cit., pp. 150–56.

13 Menon, op. cit., pp. 399–400.

14 *Documents on Kashmir Problem*, Discovery Publishing House, New Delhi, 1991, vol xiv, pp. 73–75.

ACCESSION DRAMA

To remove the misconception that the Indian government is using the prevailing situation in Jammu and Kashmir to reap political profits, the Government of India wants to make it very clear that as soon as the raiders are driven out and normalcy restored, the people of the State will freely decide their fate and that decision will be taken according to the universally democratic means of plebiscite or referendum.

– Jawaharlal Nehru's Letter to the UN Secretary-General

Sheikh Abdullah was a guest at Jawaharlal Nehru's residence in New Delhi when final discussions were being held on Hari Singh's letter seeking accession in return for immediate military asistance against the marauding Pathan tribal raiders. He had arrived from threatened Srinagar. The significance of his presence soon became clear. The maharaja had waited till the last moment before agreeing to sign away his independence. His letter was dated 24 October 1947, when the truck-borne raiders signalled their advance by disconnecting the generators of Mahura power station and extinguished the lights in Srinagar. They had broken through the last defensive line of state troops and were fifty miles away on a motorable road, two day after crossing the border with Pakistan.

Notwithstanding the urgency of the threat, New Delhi took time to respond. With only three months' experience of office in a period beset by communal carnage, the Nehru government was faced with a decision frought with unprecedented national and international implications. It had to deal with divergent pressures and high expectations. Opinion-makers at home and abroad had to be convinced that the Muslim majority of Jammu & Kashmir did not support the two-nation theory on which Pakistan had been carved out of British India; that accession to India would promote secularism and democracy both in the state and throughout India.

MOUNTBATTEN'S ROLE

The head of state, Lord Louis Mountbatten, was involved. Though no longer enjoying the powers of viceroy, he remained governor-general of the Dominion of India after 15 August 1947. (India was a Dominion of the British Crown until it adopted its own Constitution in 1950.) Consequently, New Delhi was expected to keep London informed of major policy decisions and heed its views. The governor-general kept in touch with London through regular reports to the king. Nehru was persuaded to believe that Whitehall would be impartial but it soon transpired that its approach was unsympathetic. It had wider strategic Cold War considerations in which Pakistan was seen as potentially more cooperative than India in defending the region against the Soviet Union. This was formalized when Pakistan became a member of the CENTO and SEATO Anglo-American military pacts against the Soviet Union.

Mountbatten's experience and personality lent him additional clout. In view of his experience of high-level military command during the Second World War, he was asked by the Indian cabinet to chair its crucial defence committee. His insistence that the formalities of accession be completed before troops were sent to Kashmir contributed to the delay. Otherwise, he argued in a lengthy *aide-memoire* dated 25 February 1948, it would appear that India was sending troops into what was now an independent country and lead to war with Pakistan. Nehru differed but went along. He told parliament later (March 1951) that 'irrespective of accession we would have had an obligation to protect the people of Kashmir against aggression', but he too had reasons to delay accession until Hari Singh agreed to declare that Abdullah would head his administration. This, he felt, was essential to demonstrate to the world that the state's accession to India had popular support. More important, it would reinforce secularism at home.

THE PLEBISCITE TRAP

Playing on the theme, Mountbatten proposed a procedure that would haunt New Delhi far into the future: plebiscite under UN auspices. Nehru later modified the commitment to: 'The question of the State's accession should be settled by reference to the people.' However, in a radio broadcast to the nation on 28 October, after the accession, he added the crucial phrase 'under U.N. auspices'. He was keen to establish newly-independent India's credentials as a responsible democratic member of the UN. However, as subsequently noted by his personal secretary, M.O. Mathai, 'Neither Mountbatten nor Nehru and other Indian leaders had the foggiest notion of how the U.N. functioned'.[1] One leader, Sardar Patel, did however in his role as minister for Information and Broadcasting. His personal secretary, V. Shankar, records a last-minute effort to delete the phrase:

> Sardar used to insist on seeing the text of important broadcasts including those of before 8.15 p.m. Sardar read it and noted the embarrassing commitment. He tried to contact Pt Nehru but the latter had left for the Broadcasting House. Sardar then commissioned me to go to Broadcasting House and ask Pt Nehru to delete the offending phrase "under U.N. auspices" but to retain the commitment, namely that the wishes of the people would be ascertained. I made haste to go to the Broadcasting House but by the time I reached there, Pt Nehru had already begun his broadcast and in a few minutes the deed was done.[2]

Differences between Nehru and Mountbatten on the plebiscite proposal developed further. The governor-general was giving priority to making a commitment on plebiscite under UN auspices while the prime minister insisted that the tribal raiders (this was before Pakistani troops entered the war) be cleared from Kashmir before the question of ascertaining the wishes of the people arose. Mountbatten associated Pakistan with the proposal to involve the UN at a meeting between Nehru, the Pakistani prime minister, Liaquat Ali Khan, and himself, in Lahore on 9 December. According to his report to the king, the meeting was occasionally stormy with Nehru saying he would 'throw up the Prime Ministership and take a rifle himself, and lead the men of India against the invasion ... I realized the deadlock was complete and the only way out was to bring in some third party in some capacity or other. For this purpose I suggested that the United Nations Organization be called upon.'[3]

On 31 December 1947, India complained to the Security Council under Article 35 of the UN Charter about the assistance being given by Pakistan to the raiders and warned:

> The Government of India request the Security Council to call upon Pakistan to put an end immediately to the giving of such assistance, which is an act of aggression against India. If Pakistan does not do so, the Government of India may be compelled, in self-defence, to enter Pakistan territory in order to take military action against the invaders.

Anxious as ever to promote India's reputation in the world body, Nehru again mentioned plebiscite in a letter to the secretary-general:

> To remove the misconception that the Indian government is using the prevailing situation in Jammu and Kashmir to reap political profits, the Government of India wants to make it very clear that as soon as the raiders are driven out and normalcy restored, the people of the State will freely decide their fate and that decision will be taken according to the universally democratic means of plebiscite or referendum.[4]

Nehru's idealism was his misdoing. In one of his last reports to the king, before leaving India, Mountbatten said Nehru was shocked to find that power politics and not ethics were ruling the UN. Nehru specified his suspicions in a letter to his sister, Vijayalakshmi Pandit, on 16 February 1947: 'The USA and the UK have played a dirty role, the UK being the main actor behind the scenes.' Relations between New Delhi and London had not improved when Mountbatten returned home on 21 June 1948.

DRAMATIC DECISION

The final decision on accession was taken in Nehru's residence, in circumstances that had the flavour of high drama with an element of pre-arrangement to ensure the presence of the principal actors. V.P. Menon flew back from Jammu to New Delhi with Hari Singh's theatrical letter requesting accession, bringing the state prime minister, Mehr Chand Mahajan, with him. They drove directly from the airport to the residence. In the living room, an overwrought Mahajan insisted that troops be sent immediately to Kashmir and got upset when Nehru spoke of the difficulty of sending troops quickly. Mahajan replied, 'Take the accession and give whatever power you desire to the popular party. The army must fly to save Srinagar this evening or else I will go to Lahore and negotiate terms with Mr Jinnah.' Nehru reacted angrily and asked Mahajan to leave, but Patel, who was also present, intervened. At this point a slip of paper was handed to Nehru. It was from Abdullah who was in an adjacent room. In the circumstances, Mahajan was grateful even to his bête noire. In his recollections, he records: 'He [Abdullah] now strengthened my hands by telling the Prime Minister that military help must be sent immediately ... The Prime Minister's attitude changed on reading this slip.'[5]

Abdullah's recollection of this meeting confirms Mahajan's threat to meet Jinnah in Lahore and Nehru's angry reaction, but differs in detail. He recalls: 'Jawaharlal lost his temper, "If you favour an agreement with Pakistan, leave at once." He stormed out of the room. I tried to soothe him by assuring him that the National Conference supported this decision. Jawaharlal shot back into the room where Mahajan was sitting and told him that Sheikh Abdullah supported the accession.'[6] Until the raiders' attack, Abdullah had kept the options open.

LIMITED ACCESSION

Although offering accession, Hari Singh did not lose his self-assurance. Written into the Instrument of Accession were strict limitations on the areas of governance to be ceded to the Government of India, he retaining authority over domestic affairs. The document was crafted with care. Limiting the Centre's authority to three overall subjects, defence, external affairs, and communications, it spelt out the departments 'with respect to which the Dominion Legislature may make laws for this State', and by inference those it could not. It stated specifically that the accession was subject to the terms laid down and they could not be altered without his consent. The Instrument was dated 26 October 1947.

Hari Singh, however, had little time to savour the fruits of his rearguard action. Ironically, the principal beneficiary was Sheikh Abdullah whose case for autonomy and special status for Jammu & Kashmir was based on the accession document. (The full text is provided in Appendix I.)

Another facet of the special status that would haunt New Delhi emerged the following day. Formally accepting the accession, Mountbatten added a letter to the maharaja announcing that it would be temporary until endorsed by a reference to the people. The letter, badly drafted in comparison with Hari Singh's draftmanship, stated:

> Consistently [sic] with their policy that when the issue of accession has been the subject of dispute the question of accession should be decided in accordance with the wishes of the people of the State, it is my Government's wish that as soon as law and order have been restored in Kashmir and her soil cleared of the raider, the question of State's accession should be settled by reference to the people.
>
> Meanwhile, in response to Your Highness's appeal for military aid, action has been taken today to send troops of the Indian Army to Kashmir to help your own forces to defend your territory and to protect the lives, property and honour of your people. My Government and I note with satisfaction that Your Highness has decided to invite Sheikh Abdullah to work with your Prime Minister.[7]

OUTSTANDING OPERATION

The decision may have been taken too late but for the speed with which the troops were airlifted to Srinagar the following morning and the organized help they received from National Conference volunteers on the ground. When the first aircraft flying the first contingent of Indian troops took off from Delhi, the pilot was instructed to proceed to Jammu if the raiders had reached the Srinagar airfield. Their advance had however been slowed by the rape of Baramulla. Even so, the advance units would have been stranded at the airfield had the National Conference not organized porters to unload supplies, volunteers to protect bridges and installations from sabotage, and maintain order, besides, most crucially, buses to ferry them towards Baramulla. An armed civil militia had been raised to patrol Srinagar and its environs, and guide the army units.[8] Sheikh Abdullah inspired the volunteers while Bakshi Ghulam Mohammad became known for his organizing ability. The tragic, mistaken killing of six members of the militia by Indian soldiers near Srinagar airfield was not publicized.

In the absence of the maharaja's police and administration, it was a unique cooperative operation of military and volunteer civilian forces. Many however paid the price of delay, including the commander of the first detachment of soldiers to rush blindly towards Baramulla. Lt Col Ranjit Rai and many of his men fell when they encountered well-armed superior forces. A sign marks the spot:

> In the ever green memory of the brave soldiers of the Sikh Regiment who gave their lives so that Kashmiris might live in freedom. They were the first Indian troops to come to their rescue on October 27, 1947. On this fateful hill was fought their first engagement.

---

1 M.O. Mathai, *My Days With Nehru,* Vikas Publishers, New Delhi.

2 V. Shankar, *My Reminiscences of Sardar Patel,* vol. i, Macmillan, New Delhi, 1974.

3 H.V. Hodson, *The Great Divide: Britain. India–Pakistan,* Hutchinson, London, 1969, pp. 462–65.

4 Joseph Korbel, *Danger in Kashmir,* Princeton, New Jersy, 1954, p. 98.

5 Mehr Chand, Mahajan, *Looking Back: An Autobiography,* Asia Publishing House, New Delhi, 1963, p. 151–52.

6 *Flames,* p. 95.

7 *Documents on Kashmir Problem,* vol. xiv, pp. 75–76.

8 As recalled in the Preface.

9 Mir Qasim, *My Life and Times,* Allied, New Delhi, 1992, p. 39.

DIFFERENCES EMERGE

If the average Muslim feels that he has no safe and secure place in the Union then obviously he will look elsewhere.

– Jawaharlal Nehru to Hari Singh

An occasion designed to be a moment of triumph for Jawaharlal Nehru and Sheikh Abdullah proved to be the first step towards downfall. Nehru tried to clear the rocky road to associate Jammu & Kashmir with the Indian Union by persuading Maharaja Hari Singh to agree to appoint Abdullah as what was described as head of his Emergency administration. The appointment, however, brought to the surface conflicting, deep-rooted suspicions, with communal overtones. Policy differences became sufficiently serious for Nehru to detach the state from Patel's Ministry of States and for Patel to offer to resign from his government. The resignation was not pressed, but divided signals caused confusion. The most serious outcome was to damage the mutual trust and confidence between Nehru and Abdullah that had strengthened secularism and contributed to accession. It also led a frustrated Abdullah to consider the option of independence.

Abdullah's designation was to be a brief interim step towards his appointment as prime minister of Jammu & Kashmir in place of Mehr Chand Mahajan. It was intended to enable the National Conference to implement the vitally-needed reforms it had promised and satisfy its claim to special status in the Union. The wider national objective was to reinforce secularism at home and demonstrate to foreign critics that India had helped the emergence of popular governance in the state. Nehru however miscalculated. The embittered maharaja was not prepared to hand over power so easily to his arch-opponent. From his palace in Jammu, he deployed all the weapons in his armoury against Abdullah. Promoting extremist Hindu passions against the move to place a Muslim in power in what had been a Hindu-ruled state for a hundred years proved potent. He incited anti-Muslim violence in Dogra-dominated Jammu, provided ammunition to Hindu communal parties in northern India, and strengthened elements in the ruling Congress party led by Patel which favoured the state's full integration into the Indian Union.

THE THIRD OPTION

Angered by outbursts of criticism, magnified by the press and often communal in tone, Abdullah began to openly doubt whether joining India was in the interests of the people of Kashmir. His commitment to secularism and differences with Jinnah had ruled out accession to Pakistan. However, the third option, of an independent status guaranteed by the UN, seemed available. Nehru was on record as stating that accession to India was provisional until referred to the people.

Abdullah had endorsed accession to India in the belief that Gandhian secularism, combined with Nehru's socialism and the promise of special status, would satisfy the aspirations of his people. Now Gandhi, who had publicly criticized Hari Singh, was dead, and secularism and special status under attack. He may have raised the third option as a lever to retain special status by indicating what could happen if it was threatened. This ploy, however, had the opposite effect; it was portrayed as proof of betrayal and strengthened Patel's case against him.

Nehru tried to reassure Abdullah that Kashmir's special status would be honoured, and condemned anti-Muslim outbreaks in Jammu. However, the process of transferring power in Kashmir was slowed by

Hari Singh's intransigence and the legalistic procedures prescribed by Patel's Ministry of States. Having demonstrated its ability to run the administration when the Valley was under attack, the National Conference felt cheated. It had expected to assume charge without delay. It was embarrassed by violent Hindu communal reaction in Jammu, encouraged by Hari Singh. Attacks on Muslims there revived the appeal of Muslim communalism in the Valley. Secularism suffered a setback.

Abdullah's feelings were assuaged when Nehru belatedly forced the reluctant maharaja to issue a proclamation appointing him prime minister of the state on 5 March 1948 in place of Mahajan and later leave the state permanently for Bombay. These moves were, however, interpreted as appeasement and placed Nehru's own position and secular approach in the line of fire. Critics interpreted the secularity for which Abdullah and the National Conference had been praised as a cloak for betraying India. Some went to the extent of accusing Abdullah of secretly working for Pakistan. Hindu revivalism was identified with Indian nationalism.

Discussions in the Constituent Assembly threw up sharp differences over provisions drafted to honour the conditions laid down in the Instrument of Accession giving Jammu & Kashmir a status different from that of other states in the Union. Eventually, it was given the authority to elect its own constituent assembly and the Centre's powers in the state were limited, in what became the frequently targeted Article 370 of the Constitution of India. However, the debate revealed that many members desired to whittle down the additional autonomy prescribed for the state, Patel among them. Abdullah and his colleagues. who were members of the Constituent Assembly, were unhappy. The ironclad guarantees of autonomy they desired were not accepted, and they were upset with the Article being described as a 'temporary provision' to mollify the protagonists of integration.[1]

TRAGIC PARTING

Such a fissured compromise was doomed to widen rather than overcome differences. It contributed to the tragic parting of Nehru and Abdullah. Published documents provide a step by step record of these developments. To begin with, the imprecise language of the accession documents delayed Nehru's move to install a popular government in Jammu & Kashmir to justify the deployment of Indian troops. The sentence in Hari Singh's letter concerning transitional arrangements was worded with studied vagueness. He agreed only to set up an 'interim government and ask Sheikh Abdullah to carry the responsibilities [sic] in this emergency with my Prime Minister [Mahajan]'. The formal reply of the governor-general, Lord Mountbatten, was equally imprecise, expressing satisfaction with the maharaja's decision 'to invite Sheikh Abdullah to work with your Prime Minister'.

In effect, Abdullah was promised a vaguely-described office for a limited emergency period while, to the chagrin of the National Conference, the maharaja's authority was left undisturbed. Drafts of the crucial exchange of letters on accession must have been vetted by Patel's Ministry of States. It was Patel who had proposed Mahajan's appointment to Hari Singh. The transitional formula was described as following the pattern prescribed by the ministry in finalizing the accession of Mysore state.

The centrality of Abdullah and his National Conference in Nehru's plans for Kashmir emerged in a flurry of letters even as the threat of a collision with Pakistan loomed on the horizon. He wrote to Abdullah on 10 October 1947, 'What should be done in Kashmir is for you to determine. I have impressed upon all the advisers of the Maharaja who have seen me that the only hope for Kashmir and for him is to gain your confidence completely and follow your advice.'[2] To Mahajan on 21 October, the day before the Pathan raiders entered the Valley, he wrote:

> It is clear that the only proper solution of the Kashmir problem today lies in the fullest cooperation between the maharaja and the people of Kashmir as represented by the National Conference. That cooperation can only come when the people feel they are more or less running the show.

> That is why I suggested to you the urgency of taking some step like the formation of a provisional government. Sheikh Abdullah, who is obviously the most popular person in Kashmir, might be asked to form such a government. In law there need be no major change and the Maharaja's powers might therefore continue. But in practice the burden would fall on the new interim government.[3]

Nehru suggested that any declaration of adhesion to the Indian Union should be made only after a popular interim government was functioning. When, however, the raiders' advance had forced accession on 27 October he wrote again to Mahajan expressing satisfaction with the maharaja's invitation to Abdullah to form an interim government.[4]

MYSORE PATTERN

On the same day he wrote to Abdullah that the arrangement would follow the Mysore pattern. What this meant was 'that you form the government, including the present Prime Minister, Mahajan, who retains his title. Presumably you will be called Chief Minister ... In theory Mahajan will be just one member of the Ministry with no special powers to override the others. The Maharaja will in law retain all his powers, but in practice he should abide by the advice of the Ministry like a constitutional head ... In any event, the Maharaja should formally appoint you a Chief Minister with power to act.' He also informed Abdullah that rifles and sten guns were being sent to arm the civil population.[5]

However, Nehru's instructions were not always heeded. The arms did not reach the National Conference because the militia was seen as a threat by the maharaja. On 13 November, Nehru directly advised the maharaja that 'no satisfactory way out can be found in Kashmir except through Sheikh Abdullah' and full confidence should be placed in him. He advised against a 'half-and-half affair', meaning the dual arrangement, provided in the accession documents, to which Hari Singh adhered.[6]

On I December, Nehru wrote again to Hari Singh explaining that the prospect of a plebiscite made it essential to garner popular support:

> If there is going to be a plebiscite, then obviously we have to work in such a way as to gain the goodwill of the majority of the population, which means chiefly the Muslims ... The only persons who can effectively deal with the situation is Sheikh Abdullah ... Even if military forces held Kashmir for a while, a later consequence might be a strong reaction against this. Essentially, therefore, this is a problem of psychological approach to the mass of the people and of making them feel that they will be benefited by being within the Indian Union. If the average Muslim feels that he has no safe and secure place in the Union then obviously he will look elsewhere ...

Accordingly, the time had come to establish a stable government without further delay. Abdullah should be designated prime minister and form the government with the maharaja as the constitutional head.[7]

PATEL BACKS MAHAJAN

Neither Hari Singh nor Mahajan was persuaded. From the time he assumed office, Mahajan used his influence to bolster the maharaja's powers and authority. It was his interpretation of Sheikh Abdullah's role that initially prevailed. His description of the crucial meeting merits recall:

> A conference was held at the residence of Pandit Nehru in which Sardar Patel and Mr V.P. Menon [secretary, Ministry of States] joined. Sheikh Abdullah demanded that he should be appointed "Prime Minister of Jammu and Kashmir" and I should become a glorified dummy as a "Dewan" with no powers. I know that the Maharaja would not have agreed to the appointment of the Sheikh as his Prime Minister. After three hours' discussion it was decided that Sheikh should be designated as the "Head of the Emergency Administration" and I should carry on as Prime Minister. I know that the Sheikh

> would not only try to grab as much power as he could but also use his position and power in the State to cut me out.[8]

Nehru now suggested modification of the Mysore formula through Gopalaswami Ayyangar (minister without portfolio given charge of Kashmir affairs). Patel noted in response on 10 December:

> The proposals which you have made may ease matters from the point of view of Sheikh Abdullah, but whether they ease matters from the point of view of the Maharaja is difficult for me to say. We have to bear in mind that it is we who suggested to the Maharaja to agree to the Mysore model and unless the Maharaja is persuaded to alter it, I feel that we cannot insist on him to accept any change. We have also to take into account that it is the Maharaja who entered into a commitment with Mr Mahajan and, therefore, it is for him to decide whether or not he could release himself from that commitment. All we can do is to persuade him to change his position.[9]

Patel sent a copy of his letter to Mahajan and asked him to show it to the maharaja.

In reply. the following day, Mahajan expressed his willingness to step down but did not want to let down the maharaja. He claimed to have brought the maharaja and Abdullah 'closer than anyone else'. However, in another letter the same day, he accused the Abdullah administration of 'Hitlerian methods'. Among the methods he cited were: the High Court not being allowed to move from Srinagar to Jammu; the governor of Jammu and many officers detained; others in jail without trial; certain officers whom the maharaja suspected to be Pakistanis reinstated, and finally, 'laws are being made by Abdullah himself'.[10]

Hari Singh was obviously encouraged by Patel's letter. He wrote to Gopalaswami on 17 December that he could not deviate from the Mysore model, and while agreeing to appoint Abdullah, insisted that Mahajan would continue as his dewan. Patel conveyed this to Nehru.[11]

His patience exhausted, Nehru wrote once more to Hari Singh on 30 December: 'You have said that your decision about Mahajan is final. I am sorry to learn this because I think this is not a right decision and it cannot lead us anywhere ... in the present set-up Mr Mahajan's place is not in Kashmir State.' The situation had changed since the Mysore model had been accepted and Abdullah's authority should not be weakened. A serious complaint against Mahajan was that his administration was associated in the public mind with the occurrences in Jammu at the end of October (when Muslims were attacked). Nehru complained that the arms meant for the home guard militia in Kashmir had been distributed to RSS groups and that he was not prepared to tolerate the activities of the RSS.[12] (He had received reports that Hari Singh was financing the RSS.) Nehru added urgency to the letter by dispatching a telegram to the maharaja drawing attention to the diversion of the arms sent for the home guards in Kashmir and to attacks on Muslims in Jammu. Mahajan denied the charges about the arms, and claims that Nehru expressed his regret and said he was misinformed.

That very day Nehru complained to Patel that Hari Singh's attitude had led to a complete deadlock and that 'I have used up all the tact at my disposal' in dealing with him. Abdullah and Bakshi had Hindu and Muslim backing in Kashmir. Even in Jammu local Hindus had been won over to a degree. A gulf, however, existed between Abdullah and Hindus from Punjab and the RSS which was accused of organized killing in Jammu. There would be constant friction as long as Mahajan remained.[13]

It was Gandhi's prayer address holding Hari Singh constitutionally responsible for the Jammu killings (noted in the Introduction) that evoked an outraged response revealing Mahajan's feelings. Writing to the Mahatma that his speech had been made on a false representation of facts, he insisted that more Hindus and Sikhs had lost their lives, and more of their women had been abducted, than Muslims. Contrary to reports from the scene, he insisted, 'Even at the present moment, though aggression on the part of the Hindus has completely stopped, the Muslim population is still out of control'. Even in the Valley, local Muslims and not the raiders had been responsible for the murder of thirty per cent of the Sikhs.

His anger against Abdullah also came through. While the maharaja's government could be held responsible for communal trouble up to 30 October, after that 'the responsibility [is] of the Dictator and his government as he had been in complete control of the administration'. He concluded 'Revered Mahatmaji, your verdict has been an extremely unkind act towards His Highness during this period of distress'.

Gandhi did not reply, but according to Mahajan, at a later meeting between them, 'I very strongly objected to his action in singling me out for condemnation in this manner and in condemning the killing of Muslims without condemning the killing of Hindus by the Muslims in the town of Mirpur and other places. Mahatmaji frankly agreed with me.'[14]

---

1 See V. Shankar, *My Reminiscences of Sardar Patel*, vol. II, Macmillan, New Delhi, 1974.
2 Nehru, pp. 268–71.
3 Ibid., pp 271–72.
4 Ibid., p. 277.
5 Ibid., pp. 279–81.
6 Ibid., pp. 324–27.
7 Ibid., pp. 349–53.
8 Mahajan op. cit., p. 156–57.
9 Patel, vol. I, p. 107.
10 Ibid., pp. 111–14.
11 Ibid pp. 115–18
12 Nehru, pp. 415–18.
13 Ibid., 414–15
14 Mahajan, op. cit. pp. 158–62.

PATEL'S RESIGNATION

Your letter makes it clear to me that I must not or at least cannot continue as a Member of Government and hence I am hereby tendering my resignation. I am grateful to you for the courtesy and kindness shown to me during the period of office which was a period of considerable strain.

– Sardar Patel to Jawaharlal Nehru

Letters exchanged between Jawaharlal Nehru and Vallabhbhai Patel, and by them to Gandhi, reveal how close these two pillars of the Indian National Congress came to publicly breaking apart within two months of becoming, respectively, prime minister and deputy prime minister of independent India. They represented widely different aspects of the Congress culture, but had worked together until their differences came to a head over Abdullah and Kashmir. The crisis coincided with Mahatma Gandhi's last fast for communal amity in Delhi and was eclipsed by his assassination on 30 January 1948. Their letters testify to the role of the Mahatma in keeping them together in life and in death, and their uncommon ability to express their thoughts and feelings. Posterity is obliged to the editors for compiling and publishing Sardar Patel's voluminous correspondence.[1]

The clash surfaced on superficially minor issues, as revealed in Patel's correspondence.[2] One related to Nehru despatching a senior official to Ajmer, the scene of communal disturbances, without going through the Home Ministry. (Indications of the prime minister's dissatisfaction with the Home Ministry's response to communal issues was a sensitive issue.) The other related to Kashmir affairs, which Nehru had entrusted to Gopalaswami Ayyangar, minister without portfolio, instead of the Ministry of States, which was under Patel. On 22 December, Patel wrote to Gopalaswami complaining that he had sent telegrams directly to the premier of East Punjab and to General Thimmayya (commanding forces in Kashmir) about the Kashmir administration's request for 150 motor vehicles. The question should have been handled by the Ministry of States. In future, he added peremptorily, 'the Kashmir Administration may be asked to deal with that Ministry direct'.

Gopalaswami's tart reply underlined the mounting friction on Kashmir:

> If, as Minister Without Portfolio, I can, in cases of this kind, merely act as a post office between a Ministry with a portfolio and persons outside, the situation is one which I cannot regard as consistent with my position as Member of the Cabinet ... I am the last person to wish to poach into any other Ministry's preserves and shall proceed to disconnect myself and my Ministry from all matters relating to Kashmir, including the negotiations in progress connected with the setting up of an Interim Government there.

Patel replied that his letter was concerned with transactions of ordinary administration and that 'there was no question of it affecting in any way the conduct of negotiations over which you are engaged; that the Prime Minister is already managing with your collaboration in consultation with me whenever necessary in supercession of the normal ministerial responsibility.'

Copies of these letters sent to him by Gopalaswami provided the spark that caused Nehru to erupt. He promptly wrote on 23 December to Patel that Kashmir raised international, military, and other issues that were beyond the competence of the States Ministry and had to be considered by various ministers. Gopalaswami had been asked to help because of his links with Kashmir. The conclusion of the letter was particularly harsh:

> I do not understand where the States Ministry comes into the picture, except that it should be informed of steps taken. In any event, I do not understand why the States Ministry should intervene and come in the way of arrangements being made. All this was done at my instance and I do not propose to abdicate my functions in regard to matters for which I consider myself responsible.

The exchange of letters extended late into the evening. Patel replied that he had received Nehru's letter at 7 p.m., and as it had caused him considerable pain he was hastening to send his resignation. He wrote:

> Your letter makes it clear to me that I must not or at least cannot continue as a Member of Government and hence I am hereby tendering my resignation. I am grateful to you for the courtesy and kindness shown to me during the period of office which was a period of considerable strain.

According to a footnote to Patel's correspondence, his letter of resignation was marked 'draft' and was not sent, presumably because he was persuaded to drop the controversy. His reaction, however, seems to have been conveyed to the prime minister. The conflict was patched up when Nehru expressed regret at causing his old colleague pain but, nevertheless, insisting that 'it seems that our approaches are different, however much we may respect each other. If I am to continue as Prime Minister, I cannot have my freedom restricted …' Patel responded by rejecting the possibility of Nehru's resignation and assuring him of his continued help, but stating that he could not continue 'as an ineffective colleague'.[3]

GANDHI INFORMED

In view of the serious implications of the breach, both wrote at length to Gandhi, sending copies to each other. Their views were politely expressed but did not disguise differences on matters of policy and ministerial responsibility, with Patel even suggesting that Nehru's interpretation of the prime minister's powers would make him a 'virtual dictator'.

Nehru began his letter of 6 January 1948 by recalling the long history of their differences:

> It is true that there are not only temperamental differences between Sardar and me but also a difference in approach in regard to economic and communal matters. The differences have persisted over a large number of years, ever since we worked together in the Congress. Nevertheless, in spite of these differences, there was obviously a great deal in common in addition to mutual respect and affection and, broadly speaking, the same national political aim of freedom.

On the role of the prime minister, he had the special function of coordination and supervision but without unnecessary interference with other ministers. However,

> ... [a]fter having given very serious thought to this matter during the last fortnight, I have come to the conclusion that as far as possible we must avoid, at this particular juncture, any parting of ways in Government. We are too much in the transitional stage and a serious shake-up of Government may well lead to an upsetting of the apple cart. I think we should carry on for some months till the Kashmir issue is more clarified and other problems have been tackled to some extent ... If, however, this is not considered possible, the only alternative left is for me or Sardar Patel to leave the Cabinet ... If someone has to leave, I would prefer to leave.

After seeing the copy of Nehru's letter, Patel wrote to Gandhi:

> There is no disagreement on the existence of temperamental differences and different outlook on economic matters and those affecting Hindu–Muslim relations. Both of us, however, place the interests of the country above these personal differences and, aided by mutual regard, respect and love for

> each other have cooperated in a common endeavour ... It is painful and rather tragic to reflect that we cannot carry this any further, but I fully realize the strength and conviction behind the Prime Minister's stand as regards his own position ... I have found myself unable to agree with his conception of the Prime Minister's duties and functions. That conception, if accepted, would raise the Prime Minister to the position of a virtual dictator ... .[4]

Referring to the preference expressed by Nehru for being the one to leave office, Patel concluded:

> The Prime Minister is the acknowledged leader of the country and is comparatively young; he has established an international position of preeminence for himself. I have no doubt that the choice between him and myself should be resolved in his favour. There is, therefore, no question of his quitting office.

Meanwhile, the Mahatma had begun his last fast. Nehru wrote to Patel on 13 January that the fast overshadowed other matters but hoped they would be able to fix a meeting with him. Patel then wrote an emotional letter to Gandhi:

> The sight of your anguish yesterday has made me disconsolate. It has set me furiously thinking. The burden of work has become so heavy that I feel crushed under it. I now see that it would do no good to the country or myself to carry on like this any more. I might even do harm. Jawahar is more burdened than I. His heart is heavy with grief. May be I have deteriorated with age and am no more any good as a comrade to stand by him and lighten his burden. The Maulana [Congress President Azad, who had suggested he had communal tendencies] too is displeased with what I am doing and you have again and again to take up cudgels on my behalf. This is also intolerable to me. In the circumstances, it will perhaps be good for me and for the country if you now let me go. I cannot do otherwise than I am doing.

UNITED IN GRIEF

A week later, they were united in grief over Gandhi's assassination. The letters they exchanged expressed their feelings. Nehru wrote to Patel, 'Now with Bapu's death, everything is changed and we have to face a different and more difficult world. The old controversies have ceased to be of much significance and it seems to me that the urgent need of the hour is for all of us to function as closely and cooperatively as possible ... We have learnt to disagree and yet carry on together.'

Patel was deeply touched, as expressed by his eloquent reply: 'We both have been lifelong comrades in a common cause. The paramount interests of our country and our mutual love and regard, transcending such differences of outlook and temperament as existed, have held us together ... His [Gandhi's] death changes everything and the crisis that has overtaken us must awaken in us a fresh realization of how much we have achieved together and the need for further joint efforts in our grief-stricken country's interests.'[5]

The differences however persisted. Patel remained minister for states and home affairs. He could not be spared. His skills were needed to manage the affairs of the ruling Congress party and retain the support of conservative elements within it. Though reluctantly implementing Nehru instructions, they continued to pull in opposite directions on Kashmir. The gulf between them, and the confusion it caused, is frankly described in the recollections of Patel's private secretary, V. Shankar. 'With Pandit Nehru. Sardar Patel and Gopalaswami Ayyangar providing the top leadership, External Affairs and States Ministry sharing the responsibility of Kashmir affairs at the departmental level, and the Maharaja and his Government under Sheikh Abdullah pulling in different directions and at cross purposes locally, it is a marvel that things did progress at all.'

Shankar, who was close to and an admirer of his minister, provides a background to his differences with Nehru: distrust of Abdullah and reliance on Hari Singh:

> Sardar did not trust the Sheikh nor did he share Pt Nehru's assessment of his influence in the State. He felt that our case in

Jammu and Kashmir had to be met on the basis of Maharaja's executing the Instrument of Accession. The thought of antagonizing the one on whose signature on that document alone we could justfy our legal case in Jammu and Kashmir was distressing to him …

Sardar Patel also came into conflict with Pt Nehru and Gopalaswami Ayyangar owing to the personal rift between the Maharaja and Sheikh Abdullah. It can scarcely be denied that the latter wanted the maharaja's head on a charger and taking advantage of the wrong assessment by Pandit Nehru and Gopalaswami Ayyangar of the extent of his influence in the Valley he literally wanted to dictate his own terms. Sardar Patel had shrewdly come to the conclusion that Sheikh Abdullah would not be able to deliver the goods in the event of a plebiscite which, thanks to Lord Mountbatten, was the ruling consideration of the time. Consequently, he did not want to put all eggs in the Abdullah basket.[6]

1 *Sardar Patel's Correspondence, 1945–50,* in ten volumes, ed. Durga Das, Navajivan Publishing House, Ahmedabad, 1971.

2 Patel, vol i, pp. 118–22.

3 Patel, vol vi, pp. 10–13.

4 Mountbatten's self-projecting account of his meetings with Nehru and Patel as governor-general after the clash figures in the Lord Mountbatten Papers, Broadland Archives Trust. He claims he told off Patel for faulty procedure. As for Nehru, 'I told him that in my opinion not even Mr Churchill, in the heyday of his power, dared to ride roughshod over his Ministers in the way that Pandit Nehru appeared to be doing.' He then pointed out 'the right way of dealing with this kind of thing', undeterred by his lack of experience in cabinet government.

5 Patel, pp. 17–26.

6 V. Shankar, *My Reminiscences of Sardar Patel*, vol. II, Macmillan, New Delhi, 1974.

SWORD OF PLEBISCITE

Sometimes I feel that I should withdraw the accession that I have made to the Indian Union. The Union only provisionally accepted the accession and if the Union cannot recover back our territory and is eventually going to agree to the decision of the Security Council which may result in handing us over to Pakistan then there is no point in sticking to the accession of the State to the Indian Union ... There is an alternative possible for me and that is to withdraw the accession because the Indian Union will have no right to continue the proceedings ... I am prepared to lead my army personally and to command, if the Indian Union agrees, also their troops. It would certainly hearten my people and the troops. I know my country better than any of your generals ...

– Hari Singh to Sardar Patel

Winter is a cruel time in Kashmir. *Kangris,* small earthen pots with live coals, held under full-length cloak-like *pheran,* are the only protection that most people have against the freezing cold. Dependence on food and fuel, imported earlier, is high. Winter 1948 was particularly severe. The Indian Army had driven back the Pathan raiders along the road to the border town of Muzaffarabad, but could not proceed beyond Uri. This meant that the traditional supply route into the Valley was closed. The alternative route from Jammu across Banihal Pass was often blocked by snow. Essential supplies had to be flown in. Prices rose, together with complaints of corruption in the distribution network overseen by National Conference ward committees. From the outset, the Abdullah administration was beset with problems.

Expectations from Abdullah in the Valley were unlimited after his appointment as head of the Emergency Administration, and then as the state's first popular prime minister, High office, however, proved frustrating and precarious; the ground on which it was raised unstable; his principal adversary was his head of state. Maharaja Hari Singh wreaked his revenge against the man he was forced to appoint prime minister by sponsoring a communal campaign against him in Jammu, which then spread to the rest of India and was taken up in the Indian parliament. Backing from New Delhi was undermined by the conflicting approaches of Nehru and Patel, one supporting him, the other the maharaja.

Abdullah's own limitations did not help. He was no diplomat; his mass popularity engendered a sense of superiority. His rash statements often hurt his friends and strengthened his opponents. He had no administrative experience while the administration he inherited was largely loyal to the maharaja. Preoccupied as he was with the future of the Kashmir Valley, he had little following in Jammu and Ladakh, the two other provinces of the state. Also, having gained power, rivalries emerged within the National Conference. His rival in eloquence, Ghulam Mohiuddin Qarra, broke away.

The odds were weighted against Abdullah, yet he was able to retain and deepen his popularity in the Valley by pushing through the radical land reforms promised in the Naya Kashmir manifesto; reforms that brought hope to the exploited peasantry. Large estates were abolished and landownership limited to twenty-two acres, with the surplus transferred to the tiller. The sweeping reform exceeded anything attempted by the Congress and attracted the criticism of conservatives like Patel who feared it might set a precedent. It exposed Abdullah to charges of communal favouritism as most of the beneficiaries were Muslim. It, however, reinforced his popularity when he was under pressure, though party and administrative corruption limited the gains. The Abdullah government's inability to improve the foodgrain levy and distribution system it had inherited enhanced the impact of the shortages in the state after Partition and war.

Abdullah might have learnt to overcome his problems had he not had a sword of Damocles hanging over his office in the form of the offer of a UN-sponsored plebiscite in the state made by his friend Jawaharlal Nehru. Both miscalculated. Nehru saw plebiscite as an opportunity to demonstrate to the nation and the world the secular thesis he shared with Abdullah that all Muslims of the subcontinent did not accept the two-nation theory. In truth however the prospect of plebiscite, with its communal overtones, provided an emotive issue to Hindu communal parties. Abdullah's intemperate speeches on special status as a condition of accession were treated as anti-national and, by implication, evidence that Muslims could not be trusted. Sharp exchanges on the issue in parliament and in the media widened the rift.

When the plebiscite controversy revived differences on special status, Abdullah used it as a political weapon to counter moves to fully integrate Jammu & Kashmir in the Union. However, contrary to the impression created by his detractors, he did not favour plebiscite; he anticipated that it would endanger the stability of the state. He had wanted accession to India to be confirmed by the State Constituent Assembly when it was inaugurated in 1951. This was confirmed in letters exchanged between Nehru and the Jana Sangh leader, Syama Prasad Mookerjee, in January 1953. Criticizing Nehru's handling of the Kashmir issue, Mookerjee wrote, 'I was told by Sheikh Abdullah that he and his colleagues were willing to adopt this procedure [passing a resolution in the Kashmir constituent assembly in favour of accession to India] but you were not prepared to approve it'. Nehru replied: 'This is partly true, but refers to a particular time. When the constituent assembly first started functioning this proposal was considered. Our advice then was that it would not be wise to pass that resolution immediately as this would lead to the conclusion that the assembly had been called for this purpose ...'[1]

The reality is that Abdullah strongly opposed the proposal when it was first mooted. He insisted that the decision to join India had been made when the Naional Conference supported accession and helped drive out the Pathan raiders sent by Pakistan. There was no question of choosing between the two. When, however, plebiscite was proposed by the UN Security Council, it created uncertainty in the state. Supporters of Pakistan hoped to do well, expecting the vote to be determined by religion. Faced with this possibility, Abdullah projected the third option of independence.[2]

SELF-GOAL AT UN

India's formal complaint against Pakistan to the UN Security Council on 30 December 1947 proved a self-goal at home and abroad. The council did not endorse India's complaint and the debate heightened friction with the West and dependence on the Soviet veto. At home, it stoked contradictory fears. Nehru's confidence that Abdullah would win a plebiscite for India was matched by Patel's distrust and reliance on the maharaja. Passions were aroused by describing as pro-Pakistani those recalling the condition of consulting the people attached to Kashmir's accession.

The impact of the UN debate on Hari Singh was disquieting. He seemed to lose touch with reality. After roundly condemning India's foreign and defence policies, he went to the extent of threatening to withdraw accession. He began the New Year by complaining to Patel about the move to arm the Home Guards organized by the National Conference in the Valley. Describing it as dangerous, he said the weapons could be snatched away from the guards who 'are totally unfit to handle arms'. The underlying fear that his authority would be threatened was conveyed by the phrase, 'obviously a great effort to create a rival army in the State is being made'. He went on to give vent to his frustration and bitterness:

> Sheikh Abdullah and Bakshi [Ghulam Mohammad] are virtual dictators and they have complete power. I wonder what we are expected to do and what the suggestion is. Even when Mr Mahajan and I have stepped aside are we to be blamed or coerced? This seems to me only deep propaganda in disguise to

> drive me to desperation by being bullied right and left. Already there is no law here and if the present policy continues it will be worse.[3]

In successive letters to Patel on 25 and 31 January, Hari Singh insisted on being consulted before any commitment was made to the UN Security Council. He followed up with a rambling condemnation of every aspect of the union government's handling of Kashmir: the performance of the army; the reference to the UN without consulting him; the ability of the National Conference leadership to govern.

This culminated with a threat to withdraw accession and lead his own army against the enemy. (His claim to military prowess was based on the honorary rank of Lieutenant General awarded by the British Government in return for the state's contributions to the Second World War.) His letter of 31 January to Patel illustrated his state of mind:

> Sometimes I feel that I should withdraw the accession that I have made to the Indian Union. The Union only provisionally accepted the accession and if the Union cannot recover back our territory and is eventually going to agree to the decision of the Security Council which may result in handing us over to Pakistan then there is no point in sticking to the accession of the State to the Indian Union … There is an alternative possible for me and that is to withdraw the accession because the Indian Union will have no right to continue the proceedings … The result may be a return to the position the State held before accession … I am prepared to take over command of my own forces along with the forces of the Indian Army as volunteers to help the State. I am prepared to lead my army personally and to command, if the Indian Union agrees, also their troops. It would certainly hearten my people and the troops. I know my country better than any of your generals …
>
> Another alternative that strikes me is that if I can do nothing I should leave the State (short of abdication) and reside outside so that people do not think I can do anything for them … The responsibility will then be either of the Indian Union or of the administration of Sheikh Abdullah.[4]

Patel soothed Hari Singh's feelings by assuring him that he was no less anxious about Kashmir and the proceedings at the UN, but 'a counsel of despair is entirely out of place'.[5] The maharaja did not persist with the threat of withdrawing accession. Patel sent a copy of his letter to Nehru who suggested that it would be better not to respond. In another letter to Patel he criticized the maharaja for refusing to permit his Jammu stud farm to be used as a refugee camp, his army barracks for Indian troops, and for turning down advice to return to Srinagar. This was antagonizing the people of the state.

Responding to criticlism of the Indian Army, Nehru was even more disparaging about the condition of the state troops, who had deserted their posts in Ladakh, and Hari Singh's ability to lead them:

> About the [state] army I fear it can never improve if the Maharaja has anything to do with it. It is in a hopeless mess ... They, or their officers, have lost all morale and discipline and any further association with the Maharaja will worsen the position. If any effective State army is to be built up, as it must be, it must be by our own officers and men. The matter is too serious to be left to the discretion of the Maharaja. We are playing for high stakes and dare not take risks.[6]

Reactions to Abdullah's invitation to celebrate the achievement of responsible government in the state during the week beginning 7 May 1948 reflected the differences of approach couched in the politest language. According to the invitation, responsible government had been 'secured after a bitter struggle extending over seventeen years' (since 1931 when the struggle against Dogra rule began). Regretting that he could not attend due to ill-health, Patel replied, 'we need not reflect on the bitterness of the past but on the happy and cordial relations of the present and on the glory and prosperity of the future'. He wrote to Nehru that the celebrations were inappropriate when lives were being lost defending the state. Nehru advised Abdullah to tone down the celebrations, but the reasons he gave were scarcity and poverty. However, he participated in the celebrations and on return wrote to Patel that they were successful and impressive, and 'there can be no doubt that Sheikh Abdullah's popularity in Srinagar and the Valley is very great'.[7]

PATEL'S ADVOCACY

Hari Singh did not repeat his threat to nullify accession after Patel suffered a heart attack in early March. Maharani Tara Devi expressed their concern to Patel's daughter, Maniben, who looked after him: 'You are already aware how worried we must be during these days. And since we learnt of Sardar Sahib's illness our anxiety has grown.'[8] Patel however showed no lessening of interest in the maharaja's affairs, and the rift between him and Hari Singh, on the one hand, and Nehru and Abdullah, on the other, widened.

From his sickbed, Patel instructed his secretary, Shankar, to take up Hari Singh's complaint that *jagirs*, the extensive estates gifted by the Dogra rulers to their courtiers, were being resumed without payment of compensation under Abdullah's land reform measures. Shankar noted that 'it is also to be borne in mind that probably the jagirdars would be mostly non-Muslims and this measure would probably create a certain amount of discontent and ill-feeling against the Government among the minority community'.[9]

Patel's advocacy went further. Still resting in Dehra Dun, he complained to Nehru on 4 June that Hari Singh's rights were not being respected: 'I have impressed upon the Sheikh Sahib as well as Bakshi the necessity of maintaining the prestige, the rights, and privileges of the Maharaja, but the manner in which the questions of his privy purse, jagirdars, and commandeering of office accommodation of his Private Department have left on my mind a most painful impression.'[10] Nehru was not persuaded. He conceded that Abdullah was not always tactful, but Hari Singh was oblivious of the need to muster popular goodwill and 'behaves in a manner which is completely inexplicable to me and which irritates the people'. In another letter to Patel he wrote, 'My study of the Kashmir situation has led me to believe that the Maharaja cannot play. He just does not know how to.'[11]

Abdullah could not suppress the grave charges he nurtured

against the maharaja at a meeting between them on 5 August. As related by Hari Singh in a long note to Patel, the charges included atrocities by the state troops and massacre of Muslims in Jammu, in which Abdullah 'started hinting that I had a hand'. He quoted Abdullah as angrily telling him, 'I have got to turn the minds of Muslims of the State from Pakistan to the Indian Dominion. If the Muslims feel their lives are not safe and things are not done the way I want them to be done there is no use my carrying on and I had better resign.'

To the suggestion that matters be left to the Union Ministry of States (headed by Patel), Abdullah was quoted as saying: 'If the States Ministry wants to drown myself in the Dal [lake], I for one am not going to do so. I will resign and tell the people that I have done so because I have been hampered both here and in Delhi and they can go to Pakistan or the Indian Dominion as they like.'[12]

Hari Singh's efforts to retain the inherited symbols of a dying era now verged on the pathetic. He requested Patel to see that the gun salutes in the state on his birthday, Yuvraj Karan Singh's birthday, 'departures and arrivals of myself and Her Highness', and religious festivals, were fired by the Indian army as he no longer exercised control over the state forces. V. Shankar dutifully replied that the appropriate instructions had been issued.[13]

OPEN ANIMOSITY

The animosity between Patel and Abdullah was no longer disguised. The home and states minister took strong objection to the views expressed by Abdullah at a press conference in Delhi on 25 September. He objected to his criticizing Hari Singh who, he insisted, had behaved constitutionally as head of state and could not defend himself. He was upset with his mention of Hindu fanaticism in Punjab. What however most angered Patel was Abdullah's reported reference to 'the Maharaja's friends in Delhi and certain people who believed in surrendering Kashmir to Pakistan'. He took this as a reference to himself. Patel protested to Nehru and wrote an angry letter to Abdullah.

Patel's letter touched off Abdullah's suppressed anger with the

Union States Ministry and the maharaja. He was barely polite in his reply of 7 October:

> I am astonished to have it from you that there is "practically no restriction or objection from the Maharaja in regard to the many schemes of reforms" which I have introduced or am introducing. Nor did I expect from you the remark that "today the Maharaja is powerless"... Nothing indeed is further from the facts than the complacency contained in this assertion and I may be pardoned if I have to say that the States Ministry should be so ignorant of the real position.

Abdullah recalled obstructions to the promised reorganization of the state forces. It had been agreed, he said, that 'when the present emergency is over and the Indian forces are withdrawn, the State will be left with a properly organized army to fall back upon', but nothing had been done. As the state forces had been 'a close preserve of the favourites of the ruling family', it had created problems, which was why he suggested that it be placed under a minister of his government. This was not accepted.

What rankled most was that 'that the unmistakable part which the Maharaja and his satellites took in the general massacre of Muslims in Jammu are but insufficiently appreciated'. The letter recalled a note sent earlier in which Abdullah had charged that as Hari Singh and his entourage fled from Srinagar to Jammu when the Pathan raiders attacked, 'from the [Banihal] tunnel there was enacted in every village and town through which he passed an orgy of arson and loot and the murder of Muslims. In Jammu, the killing of Muslims all over the province continued unabated for weeks under his very nose ... As against this, I and every member of the National Conference in Kashmir province at that moment of grave peril were fighting the raiders and protecting the life and honour of the microscopic minority here'. (It was actually Maharani Tara Devi, rather than the bemused maharaja, who had incited their Dogra followers to take revenge.)

The maharaja had turned down his appeal to ban the RSS which was responsible, but still he was expected to restore public confidence.

He had recalled that Gandhiji was so moved by this tragedy that he several times at his prayer meetings referred to the carnage in Jammu. 'I feel intensely on these matters,' Abdullah concluded, 'we are engaged in a life and death struggle. This is not a time to mince matters.'

Although couched in temperate language, Patel's response hit where it hurt most. He taunted, 'I am also surprised that you, who had a different attitude towards H.H. when you were in jail, as typified in your letter to him a copy of which is with me, should now speak in such terms of him'. (For the text of the letter, see Chapter 12) He continued:

> You have again harped upon incidents which, I thought, you had discreetly avoided persisting in, viz. the allegations against His Highness about atrocities. You do not seem to realize that both you and we ourselves owe the technical correctness of our position in regard to Kashmir to the Maharaja's signing the accession and calling upon you to form the ministry. Without that, neither we nor you would have been where we are.[14]

Patel explained that his ministry rather than the maharaja was responsible for holding up the Kashmir government's moves to resume *jagirs* (under the Naya Kashmir programme) because it had all-India considerations 'from which you may be immune but which we are bound' (an argument that strengthened Kashmir's case for greater autonomy).

Patel reinforced his complaints against Abdullah by noting to Gopalaswami Ayyangar that Jammu & Kashmir 'seems to be an independent State and the Government of India appears to have abdicated their functions'. Nehru was however unconvinced. While agreeing that Abdullah had been 'very indiscreet' in publicly criticizing the maharaja, he insisted that 'Sheikh Abdullah is, I am convinced, a very straight and frank man. He is not a very clear thinker and he goes astray in his speech as many of our politicians do ...'

HARI SINGH BANISHED

Nehru saw that the situation was getting out of hand: 'I feel that it is no longer safe for us to allow matters to drift,' and finally asserted his prerogative as prime minster. In a letter to Patel on 17 April, he insisted that 'the Maharaja take some kind of leave and not remain in Kashmir'. The letter contained serious charges against Hari Singh based on intelligence reports. He was financing 'a growing Hindu agitation in Jammu province for what is called a zonal plebiscite. This is based on the belief that a plebiscite for the whole of Kashmir is bound to be lost and therefore let us save Jammu at least ... If we want Jammu province by itself and are prepared to make a present of the rest of the State to Pakistan, I have no doubt we could clinch the issue in a few days. The prize we are fighting for is the Valley of Kashmir.'[15]

This time Patel did not offer to resign and carried out the instructions, though making Hari Singh's exit as painless as possible. He invited the maharaja and his family to dinner of 29 April. Yuvraj Karan Singh recalls the scene:

> After dinner my parents and the Sardar went into another room, and it was there that the blow fell. The Sardar told my father gently but firmly that although Sheikh Abdullah was pressing for his abdication, the Government of India felt it would be sufficient if he and my mother absented themselves from the State for a few months ... I should be appointed Regent by my father to carry out his duties and responsibilities in his absence. My father ... emerged from the meeting ashen-faced ... My mother went to her room where she flung herself on to her bed and burst into tears.[16]

Hari Singh took to horse-racing in Bombay. Only Karan Singh returned to Kashmir where, as *sadar-i-riyasat* (governor under the then state constitution), he would sign the papers deposing and imprisoning Abdullah but he did not inherit the title maharaja, which was abolished.

---

1 Nehru, vol. 22, pp. 179–80.
2 Recalled by P.N. Jalali, a confidante of Abdullah at the time.
3 Patel, vol. I, p. 147.
4 Ibid., pp. 158–64.
5 Ibid., pp. 165–66

6 Ibid., p. 201
7 Ibid., pp. 184–89.
8 Ibid., p. 174.
9 Ibid., pp. 182–83
10 Ibid., pp. 192–84
11 Ibid., pp. 200–1, 203–05.
12 Ibid., pp. 212–15.
13 Ibid., pp. 225–26.
14 Ibid., pp. 227–45 for text of letters exchanged.
15 Ibid., pp. 261–65.
16 Karan Singh, *Heir Apparent*, p. 92.

VISION OF INDEPENDENCE

We are proud to have our bonds with India, the goodwill of whose people and Government is available to us in unstinted measure . . . The Constitution of India . . . has treated us differently from other constituent units. With the exception of the items grouped under defence, foreign affairs and communications in the Instrument of Accession, we have complete freedom to frame our Constitution in the manner we like . . . while safeguarding our autonomy to the fullest extent so as to enable us to have the liberty to build our country according to the best traditions and genius of our people.

– Sheikh Abdullah's address to the
Jammu & Kashmir Constituent Assembly

Converting Kashmir into the Switzerland of the East was the dream shared by Maharaja Hari Singh and Sheikh Abdullah. As noted earlier, in the last days of Hari Singh's brief rule of an independent Jammu & Kashmir, his deputy prime minister, R.L. Batra, proudly announced to the press in New Delhi that 'the Maharaja has told me that his ambition is to make Kashmir the Switzerland of the East—a State that is completely neutral'. Even after being forced by the Pathan invasion to accede to India, he tried to salve as much of his dream as he could by placing tight limits on New Delhi's authority in the Instrument of Accession.

Switzerland's history of neutrality between warring neighbours and its tourist attractions had long been a model. Its people, too, spoke different languages. The state of Jammu & Kashmir was also known for its picturesque lakes, gardens, and mountains, among the highest in the world, to which so many poets and writers had testified. It had, however, been less successful in protecting itself from foreign invasion and local exploitation. Poverty, inaccessibility, and strategic considerations had kept it a land of distant beauty attracting the few but not a tourist resort for the many.

Abdullah's version of the dream began, ironically, with the desire for *azaadi* or freedom from the feudal oppression represented by Hari Singh, but developed into the ideal of neutral independence. In May 1949, a report in London's *Sunday Observer* attracted notice in New Delhi. It reported Abdullah as saying:

> Accession to either side cannot bring peace. We want to live in friendship with both Dominions [India and Pakistan]. Perhaps a middle path between them with economic cooperation with each other will be the only way to do it. However, an independent Kashmir must be guranteed not only by India and Pakistan, but also by Great Britain, the US and the UN.

The idea was not new. During the initial discussions on Kashmir at the Security Council in 1948, the Argentinian delegate, Dr Jose Arce, said, 'The Kashmiri people may well decide not to accede to India but to be independent'. Later, in 1951, Dr T.G.P. Spear, a Cambridge University historian who had once taught in India, suggested that the Valley be made an independent state guaranteed by the UN as well as by India and Pakistan, and be policed by UN troops.'

ABDULLAH'S ROAD-MAP

Most of these suggestions, as well as others emanating from later UN discussions, focused on the Valley, leaving the rest of the state to India and Pakistan. Abdullah's vision expanded from the Valley to the entire state. Even as prime minister of the state, he returned to the theme. In his inaugural address to the State Constituent Assembly in May 1951, he spoke of the attractions 'of making ourselves an eastern Switzerland', but dismissed the idea as unfeasible. His words were pregnant with meaning:

> We have to consider the alternative of making ourselves an eastern Switzerland, of keeping aloof from both States [India and Pakistan], but having friendly relations with them. This may seem attractive in that it would appear to pave the way out of the present deadlock. To us as a tourist country, it would also have certain obvious advantages. But in considering independence we must not ignore practical considerations. Firstly, it is not easy to protect sovereignty and independence in a small country which has not sufficient strength to defend itself on our long and difficult frontiers bordering so many countries. Secondly, we do not find powerful guarantors among them to pull together always in assuring us freedom from aggression.

He recalled in this context, the tribal invasion of Kashmir and said there was no guarantee against a repetition of such aggression.

Abdullah's address was a carefully crafted statement of the balance he hoped to achieve between the desire for *azaadi* and the need for links with India. A road map for the future, it emphasized the need to safeguard Kashmir's special status and indicated how the balance could be upset as it had been:

> We are proud to have our bonds with India, the goodwill of whose people and Government is available to us in unstinted measure ... The Constitution of India ... has treated us differently from other constituent units. With the exception with of the items grouped under defence, foreign affairs and communications in the Instrument of Accession, we have complete freedom to frame our constitution in the manner we like ... while safeguarding our autonomy to the fullest extent so as to enable us to have the liberty to build our country according to the best traditions and genius of our people ...

The address was also remarkable for dealing frankly with the sensitive issue of the future of Muslims in a Hindu-majority nation and underlining the role of secularism. Its praise for the Indian constitution, promulgated the previous year with Article 370 providing for Kashmir's special status, could scarcely be improved upon:

> The Indian Constitution has set before the country the goal of secular democracy based upon justice, freedom and equality for all without distinction. This is the bedrock of modern democracy. This should meet the argument that the Muslims of Kashmir cannot have security in India, where the large majority of the population are Hindus ... The Indian Constitution has amply and finally repudiated the concept of a religious State, which is a throwback to medievalism ... The national movement in our State naturally gravitates towards these principles of secular democracy. The people here will never accept a principle which intends to favour the interests of one religion or social group against another.

This did not mean overlooking his fears of the threat of Hindu communalism in India, while expressing the hope that Kashmir would help to counter it:

> Certain tendencies have been asserting themselves in India which may in the future convert it into a religious State wherein the interests of Muslims will be jeopardized ... The continued accession of Kashmir to India should, however, help in defeating this tendency.

Pakistan, however, provided no answer:

> The claim of being a Muslim State is of course only a camouflage. It is a screen to dupe the common man, so that he may not see clearly that Pakistan is a feudal State in which a clique is trying ... to maintain itself in power. In addition to this, the appeal to religion constitutes a sentimental and wrong approach to the question.

He did not overlook his conflict with Hari Singh:

> After attainment of complete power by the people, it would have been an appropriate gesture of goodwill to recognize Maharaja Hari Singh as the first constitutional Head of State. But I must say with regret that he has completely forfeited the confidence of every section of the people. His incapacity to adjust himself to changed conditions and antiquated views on modern problems constitute positive disqualifications for him to hold the high office of a democratic Head of State.

This remarkably perceptive survey of the forces impinging upon the delicate constitutional balance achieved by Jammu & Kashmir in the Indian Union represented the challenge Abdullah saw facing him as prime minister of the state. He was at the peak of his career and it provides a key to understanding previous events and subsequent developments. (The complete text of address is reproduced in Appendix Two.)

MEETING WITH US DIPLOMATS

When Abdullah spoke of not finding 'powerful guarantors', he spoke from experience. While on the Indian delegation to the UN in early 1948, he had blamed Pakistan for the tribal invasion of Kashmir that the Security Council was debating. Until then he and his colleagues had been discussing whether to join India or Pakistan or be independent. It was under these circumstances that 'both the Maharaja and the people of Kashmir requested the Government of India to accept our accession'. He praised Nehru for making accession subject to ratification by the people after Kashmir had been freed from the marauders.[2] Thus, the third option of independence was kept on the table.

Abdullah had been invited to join the Indian delegation to show the Security Council that accession of Jammu & Kashmir to India had popular support. Pakistani spokesmen insisted that it was his proximity to Nehru that influenced his backing for the decision. His response was characteristic:

> It is said that Sheikh Abdullah is a friend of Jawaharlal Nehru. Yes, I admit that. I feel honoured that such a great man claims me as his friend. And he happens to belong to my own country; he is also a Kashmiri and blood is thicker than water. But that does not mean that because of his friendship I am going to betray the millions of my people who have suffered along with me for the last seventeen years and sacrifice the interests of my country. I am not a man of that calibre.

Though not disclosed at the time, while in New York Abdullah met Warren Austin, the US representative at the UN. Austin sent the following message to US Secretary of State, George Marshall, on 28 January 1948, as recorded in State Department papers subsequently made public:

> It is possible that principal purpose of Abdullah's visit was to make it clear to US that there is a third alternative, namely independence. He was overly anxious to get this point across ... He did not want his people to be torn by dissensions between Pakistan and India. It would be much better if Kashmir were independent and could seek American and British aid for development of country. I, of course, gave Abdullah no encouragement on this line and am confident that when he left he understood very well where we stand on this matter.[3]

George Marshall set out the official line in a telegram to the US embassy in New Delhi on 4 March 1948:

> Re various proposals for Kashmir independence, we had in the past, as you know, followed the line that princely states be incorporated in either India or Pakistan on assumption that balkanization of Indian subcontinent would jeopardize and complicate economic transition and create conditions of instability ultimately adverse to broad US interests [in] that area. Our current thinking re Kashmir is influenced by these considerations subject to proviso that should concept of independence appear to be basis of GOI-GOP [India– Pakistan]

> peaceful settlement of Kashmir issue, we would probably not oppose such a solution, but would certainly take no initiative in supporting it.

However, there is evidence that Abdullah continued to sound out Western response to the third option. On 29 September 1950, he met the US ambassador to India, Loy Henderson, who cabled the State Department on his two secret meetings. The message shows Abdullah trying to adjust to American Cold War pressures by denying, presumably in response to questions, that he was pro-communist. He had broken up large estates without compensation (for which Naya Kashmir had taken pride) to deny communists the credit. On the question of independence, Henderson's telegram added:

> In discussion [of the] future of Kashmir, Abdullah was vigorous in restating that in his opinion it should be independent; that an overwhelming majority of the population desired their independence; that he had reason to believe that some Azad Kashmir leaders desired independence and would be willing to cooperate with leaders of the National Conference if there was reasonable chance such cooperation would lead to independence. Kashmir people could not understand why UN consistently ignored independence as possible solution for Kashmir. Kashmir people had language and cultural background of their own. The Hindus by custom and tradition differed widely from Hindus of India, and the background of Muslims quite different from Muslims of Pakistan. Fact was that population of Kashmir homogenous in spite of presence of Hindu minority.

Asked by the ambassador whether an independent Kashmir could remain stable without the support of India or Pakistan, Abdullah was reported to have replied that it would need US assistance, directly or through the UN. He added:

> Adherence of Kashmir to India would not lead in the foreseeable future to improving miserable lot of the population.

> There were so many areas of India in urgent need of economic development, [he was convinced that Kashmir would get relatively little attention]. Nevertheless, it was preferable for Kashmir to go to India than to Pakistan. It would be disastrous for Kashmir to be brought under control of [a] government with [a] medieval outlook.[4]

At the same time, Abdullah did not go along with Western proposals for a plebiscite under a divided authority in the state. When the UN representative, Dr Frank Graham, and his team met him in Srinagar in July 1951, he argued that legally the authority of the maharaja should be restored over the entire state before a plebiscite could be held. Before meeting Graham, he had been briefed about discussions between Nehru and the UN representative.[5]

Walter Crocker, then Australian high commissioner in New Delhi, recalls Abdullah favouring independence when they met during a visit of his to Kashmir in 1952.[6] These discussions were not publicized, but press reports of Abdullah's meeting in Srinagar in 1952 with Adlai Stevenson, then a high-profile candidate for the US presidency, touched off a public storm. Abdullah's version of the meeting in his memoirs is that as he was an honoured guest, he was invited to lunch. 'When he [Stevenson] reached Delhi the correspondents asked if he had met me. In his garrulous manner he said, "of course, three times". That was enough for the press, and particularly for the Left, to raise hell.'

SUSPICIONS AROUSED

The US stand on Kashmir in the Security Council was seen as hostile, especially as interpreted by the acerbic Krishna Menon when representing India at the UN. Reports of US moves to associate Pakistan with Western military alliances were seen as a mounting threat by New Delhi. In this context, contacts with Western diplomats on Kashmir could not but arouse suspicion.

On 13 July 1953, the US ambassador in New Delhi, George Allen, cabled the State Department for instructions, reporting that 'Indian leaders certain to show concern over reports that individual

Americans have encouraged Abdullah to favour independence for Kashmir and have held out hope of US economic assistance, possibly in return for air bases ... There has been veiled implication that Stevenson was charged with special mission by present US administration. Nehru appears convinced of this and may have originated reports.'

In response, the ambassador was asked to assure the prime minister that the 'US Government made no suggestion, officially or unofficially, [to] encourage Kashmir government [to] seek satisfaction [on] any set of demands. You may assure Nehru [that] Stevenson [was] given no mission to discuss Kashmir with Abdullah or anyone else.' American embassy staff were asked to refrain from visiting Kashmir.[7]

---

1 Cited by P.N.K. Bamzai, *Kashmir and Power Politics,* Metropolitan Books, Delhi, 1966, pp. 195–96.

2 *Documents on Kashmir Problem,* II, pp. 210–26.

3 *Foreign Relations of the United States 1948,* vol. v, pt I, Washington DC, 1975, p. 294.

4 Ibid., vol. v, pp. 1433–35.

5 Sandeep Bamzai, *Bonfire of Kashmiryat: Deconstructing the Accession,* Rupa, Delhi, pp. 201–06.

6 W.R. Crocker, *Nehru: A Contemporary's Estimate,* George Allen & Unwin, London, 1966, p. 96.

7 *US Foreign Relations 1950,* vol XI, pp. 1953–54.

HINDUTVA CAMPAIGN

It is very well for the people of India to think that communalism has been finally eliminated. but no one can deny that the communal spirit still exists in India. Many Kashmiris are apprehensive as to what will happen to them and their position if, for instance, something happens to Pandit Nehru.

– Sheikh Abdullah at Ranbirsinghpura

As the plebiscite sword of Damocles continued to dangle over Jammu & Kashmir it gave rise to disruptive fears and reactions, and the UN-sponsored ceasefire of 31 December 1948 left the Indian Army unhappy. Its plans to drive up to Muzaffarabad and other points of ingress into the Valley, over which much blood and money had been shed, had been frustrated. Even earlier, instructions from New Delhi had indicated a reluctance to extend Indian control beyond the Kashmiri-speaking area loyal to the National Conference. This reluctance was confirmed by Lt Gen. S.K. Sinha (now Governor of Jammu & Kashmir) in his *Operation Rescue: Military Operations in Jammu and Kashmir 1947–49.*[1] The initial plan was to hold a plebiscite immediately after the Pathan raiders were driven out of the area. Abdullah's standing would then ensure that the result would favour India. The situation, however, changed when Pakistan entered the war, and the prolonged debates in the UN Security Council altered the configuration of the proposed plebiscite.

Political reactions were more serious. In the Valley, the lingering pro-Pakistan elements of the Muslim Conference renewed their campaign against the National Conference. In Jammu province, it heightened Hindu insecurity at the possibility of the state joining Pakistan by majority (Muslim) vote. This led to a move for separate plebiscites in Jammu & Kashmir that strained communal relations and resistance to a government dominated by the National Conference. Maharaja Hari Singh fuelled the fire: Jammu was after all the seat of the Dogra dynasty.

Before Partition, Jammu province had a Muslim majority. According to the 1941 census, seventy per cent of the population were Muslims, and over ninety per cent in Kashmir. After the ceasefire however, Hindus were in a majority in the areas of Jammu under Indian authority. Much of the Muslim-dominated region of Poonch and Mirpur, adjoining Pakistan, was retained by the Pakistan army. Many Muslims had also moved from Hindu-dominated areas in the wake of the Partition killings in neighbouring Punjab. Unlike the Valley Muslims, they had not inherited the secular traditions of *kashmiryat.* Among them was Chaudhry Ghulam Abbas, founder of 'Azad Kashmir'.

As noted in an earlier chapter, one of Abdullah's first efforts in his newly assumed office of head of the state administration was to restore communal peace in Jammu city and assuage the hurt of terrorized Muslims, a move that won Gandhi's praise. He realized that the uncertainty created by an impending plebiscite was generating instability.

Reacting to Hari Singh's speech at the opening of the Jammu radio station on 1 December 1947, in a letter to Nehru, he described the maharaja's description of accession as 'a decision arrived at in a state of emergency owing to acts of aggression' as unfortunate. It implied that the accession was involuntary. He complained that Hari Singh directed his prime minister (Mahajan) to take steps to form an interim government without wishing to consult anyone else: 'My position as head of administration in the context of this directive seems to be entirely meaningless.'

The policy of 'the Maharaja and his clique' was to foist Hindu domination on the state 'for which purpose they bank upon local communalists as well as those elements in India who are against the setting up of a secular state for which you and Gandhi are fighting so bitterly in India'. It was then that he suggested that the maharaja be asked to abdicate in favour of his son, leaving the governance of the state to a Council of Regency. (Little-known details about Abdullah's letters, the proceedings of the National Conference, and political developments during this period are disclosed by Sandeep Bamzai, who had access to the papers of his grandfather, K.N. Bamzai, who some of us knew as Jawaharlal Nehru's confidante and adviser on Kashmir.)[2]

COMMUNAL PRESSURES

Even after Hari Singh had been banished to Bombay and his principal adversary in the Indian government, Sardar Patel, had died on 15 December 1950 after protracted illness, pressures on Abdullah continued to mount. Centred in Jammu, the campaign against him was spearheaded by Hindu communal organizations throughout India. Differences between Hindu Jammu and Muslim Kashmir were magnified and long-winded UN Security Council discussions on plebiscite rubbed in the salt.

Abdullah had cause for concern when political developments in India indicated a change in the equation between Nehru's commitment to secularism and the more orthodox, religious-oriented elements in the Congress party. Patel had managed to secure the election of the like-minded Dr Rajendra Prasad as the first president of the Indian Republic in preference to Nehru's choice of the veteran C. Rajagopalachari. Also, in 1951, the overtly pro-Hindu Purushottam Das Tandon had been elected Congress president in the face of Nehru's strong opposition. His views of Tandon, who had been president of the UP state Congress, were expressed in a letter to Pandit G.B. Pant, then chief minister of the state: 'Tandon ... is continuously delivering speeches which seem to me opposed to the basic principles of the Congress ... communalism has invaded the minds and hearts of those who were pillars of the Congress in the past.'[3] Nehru was obliged to threaten to resign before the party replaced Tandon as president in September 1951. Meanwhile, that very year, the founding of the Bharatiya Jana Sangh gave new life to the Hindutva forces.

By 1952, Abdullah's speeches began to reflect the divergent strains on him. At a public meeting in Srinagar on 8 May he praised the Indian Army for protecting the life and honour of Kashmiris, and the Indian people for symbolizing their sympathy by sending packets of salt to the Valley. The ideal of secularism, he said, had been sanctified by the blood of martyrs. On 31 July, observed as Martyrs' Day in Kashmir, he declared, 'Our relationship is not that of master and slave, but it is a free and voluntary association of partners in a joint task which bestows common and equal advantages on both'.[4]

ON THE VERGE

Frustration seemed to take over when Abdullah spoke at the district town of Ranbirsinghpura, near the ceasefire line in Jammu, on 11 April 1952. It was a speech that was to dog his future.

The *Hindu* of Madras reported him as insisting that Kashmir's accession to India would have to be of a restricted nature so long as communalism had a foothold on the soil of India. He described arguments in favour of full application of the Indian constitution to Kashmir as 'unrealistic, childish and savouring of lunacy'. His reasoning was:

> We want to join India without any kind of mental reservations. But how can we do so as long as we are not convinced about the complete elimination of communalism in India? We are prepared to welcome application of India's constitution to Kashmir in its entirety once we are satisfied that the grave of communalism has been finally dug in India. Of that we are not clear yet.
>
> It is very well for the people of India to think that communalism has been finally eliminated. But no one can deny that the communal spirit still exists in India. Many Kashmiris

> are apprehensive as to what will happen to them and their position if, for instance, something happens to Pandit Nehru. We do not know. As realists we Kashmiris have to provide for all eventualities. That is why I say that those who want Kashmir to lose its separate identity are talking without any conception of the practicalities that face us today …
>
> I would like to warn those who talk lightly of Kashmir's complete accession to India in all subjects that they are fanning fires of conflict once again. For if there is no special status for Kashmir in the Indian constitution, how can we go to the Muslims in Kashmir and convince them that India does not intend to interfere in the internal affairs of Kashmir? I am not saying that India will interfere in our internal affairs but there is something called sentiment which has to be recognized. We have accepted India in regard to defence, foreign affairs and communication and not in respect of other subjects because we wanted some kind of autonomy for ourselves in internal matters. Now some people here and in the Indian press also have started questioning our very fundamental right to shape our destiny in our own way. They do not tell us what will happen to Kashmir if there is a resurgence of communalism in India and how in those circumstances we are to convince the Muslims of Kashmir that India does not intend to swallow up Kashmir.

If Abdullah had assumed that his predicament would be appreciated, he was mistaken. The Ranbirsinghpura speech, especially his reference to Nehru's departure, was interpreted as confirming a potential threat of separatism; a fear whipped up by the plebiscite proposal. His attack on Hindu communalism was seen as excessive and hurtful to India's reputation.

Nehru was upset despite the inverse compliment paid to him. By exaggerating the strength of Hindu communal forces, he had provided sustenance to them and encouraged criticism of India abroad when the Security Council was considering Kashmir. He wrote to Abdullah on 16 April:

> I have felt deeply about Kashmir because it represented to me many things and many principles. It has always been an axiom with me, quite apart from the constitutional position and the like, that the people of Kashmir must decide their own fate. For me the people of Kashmir were basically represented by you. If you feel as you do then the link that has bound us together necessarily weakens and I have little heart to discuss such matters.[5]

Abdullah tried to make up. He told a gathering in Srinagar that his speech had not been correctly reported. On 23 July he met Congress members of parliament in New Delhi for over an hour to try to clear the doubts created by the Ranbirsinghpura speech. He is reported to have said that the well-established friendship and confidence between Indian and Kashmiri leaders was not so brittle as to be shattered by one incorrectly reported speech. There was no question of Kashmir trying to maintain an independent status; small states could not survive in the modern world.[6]

THE DELHI AGREEMENT

That very month, Nehru evolved a formula he hoped would address fears about erosion of Kashmir's special status. On an issue that was symbolic and controversial, the Delhi Agreement authorized the state to fly its own flag (the red flag with plough of the National Conference) provided it did not fly higher than the union tricolour. Equally significant, Article 356 of the Indian Constitution empowering the president to assume the governance of a state and Article 360, dealing with financial emergencies, would not be applicable to Jammu & Kashmir.

A striking victory for the National Conference was acceptance of its demand for the end of dynastic Dogra rule. The office of maharaja of Jammu & Kashmir was abolished. A *sadar-i-riayasat* elected by the state assembly would take over from Hari Singh as head of state, and would not be nominated by the president of India, like governors of other states, but hold office 'during the pleasure of the President'. To smooth the transition, as advised by Nehru, Abdullah agreed to appoint his eighteen-year-old son, Yuvraj Karan Singh, as the first *sadar*. He believed that he could manage him, but realized too late that Karan Singh would wreak his revenge.

As a concession to the Naya Kashmir programme for land reforms without compensation, the Fundamental Rights enshrined in the Indian Constitution would not be made applicable to the state. (The Right to Property provided in the Indian Constitution, which made payment of compensation obligatory, was later rescinded by parliament.) The Indian Supreme Court would have appellate jurisdiction.

Abdullah, however, was not satisfied. He is reported to have told the National Conference party working committee that the relationship with India must be transitional and that the state constitution should only be finalized after the dispute over the state between India and Pakistan was settled. He was unwilling to accept the Supreme Court's jurisdiction, arguing that no one in India was prepared to respect the state's autonomy and there was a unanimous desire to integrate it with the union. This made it impossible to persuade Muslim opinion to accept permanent accession. Indicating the way his mind was working, Abdullah quoted Nehru as vaguely mentioning the possibility of a Sikkim or Bhutan type of relationship with India and insisted on alternative solutions being worked out.[7]

A serious rift in the National Conference leadership now emerged. Bakshi Ghulam Mohammad, the deputy prime minister, and others felt Abdullah was over-reacting. A resolution supporting the Delhi Agreement was adopted by majority vote.[8]

LAST DEFENCE

Mounting criticism of Abdullah and his own policies in parliament provoked from Nehru, on 7 August 1952, an outstanding speech on his vision of the path-breaking, mutually-accommodative relationship he was trying to forge with Kashmir (as noted in the Preface). To counter pressure for the state to be bound more closely to India, he declared that it was for its people to decide whether or not they wished to stay within the union. In response to the demand for action to integrate Kashmir, he declared:

> With all deference to Parliament, I would like to say that the ultimate decision will be made in the minds and hearts of the men and women of Kashmir and not in this Parliament or at the United Nations ... Many things have happened in Jammu and Kashmir which I do not approve of; but there it is. I have no doubt that many things have happened and will happen that neither my honourable friends on the opposite side of the House nor I will approve of. But what is our approach going to be?
>
> You can criticize Sheikh Abdullah. Sheikh Abdullah is no god. He commits many errors and will commit more. He is a brave man and a great leader of his people. That is a big enough thing. He has led his people through weal and woe and has led them when facing grave disaster ... If he has failings, if he has made a mistake here or there, if he has delivered a speech which we do not like, what of that? Bigness is bigness in spite of a hundred mistakes ...
>
> If the people of Kashmir do not wish to remain with us, let them go by all means; we will not keep them against their will, however painful it may be for us. That is the policy that India will pursue and it is precisely because India stands for such a policy that people will not leave her. People will cleave to her and come to her. Our strongest bonds with Kashmir are not those that are retained by our army or even by our Constitution, to which so much reference has been made, but those of love and affection and understanding, and they are stronger than the Constitution or laws or armies.[9]

It was too late, however, to bridge the gap between Hindu communalism, coated with a sense of endangered nationalism, and an increasingly frustrated, combative Abdullah. Instead of the cleaving he hoped to inspire, both sides were drawing further apart. The gap was widened further when, joined by the Jana Sangh in the rest of India, the Praja

Parishad launched a massive movement in Jammu to protest against the Delhi Agreement. Carrying the national flag and Union President Rajendra Prasad's portrait before them, the demonstrators' chant reverberated far beyond Jammu:

> *Ek desh mein do vidhan; ek desh mein do nishan; ek desh mein do pradhan: Nahin chalenge, nahin chalenge.*
> (Two constitutions, two flags, two heads of state in one country will not be tolerated.)

NEHRU UNDER THREAT

Now Nehru was deeply concerned. The Praja Parishad agitation, taken up nationally by the Jana Sangh and other Opposition groups, was developing into a threat to him personally. Communal passions were being aroused throughout India, but it was difficult to take action when the protest appealed to nationalist sentiment. Also, Abdullah's failure to respond to the Delhi Agreement olive branch, made him reluctant to allow further talk of Kashmiri independence.

Apart from the communal tensions it would promote in India, he was worried by the possibility of involvement in Cold War intrigues of such a strategically-situated area. Moves to integrate Pakistan into Western military alliances were becoming known. This was seen as influencing US and British representatives at the UN to be partial towards Pakistan. The architect of India's non-aligned status, he could not afford Kashmir become a cockpit of Cold War conflict, a phrase popular in New Delhi at the time.

Nehru did not then go public on an issue arousing so much passion. He expressed his concern in his regular letters to state chief ministers. On 4 December 1952, he wrote:

> The far-reaching land reforms in the State have naturally not pleased some of the old landlord elements and they have joined the agitation against the government there. In this they are being helped directly by some communal elements in other parts of India ... In the name of closer association with India,

> they are acting in a manner which might imperil that very association.

Two weeks later, his letter was more specific, linking the Jammu agitation with reactions to the influx of refugees from what was then East Pakistan and the campaign to ban cow slaughter: 'The people at the back of these agitations belong to communal organizations like the Hindu Mahasabha, the Jana Sangh, the RSS and the Ram Rajya Parishad. Appropriately, Master Tara Singh and his Akali Dal have lined up with them.'

Then, again, on 27 January 1953, stressing the contradictory aspects of the movement:

> The Jammu agitation, about which I have written to you previously, is again a remarkable instance of folly or mischief. [It] plays into the hands of Pakistan. It is clear that the objective of these organizations is not confined to Jammu and that they are aiming at bigger quarry. Their dislike of the Government of India and the secular policy that it pursues is so great that, in order to injure it, they are prepared even to harm our relationship with Jammu and Kashmir State.[10]

The prime minister's instructions to take firm action against communal sympathizers of the Jammu agitation in Delhi, Punjab, and UP, however, proved largely ineffective. In a replay of similar situations earlier, the Union Home Ministry had different priorities. Headed by the enfeebled Kailas Nath Katju, following the death of Vallabhbhai Patel, it failed to deter the movement.[11] With Abdullah pushed into the opposite corner by the Jammu agitation, conflicting pressures were driving the old comrades apart.

After a three-hour session with Abdullah, Ian Stephens, then editor of the Calcutta *Statesman*, gained the impression of an outstanding, if troubled, leader:

> The impression left on my mind after three hours in a poplar - bordered Srinagar garden with the Prime Minister of Indian-

held Kashmir ... was a courageous, forthright, vigorous man, intelligent, though without intellectual range, gifted with a strong personality and therefore probably an inspiring leader of the downtrodden.

He was obviously non-communal, whole-heartedly so. He spoke with pride of a pleasant reality I had noticed: that in and around Srinagar, no doubt because of his administration's efforts, Hindus, Sikhs and Muslims mingled in cordiality. Pre-eminently he appeared to me a Kashmiri patriot full of zeal to impress his countrymen's plight, preoccupied with the vale, the centre and motive of his whole political life, but concerned with the rest of the subcontinents's affairs ...

Evidently, he thought now if not before, that in many Hindu Congressmen, a façade of secular tolerance had an actual communalism as narrow as any in Pakistan, indeed perhaps worse, because of the caste system.[12]

---

1 See my *Kashmir The Wounded Valley*, p. 147 and Navnita Chadha Brhera, *Demystifying Kashmir*, Pearson Longman, The Brooking Institution, Washington, 2006, pp. 30–34.

2 Cited by Sandeep Bamzai, *Bonfire of Kashmiryat: Deconstructing the Accession*, Rupa, New Delhi, 2006, pp. 17–21. Although letters from Nehru are published in the *Selected Works of Jawaharlal Nehru*, letters to him are not accessible apart from copies retained by others. In his memoirs, Abdullah complained that he had requested Nehru for permission to publish his letters to him, Maulana Azad, and Rafi Ahmed Kidwai after Bakshi had referred to them, but to no avail. *Flames*, p. 126. The ban remains.

3 Cited by S. Gopal, *Jawaharlal Nehru: A Biography*, Vol. II, p. 92.

4 Cited by S. Vashisht, *Sheikh Abdullah: Then and Now*, Maulik Sahitya Prakashan, Delhi, 1968, pp. 61–62.

5 Cited by S. Gopal, *Jawaharlal Nehru: A Biography*, Vol. II, p. 120.

6 S. Vashisht, op. cit., p. 89.

7 Sandeep Bamzai, op. cit., pp. 169–70.

8 See P.N.K. Bamzai, op. cit., pp. 206–12. The Bamzais differ in their interpretation of Abdullah's role.

9 Jawaharlal Nehru's Speeches 1949–54, pp. 107–25.

10 Jawaharlal Nehru, *Letters to Chief Ministers*, vol. III (1952–54). Oxford University Press, New Delhi, 1987, pp. 192, 198, and 230.

11 See S. Gopal, op. cit. pp. 125–27 for Nehru's weakness in handling Ministry of States.

12 Cited by Gul Mohd Wani, *Kashmir Politics: Problems and Prospects*, Ashish Publishing House, Delhi, 1993, pp. 57–58. Ian Stephens was a strong supporter of Pakistan's case on Kashmir in his writings, notably in *Horned Moon*, London, 1953.

LAST WARNING

It is always painful to part company after long years of comradeship, but if our conscience so tells us, or in our view an overriding national interest requires, then there can be no help for it . . .

– Jawaharlal Nehru to Sheikh Abdullah

In December 1947, Sheikh Abdullah was hailed by Mahatma Gandhi and Jawaharlal Nehru for rescuing secularism from the forces of Hindu communalism and countering Pakistan's efforts to exploit Islamic fervour to takeover of Kashmir. He had supported its accession to India. Five years later, his detractors were pillorying him in the Indian parliament and press as anti-national, pro-Pakistan, even communal. The final act was played out in the first eight months of 1953.

The souring of the cameraderie between Nehru and Abdullah—their views on secularism and social change had forged the link between India and Kashmir—mirrored the transformation. Reacting to the spreading Jammu movement against the special status of the state, orchestrated by Hindutva parties, Abdullah pushed for greater independence. Nehru saw his dream of Kashmir confirming India's commitment to secularism dissolving. Then fate played a hand. The death of their common arch-critic, Jana Sangh President Syama Prasad Mookerjee, while under detention in Srinagar, heralded the end of the affair. The final act was scripted by the chief spook of the Union Home

Ministry, Bhola Nath Mullick, who had been appointed director of the powerful Intelligence Bureau by Sardar Patel before his death.

The impending tragedy can be followed, scene by scene, from the letters exchanged by the principal characters in the closing months to project or defend their views. Nehru writes repeatedly and at length to all concerned, including Syama Prasad, expressing anxiety that the spread of the Jammu agitation threatens to revive communal polarization in India, strengthens anti-Indian feelings in Kashmir, and hurts India's case at the UN. The Jana Sangh president is unconvinced, insisting that the prime minister is strengthening the threat posed to national unity by Abdullah. (Nehru's letters take up the best part of volume 22 of his *Selected Works;* brief extracts with dates and page numbers in parenthesis from a selected few are quoted below.)

FLURRY OF WARNINGS

The year begins with Nehru writing to Abdullah: 'There can be little doubt that the whole genesis of the Jammu movement has little to do with Jammu problems. It is definitely a subversive movement of the most reactionary communal type aiming at something much bigger than Jammu. (160) He suggests they meet to discuss the problem. There is no hint of differences in their approach.

The language of a letter to Kailas Nath Katju on 4 January (Katju was now home minister), betrays intense anxiety and anger. The Jammu situation, Nehru writes, 'is an attempt of the most poisonous kind to upset the entire policy of Government, not only in Jammu and Kashmir, but in India as a whole ... Syama Prasad Mookerjee is playing a very clever and, what I consider, a very dirty game. I think we should realize that and give him no quarter.'

As before, Nehru is critical of the Home Ministry. It is slow to take action and some officials are sympathetic to communal organizations. He did not recall his differences with Patel on this account, but traces the problem back to the traditions set by the Political Department in viceregal days (when it was more concerned with intrigue and influence in the princely states than inculcating democratic values).

The Home Ministry 'should be made to sit up and informed clearly what our policy is ...' (170–72) .

He is back to advising Abdullah on 5 January to avoid provoking Jammu and Dogra sentiments in decisions concerning the sequestration of excess land and Hari Singh's orchards, and the need to finalize the Delhi Agreement signed between New Delhi and Srinagar (172–76). The advice would be repeated because the delay and Abdullah's intemperate speeches were providing ammunition to the Jammu agitators. Then to Syama Prasad on 10 January to point out that the violent Praja Parishad agitation was hurting India's case at the UN and how Kashmir could not be treated in the same way as other states (178–81).

With the volunteers from outside adding muscle to the agitation, Nehru writes two letters to Bhimsen Sachar, chief minister of East Punjab, on 22 and 25 January, urging him to stop entry of Praja Parishad supporters into Jammu: 'It seems to me that we have not fully realized the extent and implications of what lies behind the Jammu agitation. It is obviously a more widespread affair than perhaps most people imagine and is being used by communal elements for other purposes (182–84).

On 25 January, the eve of Republic Day, he sends a note to the Home Ministry to ensure that the Delhi administration remained alert to the threat 'being made on behalf of the communal organizations like the Jana Sangh, RSS, and Akali Dal to create trouble in Delhi on the basis of the Jammu Parishad agitation (185).

Nehru returns to the theme of mollifying Jammu sentiment in another letter to Abdullah on 30 January. Suggesting the appointment of a commission to look into issues in which the needs of Kashmir and Jammu differ, he advises: 'It is clear that a considerable section of the people in Jammu province have been unfortunately moved by this misconceived agitation. They have to be won over and not merely suppressed ... I am very glad, therefore, that in your speeches you have made the right kind of appeal ... The recent display of the union flag on Republic Day had a good effect in Jammu. It would be a good thing if the national flag was put up in one or two places together with the state flag (188–90).

Exchanges with Syama Prasad became sharper, with no diminution of mutual hostility. Reacting to the Jana Sangh president's accusation that he was bringing the country to the brink of disaster, Nehru replies on 3 February: 'I am equally convinced that the policy you have pursued in regard to Jammu and Kashmir and certain other matters is completely harmful to India's interests and to the ideals we have always proclaimed.' If allowed to expand, the Praja Parishad agitation 'would bring disaster in its train ... Believing this, as I do, the only course I can follow is to resist this utterly misconceived agitation' (191–94). A week later he adds, 'I have before me a detailed list with full particulars of over a hundred officers, high and low, including district magistrates, superintendents of police and constables, who have been more or less seriously injured by the crowds of so-called *satyagrahi*. That is hardly an evidence of a peaceful agitation' (197).

APPEAL REJECTED

On 10 February, Nehru appeals to Abdullah to give full effect to the Delhi Agreement: 'It would help us greatly if some indication came from your government about the early implementation ... That would partly disable any big agitation' (196). However, the spread of the Jammu agitation was pushing Abdullah in a different direction, as conveyed in a confidential note to Nehru disclosed by Sandeep Bamzai in *Bonfire of Kashmiryat*. Bamzai had access to papers left by his grandfather, K.N. Bamzai, Nehru's unofficial link with Kashmir developments, and elements of the note are footnoted in the Nehru Correspondence. The note quotes Abdullah as writing:

> Even the Delhi Agreement is not going to satisfy certain elements in India ... I cannot continue to keep people in the Valley on tenterhooks. So far the people in the valley have been silent because they know that I will not barter away their interests. Moreover, how can we have peace in the State if the solution which India and Kashmir adopt is not acceptable to

> Pakistan ... If today Jammu has rebelled, it is not far off when we will lose all sympathy in the valley. In the circumstances, independence is best because Pakistan would never agree to a unilateral arrangement and our borders will always be attacked by them. Tell Panditji to have a solution which will be honourable to all—Pakistan, India, Kashmir and to him.

According to the confidential note, Abdullah made district-wise suggestions for separating an independent Kashmir from Jammu and Ladakh that would remain with India. Kashmir would consist of Uri, Titwal, Gurais, Zojila, Tragbal, and the Jammu side of Ramban (Doda district).

This presumably represented Abdullah's first preference. He also suggested a variety of solutions in a separate note entitled 'Possible Alternatives for an Honourable Settlement between India and Pakistan on the Kashmir Issue'. These included proposals floated earlier: for the entire state to be independent, guaranteed by India, Pakistan, and the UN; the entire state to be under UN trusteeship for ten years, after which the people could opt for either India or Pakistan; the entire state be a condominium of India and Pakistan.[1]

Nehru could see no way out. On 1 March he writes despairingly to Maulana Azad:

> I fear that Sheikh Sahib's mind is so utterly confused that he does not know what to do. All kinds of pressures are being brought to bear on him and he is getting more and more into a tangle. There is nobody with him who can really help him very much, because he does not trust anyone fully, and yet everyone influences him ... My fear is that Sheikh Sahib, in his present state of mind, is likely to do something or take some step, which might make things worse. [210]

The continued expansion of the Jammu agitation increases pressures on both. A large demonstration is staged in Delhi on 6 March leading to the temporary arrest of Syama Prasad, N.C. Chatterjee, president of the

Hindu Mahasabha, and Nandalal Sharma of the Ram Rajya Parishad. Nehru erupts in parliament, 'When honourable members go and break the law deliberately, when honourable members side with the enemies of this country ... let us have a full discussion. Let us see who is right and who is wrong.'

The discussion is held on 25 March. The prime minister delves into history to reinforce his attack on Hindutva parties, describing their policies as 'highly pernicious and malignant'. Recalling the contribution of communalism to unhappy phases of India's history, he sees it as

> poison that has injured us in the past many a time, that has brought down India, which has split India, which has led India to civil war, which has degraded India and which has humiliated India. And it comes out again and again ... What I am afraid of is this attempt, this repeated attempt, to rouse up certain passions of the people, to rouse up certain prejudices in the people, to play upon them, to exploit them in the name of the country, in the name of nationalism ... We can never forget what we have seen in this city of Delhi and other places around it ...

and in defence of his Kashmir policy:

> It is admitted that accession or no accession, we are not going to hold on to Kashmir against the will of the people of Kashmir, it just does not matter if there is accession or not. I make it perfectly clear that I am not going to hold on by force of arms ... We are there because the people of Kashmir wanted us to be there, or a majority of them. If they do not want us, out we come, whether the accession is legally binding or is complete or incomplete ... Therefore, adopting a policy which weakens our position in the minds of the people of Kashmir is not for strengthening our hands ... It is patent that the policy of the Praja Parishad, as pursued there, weakens our cause nationally and internationally, in Kashmir and elsewhere.

This conveyed an assurance that India's Kashmir policy had not changed. Abdullah is not, however, convinced that it can be sustained. The mounting communally-inspired campaign for fuller integration was generating a backlash among Muslims in the valley. Persisting in trying to distance Kashmir's relationship with India, he did not respond to the prime minister's invitation to come to Delhi for talks, but sent his principal aides.

NEHRU'S LAST LETTER

The need for Nehru to avert a collision that could derail his government was urgent. On 28 June, six weeks before Abdullah was dismissed, Nehru's letter to him warns of possible consequences while appealing for mutual understanding. It begins by reiterating his invitation for talks which would include Bakshi Ghulam Mohammad (who had been in touch with Nehru) and Mirza Afzal Beg (a hard-line adviser of Abdullah), and regretting his inability to go to Kashmir due to pressing engagements. Then followed an analysis of the reasons that were driving them apart and that he had no option but to respond, irrespective of their friendship:

> Nothing is more depressing than confused thinking in any vital matter ... I have thus far kept my mind fairly clear on the Kashmir issue in spite of its difficulties ... But lately I have not at all been clear as to what you have been thinking and naturally that has a powerful effect on my own thinking ... I know that during the last three or four years doubts have arisen in your mind and we have discussed them. We did not agree about some things and, on one or two occasions, I even told you that I did not wish to come in your way if you differed from me on any vital matter. If so, we naturally have to think what out separate courses of action should be. However, we generally agreed about the policy that should be pursued and there the matter rested ...
>
> Recent developments have, however, led me to think that you have either changed your mind completely or are not clear about your thinking ... You told me that there were only

> two courses open for Kashmir: either full integration or full autonomy, whatever that might mean. I did not agree with you in this, nor do I agree with you even now because there are many other middle courses ...
>
> We have argued enough and must accept each other's present conclusions and then discuss the future on that basis. If that unhappily leads to divergence with all its consequences we fashion our respective courses accordingly ... Thus far, I have proceeded on the basis of friendship and confidence in you and have been vain enough to expect the same approach from you. Whether that is justified or not is for you to say. Individual relations should not count in national affairs and yet they do count and make a difference.
>
> To me it has been a major surprise that a settlement arrived between us should be bypassed or repudiated, regardless of the merits. That strikes at the root of all confidence, personal or international. No treaty would be worth the paper it is written on if it was to be repudiated soon after. So far as I am concerned, no power in the world would make me go back on the pledge I gave in that [Delhi] Agreement. If my Parliament or my people in India repudiate that, they repudiate me ... My honour is bound up with my word ... It is always painful to part company after long years of comradeship, but if our conscience so tells us, or in our view an overriding national interest requires, then there can be no help for it ...

The letter mentions other charges that strengthened the case against Abdullah. One, particularly hurtful, is that he was moving away from secularism:

> My Government has stood, as you have so consistently stood, for a secular democracy. I do not know what your feelings are on this subject now. But I fear the tendency in Kashmir is to keep away from it. Unfortunately that will have its reactions in India as such tendencies in India have their reactions in Kashmir.

The other referred to differences in Abdullah's cabinet and the National Conference that would pave the way for his dismissal:

> What I have felt lately has been that your Government is very far from harmonious and in fact pulls in different directions, that you organization is also disintegrating in the same way. If this process continues, I have little doubt that Kashmir would relapse into utter backwardness, as far as political life is concerned.

PAINED REFUTATION

On 4 July, Abdullah responds with a hurt point-by-point refutation, the text of which is made available by Sandeep Bamzai. Referring to Nehru's invitation, he writes that he could not leave Srinagar at the time; Bakshi and Beg could explain why. Then, rejecting the charge that he was becoming confused:

> I have not been able to understand how you have the impression that I was lacking in this clarity. It is possible that some people may consider a particular line of thought to be the only clear one while others may hold a different line and similarly believe that to be more clear. I have now been in intimate touch with Kashmir and its people for the last 22 years. I have never been hazy in regard to this objective and therefore there is no confusion in my mind.

Nehru's criticism of his views on autonomy evoked the most forthright statement Abdullah had made on the sensitive subject:

> Objectively, the State is subject to pulls from India and Pakistan. The external pressure naturally creates internal reactions in terms of divided loyalties. In order to neutralize these reactions, we had devised a formula and considered a restricted relationship with India as a suitable course conducive to internal consolidation. We believe that the accession of the State to India on the terms of the Instrument of Accession would provide the necessary opportunities of allaying the fears of various sections of the people of the State ...
>
> To my mind the middle course that you have referred to in your letter has been the one that we desired in our

> relationship with the Indian Union. You have spoken about guarantees. We certainly believe that the terms of the Indian Constitution provided an adequate guarantee which we felt would enable us to work for internal solidarity. But I would like to point out to you the discrepancies that we have come to notice from time to time in the attitude of the Government of India.
>
> When Article 370 was devised, we felt assured by the statement of Sardar Patel that the Instrument of Accession would be the final basis of the Indo–Kashmir relationship. Subsequently, when the Delhi Agreement came up before the Council of States [Rajya Sabha] on August 5, 1952, Shri Gopalaswami Ayyangar stated that Article 370 was not a permanent feature of the Constitution and "when the time came" this provision could be wiped off from the Constitution. This clearly shows that ... such assurances come with a good deal of mental reservation ...
>
> The ground has been shifting from time to time ever since the Instrument of Accession was signed and it has been made abundantly clear to us that ultimately the special position accorded to our State in the Indian Constitution would be taken away. You can well imagine the reaction of such a threat to the local rights and privileges of the majority community, particularly at a time when they are subjected to much psychological pressure from many quarters which threaten to undermine their very faith in the ideals that made them turn towards India.

Abdullah points to the frustration caused by the continued discrimination against Muslims in the state forces and the post and telegraph services. They felt that 'in spite of you ... the ideals of secular democracy are not much in evidence so far as Kashmiri Muslims are concerned ... I have been attempting to balance opposing points of view in Kashmir and I derived my strength from what I supposed was an assurance that the State's accession to India would result in a fair deal to all sections of the people. But unfortunately that goal has not been achieved.' He describes the charge of disruptive tendencies in the administration and organization as baseless.

To the suggestion that hurt him most—that he was moving away from his commitment to secularism—Abdullah responds:

> I feel greatly grieved and hurt when even friends like you start doubting and misunderstanding me. My conviction in the principle I have been upholding all along has not faltered even when I had to face heavy odds. I may remind you that it was a difficult decision to take when I proposed conversion of the Muslim Conference to National Conference. Even when we were faced with what seemed an inevitable fate in 1947, I did not turn my face on these principles but fought [for] them.[2]

The letter ends with a plea for mutual understanding:

> I can, however, assure you that I fully realize your position and you cannot expect me to do or say anything which would weaken it. My honour is linked with yours and I would request you to understand my position. I can be helpful to you only if I am in a position to deliver the goods.

There was however no space left for mutual understanding. The issues brought to national attention by the Jammu agitation over the Delhi Agreement raised the divergent expectations of Nehru and Abdullah to the surface. One expected Kashmiris to agree to be integrated into the Indian Union, like other regional identities, after accommodating and overcoming interim obstacles. The other saw the link with India as a partnership in which certain powers were conceded to the Union government for mutual benefit, but internal sovereignty was retained. This was the approach Abdullah had outlined in his inaugural address to the Jammu & Kashmir Constituent Assembly.[3]

Another consequence of the Hindutva-generated Jammu agitation was to narrow Abdullah's horizon from preserving the special status of Jammu & Kashmir to increasingly projecting the negative Muslim reaction in the valley. Interpreted by his critics as evidence that he was becoming communal, he maintained that he was drawing attention to the impetus the agitation was providing to the revival of pro-Pakistani sentiment. Nehru, however, saw Abdullah's reaction as emphasizing communal discord and aiding Pakistani propaganda.

---

1 Sandeep Bamzai, op. cit., pp. 176–79.

2 Cited by Sandeep Bamzai, op. cit., pp. 179–84.

3 For a perceptive discussion of contrary India–Kashmir expectations, see Navnita Chadha Behera, *State Identity and Violence: Jammu, Kashmir and Ladakh,* Manohar, New Delhi, 2000, pp. 90–99.

MIDNIGHT ARREST

If we gave him an opportunity to take his case to the streets he would easily arouse acute communal and chauvinistic sentiments among the Kashmiri masses, which could in turn result in serious and violent disturbances. Anti-national elements and agents were active in the valley and, given a chance, would not hesitate to plunge the State into utter turmoil.

– Karan Singh to Jawaharlal Nehru
urging dismissal of the Abdullah government

In his memoirs, Sheikh Abdullah provides a version of the developments leading to his removal as prime minister of Jammu & Kashmir that differs from Nehru's in key respects. Like Kurozsawa's classic film *Rashomon,* both are compelling. Other versions are provided by *Sadar-i-Riyasat* Karan Singh, Intelligence Bureau chief B.N. Mullick, and General B.M. Kaul. They overlap but differ in approach and motivation; together they present a murky picture of high-level intrigue.

Abdullah's is a tale of suspicion and treachery. According to him, Bakshi Ghulam Mohammad and Ghulam Mohammad Sadiq were turned against him by New Delhi (both were to subsequently become chief ministers). Referring to Nehru's visit to Srinagar on 16 May 1953, he writes, 'I noticed that Jawaharlal was not the same man; clearly his confidence was shaken. I was amazed to see him speaking quietly with Bakshi Ghulam Mohammad and his friends. Whispering in corners had started.'[1]

The Delhi Agreement and Jammu agitation had let loose forces demanding the state's complete merger with the Indian Union. He found that 'Jawaharlal Nehru and Maulana Azad were interested in the [merger] proposition, but did not agree with the strategy'. Nehru was resisting his removal at the time because it would strengthen Pakistan's psychological war against India.

THE LAST NAIL

Then came the crisis created by the death of Syama Prasad Mookerjee while in detention in Srinagar for entering the state without the entry permit required at the time. He recalls the circumstances:

> One morning I was informed by Pandit Shyam Lal, Minister for Jails [in the State Government], that Dr Mookerjee had suffered a massive heart attack. I was shocked. He died during the night of June 23, 1953. News of his death spread like wildfire. His dead body was flown to Delhi. From the start, I was not in favour of detaining him in Srinagar. But the Home Minister, Bakshi Ghulam Mohammad, had his own reasons, plus the nod from Delhi. I could not do much.[2]

On this sensitive subject, Nehru took a similar line to deflect allegations that Syama Prasad's death was a conspiracy organized by Abdullah. On return from a visit to England, he issued a statement emphasizing that Syama Prasad had been detained in a villa adjoining Srinagar's famous Nishat Bagh, with its own 'little garden with fruit trees and flowers', and was being well looked after.[3]

This was not however the assessment of Karan Singh, as *sadar-i-riyasat.* On 26 June, on the subject of Syama Prasad's death, he wrote to the prime minister:

> Apart from its grave political repercussions, it came as a great shock, particularly as we were completely unaware that he had not been keeping good health for some time. I was not informed of his illness or his removal to hospital and, most amazing of all I only learnt of his demise several hours after the body had been flown from Srinagar, and that too from unofficial

> sources. There is a widespread feeling and indeed there are strong reasons which indicate that in this unfortunate matter, the State Government, to say the least, acted in a most questionable and incompetent manner. I shall explain further when we meet.

Karan Singh had been increasingly critical of Abdullah. Earlier in June, he had sent a note to Nehru, then visiting England, urging action against Abdullah for reneging on the Delhi Agreement and questioning previous agreements with New Delhi. The youthful head of state peremptorily told the prime minister:

> This cannot be allowed, as it will make our position absolutely impossible and a grave blow to our national interests and naturally to our international position also. I need not mention the grave and widespread repercussions that will result from such a development.

Significantly, the note was sent through the Union Home Minister who was visiting Srinagar. In it, he informs Nehru that he had requested Dr Katju to 'arrange with the Government of India Intelligence Service [Intelligence Bureau] here to keep in close touch with me in correctly appraising this unstable and most unpredictable situation.' The minority community in the Valley [Hindus], he added, was feeling 'most apprehensive and distressed at the way things are moving here and there is great panic and despair among them.'[4] The need for intervention could not have been phrased more insistently.

UNDERCOVER OPERATION

The Intelligence Bureau had been active in Kashmir after the accession, with B.N. Mullick sent there by Patel in 1949. An outstanding operative, his talent for pleasing his political masters while pursuing his own agenda emerges from his memoirs. In August that year he notes that he was asked to report on allegations by Kashmiri Pandit and Jammu Dogra callers on Nehru and Patel that Abdullah was hostile to India. The report he submitted after visiting the Valley could hardly have been improved upon by the warmest of Abdullah's supporters. Nehru was so delighted that he had copies of the report distributed to Indian missions abroad.

Mullick had detailed all the reasons for trusting Abdullah. His support for accession was not forced by events; it reflected a deep ideological identity with India based on their support for 'the people's struggle against the Indian princes, as also Sheikh Abdullah's struggle against the Maharaja of Kashmir'. His regard for Nehru and Gandhi was deep and genuine; they had 'always stood for the oppressed people of the Kashmir Valley against the Dogra ruler'. Recalling Nehru courting imprisonment to defend Abdullah, he reported that 'strong bonds of unity had been forged between the Kashmiri people and the Indian people'. Abdullah's friendship and identity of views with Nehru was contrasted with his distrust of and repugnance for Jinnah.

Patel's reaction to the report was very different from Nehru's, and Mullick adjusted accordingly. He recalls:

> The Sardar then gave me his own views about Sheikh Abdullah. He apprehended that Sheikh Abdullah would ultimately let down India and Jawaharlal Nehru and would come in [sic] his real colours. His antipathy to the Maharaja was not really an antipathy to the ruler as such, but to the Dogras in general and with the Dogras he identified the rest of the majority community in India.

Notwithstanding the definitive nature of his report and the important informants he had cited, Mullick soon contradicted it in words and action. 'Future events,' he noted, 'proved that the Sardar was right and I was not. Within three years, we found ourselves fighting against Sheikh Abdullah.'[5] From then, he imported suspicion and a tinge of communalism into his interpretation of Abdullah's actions and speeches, eventually compiling the charges required to justify arresting the prime minister of Jammu & Kashmir. Nehru had concurred with his dismissal but was against arrest.

Mullick presents a detailed account of the developments

preceding that climactic event in his memoirs.[6] He recalls Nehru's visit to Srinagar in May 1953. During that visit, 'throughout the Sheikh maintained his hostile attitude towards India, though he outwardly showed respect and cordiality to the prime minister. In spite of the latter's attempt to induce him to take a reasonable attitude, the Sheikh remained recalcitrant.'

He then describes Abdullah as ignoring and insulting Maulana Azad, who was sent by Nehru to Srinagar, and states, 'The Maulana Sahib's advice to the prime minister on his return was to dismiss Sheikh Abdullah before he committed any more mischief'. Azad had written to Abdullah:

> What I am telling you now is as a personal friend. There is only one way of safeguarding the future well-being of the people of Kashmir and that is the way which we laid down in 1949 and which you had accepted. Hold steadfast to this way and be assured that you will never have to regret it.[7]

Nehru was in London for the Commonwealth Prime Ministers' Conference, and Mullick reported to him there. According to him, 'though he [Nehru] still hoped that a change for the better might still come over the Sheikh, he was very upset at the shape events were taking there and he considered that the time might come soon when certain drastic steps might have to be taken'.

He concedes, however, 'It would be wrong to conclude that Sheikh Abdullah was as yet planning to take Jammu and Kashmir into Pakistan. He was evidently angling for special status just short of independence. He knew he would have no position in Pakistan; but a semi-independent status for the Valley would give him all that he desired—security from foreign invaders, economic prosperity due to influx of tourists and munificence of India and yet no subservience to the Central Government which according to him was Hindu dominated.'

On returning to India in July, Mullick visited Srinagar to confirm intelligence reports of differences within the National Conference. According to him, 'only Afzal Beg, Mohd Shafi and a few others were with the Sheikh; all the other important leaders, that is Bakshi, Sadiq, Masoodi, Mir Qasim [who was also to become chief minister] and the Hindu leaders like Saraf, Dogra and Dhar were ranged against him'. He concluded, 'The more the Sheikh was getting isolated, the more desperate he was becoming and there was every apprehension that he would assume the role of a dictator or do some other desperate act'.

FINAL INSTRUCTIONS

In New Delhi, Mullick reported his findings to the prime minister. Intelligence activities in Kashmir were stepped up. A senior deputy director, D.W. Mehra, was deputed to Srinagar. The final instructions, according to him, were received by them on 31 July:

> He [Nehru] talked to us for nearly two hours, giving us the entire background picture of Kashmir from the earliest times to date and finally he came to the point that there was no other alternative but to remove Sheikh Abdullah and install Bakshi Ghulam Mohd in his place. He hoped that the change would be effected peacefully but he warned that we must be prepared for the worst, because the Sheikh undoubtedly had a large following in the valley and in this matter the pro-Sheikh group would be supported by the pro-Pakistani elements also. Mehra should be prepared to assume control of the Jammu and Kashmir police force and was to take over as Chief Executive under the Sadar-i-Riyasat, if that became necessary.
>
> At that point Pandit Nehru was nearly overwhelmed by emotion. Both of us, who had known him for some years, had never seen him in such a disturbed mood before. We realized that he was on the point of uprooting a plant which he had nursed with great care.

Secret instructions were then sent to army commanders in the state to be on the alert against disturbances. A cabinet minister, Ajit Prasad Jain, was asked to keep a watch in Srinagar; while another, Rafi Ahmed Kidwai, was in charge of Kashmir affairs in New Delhi. Sensitive to signs of a backlash against Indian Muslims in reaction to Abdullah's campaign for *azaadi*, Kidwai was keen to have him removed. Preparations were complete.

Karan Singh's version of the final days largely concurs with Mullick's but is phrased in less accusatory terms in regard to Abdullah.[8] He recalls stressing the dangers he had described in his note and finding Nehru disturbed and making no attempt to defend Abdullah. While insisting that he was careful not to give the impression of taking sides, he nevertheless recalls being in close contact with 'the pro-Indian group' headed by Bakshi. Another state minister he singles out for praise is Deputy Home Minister Durga Prasad Dhar (a Pandit) for playing 'a significant role in keeping New Delhi informed about the inner conflicts within the National Conference. Jawaharlal liked him and held his political judgement in high regard' (as did Indira Gandhi subsequently).

DIFFERENT VERSIONS

Abdullah gave his version of these preparations in his *Flames of the Chinar*.[9] He saw Kidwai as a close confidante of Nehru placed in charge of the toppling operation with the support of Communist leaders like Z.A. Ahmed and Harkishan Singh Surjeet. They wanted to promote the interests of Sadiq known to be close to them. Pakistan's Anglo–American supporters were also bent on his removal. He quotes from Mullick's book to confirm his conclusion that Nehru and Azad favoured complete merger, as did other national leaders like Acharya Kripalani and Jayaprakash Narayan. When Kidwai expressed his intention to visit Srinagar, Abdullah did not conceal his bitterness:

> Sickened by the double-dealings and changing loyalties of the Indian leaders, I informed Rafi Sahib that the situation had deteriorated to such an extent that it would defy all his efforts to improve it. Still, we would welcome him in Kashmir. The Jana Sangh and the Praja Parishad were demanding my arrest as the price for changing their hostile attitude to Jawaharlal Nehru. It was, therefore, agreed that I be made the scapegoat …
>
> In Delhi, preparations to overthrow my government and

> arrest me were now complete. Rafi Ahmed Kidwai and B.N. Malik were in charge of the coup d'etat ... On July 27, Karan Singh had received a secret message from Jawaharlal. Zero hour had been announced.

Abdullah's version of his dismissal and arrest on 8 August is brief. He met the *sadar-i-riyasat* at 6 p.m. and was advised to call a cabinet meeting after a week. He proceeded to Gulmarg with his wife and private secretary, R.C. Raina. They were awakened by loud knocking at the door. Raina informed him that the house was surrounded by the state army. The superintendent of police and Karan Singh's ADC entered the room and handed him a sealed envelope containing orders for his dismissal and also another memorandum signed by Bakshi Ghulam Mohammad, Pandit Sham Lal Saraf, and Pandit Girdhari Lal Dogra (all cabinet ministers) expressing no confidence in him. The final item handed over was a warrant of arrest.

The Karan Singh and Mullick versions of events overlap but the differences are significant. Karan Singh[10] quotes at length from the memorandum signed by Bakshi and the other ministers to justify the dismissal. Referring to the delay in implementing the Delhi agreement, it charged Abdullah with arbitrarily seeking 'to precipitate a rupture in the relationship of the state with India'. It picked out Baig for persistently following policies of narrow sectarianism and communalism ... Unfortunately you have been lending your support to his policies in the Cabinet and his activities in the public ... The result is that unity and secular character, the two fundamental aspects of our State, stand threatened today'.

On receiving the memorandum on 8 August, which he admits was not entirely unexpected, Karan Singh invited Abdullah to meet him before going to Gulmarg. According to his autobiography, Abdullah claimed that though there were some differences of opinion, there were no basic political or administrative differences within his cabinet, which had been exaggerated by the Indian press. He was unable to give any assurance that the cabinet crisis would be resolved. Similar to the line taken by Mullick, Karan Singh suggests that Abdullah was expecting some international pressure to secure virtually independent status for Kashmir, and that was why he was holding up implementation of the Delhi Agreement.

Accordingly, the *sadar-i-riyasat* instructed his political and legal advisers to be prepared, outdoing Mullick in his assessment of the threat:

> If we gave him an opportunity to take his case to the streets he would easily arouse acute communal and chauvinistic sentiments among the Kashmiri masses, which could in turn result in serious and violent disturbances. Anti-national elements and agents were active in the valley and, given a chance, would not hesitate to plunge the State into utter turmoil.

It was then, Karan Singh suggests, that 'We therefore decided that the Sheikh would have to be dismissed', though the decision had been taken days earlier. He was reluctant to arrest him, but 'Bakshi Ghulam Mohammed made it quite clear that he could not undertake to run the government if the Sheikh and Beg were left free to propagate their views'.

ORDER OF DISMISSAL

That very evening, Karan Singh signed the order for his prime minister's dismissal, sidestepping the normal democratic practice of testing the majority in the state assembly. After reiterating his charges against Abdullah, it declared:

> Whereas, finally, the functioning of the present Cabinet on the basis of joint responsibility has become impossible and the resultant conflicts have gravely jeopardized the unity, prosperity and stability of the State;
>
> I, Karan Singh, Sadar-i-Riyasat, functioning in the interests of the people of the State who have reposed the responsibility and authority of the Headship of the State in me, do hereby dismiss Sheikh Mohammad Abdullah from the Prime Ministership of the State of Jammu and Kashmir, and consequently the Council of Ministers is dissolved herewith.

It was late evening by the time the papers were ready, with rain falling. Karan Singh writes that he deputed his ADC, Major B.S. Bajwa, to deliver the letter to Gulmarg. He feared violence if Abdullah had got an inkling. Abdullah was however totally unaware of what was impending, which Karan Singh uncharitably interprets as being because he was 'so arrogant in the possession of power that he would never dream than anyone would dare to challenge him'.

The further details provided indicate that Abdullah was completely taken by surprise. When his ADC reached Gulmarg it was late at night:

> The Sheikh and Begum Abdullah were fast asleep. With some difficulty and much knocking he was awoken and handed the letter and a warrant of arrest. On reading it, he flew into a rage and shouted, "Who is the Sadar-i-Riyasat to dismiss me? I made that chit of a boy Sadar-i-Riyasat". By then his house was fully surrounded by the police. He was given two hours to say his namaz and pack, during which we later learnt he burnt a number of documents that he had with him.

MYSTERIOUS EMISSARY

Mullick's version, however, makes much of information that an emissary from Pakistan was on his way to Tangmarg (near Gulmarg) to meet Abdullah. Suspicions had deepened, according to him, when the Sheikh suddenly left for Tangmarg (but with no evidence given of a meeting). Then, after Karan Singh had signed the order dismissing Abdullah, A.P. Jain (Nehru's observer in Srinagar), confirmed that the Sheikh had left for Tangmarg that morning, probably to hatch his plans for a coup and so action for a change-over had been decided for that night, but on account of Bakshi's hesitation, the change-over had not till then taken place.

Mullick places himself at the centre of subsequent, fast-moving events. He informs the prime minister who is at a party in Hyderabad House. Nehru asks him to contact Mehra in Srinagar, who informs him that Bakshi is jittery and hesitant to take over till Abdullah's arrest is confirmed. At midnight, the *sadar-i-riyasat* issued orders for the arrest 'as his meeting the Pakistan emissary would constitute a grave danger to the State'. It was not till four the next morning, when Bakshi heard that a police party had left for Tangmarg to arrest the Sheikh, that he went to Raj Bhawan to be sworn in as prime minister.

Facts did not impede the Intelligence Bureau chief's zeal to smear his victim. While Abdullah was woken up from sleep in his Gulmarg house to be arrested, his account of the event is: 'Mehra reported this at about 4.30 in the morning and also mentioned that L.D. Thakur, DIG of Police, with a force of police and militia had been sent to Tangmarg to take the Sheikh into custody, as there was every danger that he would go in hiding and try to create disturbances in Kashmir with the help of Pakistanis.'

Karan Singh makes no mention of Tangmarg or the mysterious emissary from Pakistan. There are discrepancies in times, places, and descriptions in the two accounts. Was the emissary invented to rush Nehru into authorizing Abdullah's arrest after his dismissal or give him an excuse for doing so? According to S. Gopal, Nehru's official biographer, 'he certainly does not seem to have anticipated the way in which Abdullah was dismissed, by stealth of night in his absence, and his prompt arrest thereafter'. In his letter to chief ministers on 22 August, Nehru wrote, 'We learnt of these events after they had taken place'.[11]

This is confirmed by yet another version of the coup in Lieutenant General B.M. Kaul's *Untold Story*.[12] Another Kashmiri, Kaul was an ambitious army officer who had gained Nehru's confidence and was 'on leave' in Srinagar at the time. He recalls that Abdullah told him that the fate of Kashmir should be decided by its people who might opt neither for India nor Pakistan but to be independent. When asked what might be the fate of the forty million Muslims in India if Kashmir became independent, he said this was not his business. He warned that if India did not stop interfering in Kashmir, he would have to resort to other methods.

Despite his limited experience, Kaul concluded: 'He [Abdullah] appeared ruthless, haughty and the people were losing faith in him. They strongly resented Nehru's continued support to one who was toying with the lives of innocent Kashmiris ... When it is found that a democratic State can no longer sustain the pattern of life it seeks, it must amputate what is rotten and pernicious for the health of the populace.'

Kaul's version of the Tangmarg\Gulmarg emissary intelligence report also goes beyond Mullick's version in justifying the need for immediate action. According to his scenario, Abdullah was to meet certain 'friends' from across the border which was only seven miles away and, after clearing up some points with them, proposed arresting Bakshi, Dhar, and some others on trumped-up charges. He would then replace them by suitable henchmen and fortify his own position within the cabinet. Finally, he would make a statement before a press gathering declaring Kashmir to be independent and asking India (what about Pakistan?) to withdraw its forces from there.

Kaul flew back to Delhi to report to the prime minister, who apparently was not fully persuaded. His account of what followed when he returned to Srinagar to confer with Karan Singh, Bakshi, and Dhar is worthy of reproduction:

> We were in a vicious circle. If we told Nehru in advance that Abdullah was being arrested, we knew he would prohibit such a move. But a free Abdullah was threatening democracy in Kashmir, and was against our national interests. Arresting him, however, was contrary to Nehru's wishes though compelling under the situation. After some heated discussion, we all agreed that the time had come for Abdullah to go and, if he persisted in his proposed plans, he should, if necessary, be taken into custody without reference to Nehru (though the Yuvraj kept pointing out the need to tell Nehru of this step first).

As anticipated, the prime minister was furious:

> On August 9, Nehru rang up Yuvaraj Karan Singh and blew him up for allowing Abdullah to be arrested. The latter after hearing only a part of the outburst and being shaken by Nehru's

> blasting, handed over the telephone to A.P. Jain. Jain not being able to take in the tirade all by himself, passed the phone over to D.P. Dhar. It was all over now bar the shouting.[13]

However, Kaul remained close enough to the prime minister to be placed in command of the divisions defending NEFA in North-East India against the Chinese incursion in 1962. He resigned from the army after the defences collapsed. As for Mullick, perhaps Nehru should have remembered what he says he told him when they met in the prime minister's office after his appointment as director of the Intelligence Bureau. Asked by Nehru about methods of work, 'I told him,' Mullick replied, 'that the prime minister should not know the methods of collecting intelligence because these might violate all the Ten Commandments; he should be concerned only with the result.'[14]

Mullick's potent influence on Nehru and Nehru's over-dependence on him are confirmed by K.S. Subramaniam, formerly of the Intelligence Bureau, in his recent exposé on the role of the police and Intelligence Bureau in dealing with political violence. Subramaniam draws specific attention to the disinformation provided by Mullick in relation to Sheikh Abdullah.[15]

---

1 *Flame*, pp. 116–17.

2 Ibid. p. 119.

3 *Selected Works of Jawaharlal Nehru*, vol. 22, pp. 276–78.

4 *Jammu and Kashmir 1949–64; Select Correspondence between Jawaharlal Nehru and Karan Singh*, Penguin–Viking, New Delhi, 2006, pp. 114–16.

5 B.N. Mullick, *My Years With Nehru: Kashmir*, Allied Publishers, New Delhi, 1971, pp. 15–16.

6 Ibid, pp. 36–47.

7 Azad to Abdullah, 9 July 1953. Cited by S. Gopal, *Jawaharlal Nehru: A Biography*, vol. ii, p. 131.

8 Karan Singh, *Heir Apparent*, pp. 156–57.

9 *Flame*, pp. 119–21.

10 Karan Singh, op. cit., pp. 158–64.

11 Cited by S. Gopal, *Jawaharlal Nehru: A Biography*, p. 133.

12 B.M. Kaul, *Untold Story*, Barnes & Noble, New York.

13 Ibid. p. 146.

14 B.N. Mullick, *My Years With Nehru, 1948–1964*, Allied Publishers, New Delhi, 1971, pp. 22–23.

15 K.S. Subramaniam, *Political Violence and the Police in India*, Sage Publications, New Delhi, 2007, pp. 84–90.

A COOKED CONSPIRACY

Time would tell who had been disloyal to India.

– Sheikh Abdullah to Pandit Jia Lal Kilam
when jailed in Udhampur

Bakshi Ghulam Mohammad's reluctance to assume the office of prime minister of Jammu & Kashmir until Sheikh Abdullah was imprisoned was justified by events. As deputy prime minister and home minister of the state, known for political pragmatism and managerial acumen, he put in place party and police arrangements to control the fallout. He could not however rival Abdullah's popularity, and charges of betraying the link with India could scareely hurt the esteem in which the Sheikh was held in the Valley.

The disturbances that broke out as news of his dismissal and arrest spread were played down in the press. According to Mullick, nearly sixty persons were killed in police firing, mostly in Srinagar, and the agitation for the Sheikh's release continued for some time.[1] Mirza Mohammad Baig, who was also arrested with Abdullah, after his release put the toll at 1,500. According to Abdullah himself,

> The news of my arrest spread like wild fire. Violent demonstrations were held all over Kashmir. Many Kashmiris were killed in police firing. Thousands were arrested. Several

> members of the Assembly were bought over and the remainder were thrown in prison ... Lavish amounts of money were distributed by India to appease the Kashmiri Muslims. Rice was freely supplied ... A deliberate campaign of character assassination was started against me by the local and the Indian media. It was suggested that I had led the life of a debauched Moghul king. Fortunately, all this slander caused no lasting damage. Over time, people lost confidence in my enemies and realized that I was the victim of a sinister conspiracy.[2]

Bakshi had managed to gain the confidence of policy-makers in New Delhi who themselves differed on policy. He was an organization man. His skill and leadership in organizing labour support for the National Conference in the early days and in the defence of Srinagar when the Pathan *lashkars* were at its gates gave him a position next to Abdullah's. He was more accessible. However, while Abdullah was gripped by his vision of autonomy, Bakshi was pragmatic, more interested in gaining and retaining power and all it could secure for him and his family. He could be ruthless when unable to secure compliance with bribes. The massive funds he received from New Delhi were spent on some lasting projects; the lower-level tunnel at Banihal, housing projects; hydroelectric power; the benefits received by the prime minister and his family made them known as BBC or the Bakshi Brothers Corporation.

Nehru may not have always approved of his actions, but like Mullick, he was able to get inconvenient things done. For the Home Ministry and its intelligence operatives, he was 'Our man in Srinagar'. Unlike Abdullah, he was happy to provide all the facilities they wanted in the state. For Mullick, he was 'a liberal-minded and large-hearted person with his feet planted strongly among the masses ... He was completely loyal to Jawaharlal Nehru and considered himself an Indian out and out.'[3] He, however, concedes that the prime minister was 'never fully reconciled to the Sheikh's detention and from time to time raised the question of his release'. Mullick's interpretation of Nehru's concern for Abdullah is, 'this was not because the prime minister felt that any change had come over the Sheikh—actually no such change was at all discernible and the Sheikh's activities in jail became even more inimical towards India—but he was inherently opposed to any detention without trial'.

The intelligence chief's justification for his role in imprisoning Abdullah went beyond the allegations of anti-national activities. In the face of Nehru's objections, he insists: 'The Sheikh could not be released and events in Kashmir moved forward ... And a period of peace and prosperity followed. Bakshi proved to be a good leader and was ably assisted by his cabinet consisting of Sadiq, Saraf, D.P. Dhar, Dogra and others.'[4] The years 1953–57, according to him, stand out as the best period in Kashmir.

Economic conditions did improve in comparison to Abdullah's last turbulent days in office. Central aid flowed in; travel and transport to and from the Valley was facilitated by the lower-level Banihal tunnel; tourism revived. However, the economic upturn failed to assuage resentment over Abdullah's arrest, as events would show. Bakshi for his part showed signs of falling from the pedestal on which Mullick had placed him, as he concedes: 'Bakshi was forced to become more and more autocratic. Taking advantage of the situation, some of his protégés and some members of his family indulged in some shady deals which started affecting Bakshi's personal reputation.'[5] The chief minister sponsored a so-called volunteer Peace Brigade that became notorious for harassing people. His cousin, Abdul Rashid, appointed general secretary of the National Conference, was a conduit for receiving funds. Soon the Bakshi Brothers Corporation (BBC) became widely known for venality.

Bakshi continued to resist the release of Sheikh Abdullah, notwithstanding advice to that effect from Jawaharlal Nehru and the outspread of pro-Abdullah sentiment in the Valley. He had him moved to a sub-jail in the village of Kud, outside the Valley, beyond Banihal. New Delhi was kept happy by initiating the process of eroding Kashmir's special status. The Jammu & Kashmir Constitution was adopted by the State Constituent Assembly on 17 November 1956, and took effect on 26 January 1956, seven years after the Constitution of India. It described the state as an 'integral part of the Union of India', and endorsed measures to consolidate its ties with the rest of the country. In addition to administrative linkages, the jurisdiction of the Supreme Court was extended to the state, a measure opposed by Abdullah. Opposition was crushed, as sympathetic political leaders from outside came to realize. The well-known socialist MP, Asoka Mehta, was roughed up in Srinagar when expressing his criticism. His colleague, political commentator Balraj Puri, was manhandled in Jammu that very month.

Prominent members, unhappy with the National Conference becoming associated with the Bakshi regime, hived off. Sheikh Abdullah's constitutional adviser, Mirza Afzal Beg, formed the Plebiscite Front to keep alive the promise that accession to the Indian Union would need to be ratified by a reference to the people. The respected Maulana Syed Masoodi sought to bring Bakshi's misdoings to New Delhi's attention. He had been general secretary of the National Conference until evicted by Bakshi (and was later to become member of parliament). Masoodi found a sympathizer in Mridula Sarabhai, of the affluent Ahmedabad Sarabhai family, who devoted herself to the Abdullah cause. Bakshi however had the support of Mullick who continued to wage his own war against Abdullah. This brought her into his sights and he found 'her house in Delhi became a haven for the activities of the Plebiscite Front leaders, some of whom even made contacts with the Pakistan High Commission from this place. They took advantage of her munificence and made her part with a considerable amount of money.'[6]

The popular upsurge in the Valley affected National Conference leaders who had distanced themselves from Abdullah. They included Ghulam Mohammad Sadiq and Mir Qasim, whom Bakshi included in his cabinet (both would be future chief ministers associated with the Indian National Congress). They were surrounded by a menacing crowd when on their way from Shopian to Srinagar, barely escaping with their lives. According to Mir Qasim, 'Srinagar was in total chaos. Bakshi Saheb's own house, despite the police guard, was under attack. He was nervous and wanted to step down.'[7]

Faced with a fait accompli, Jawaharlal Nehru showed familiar traces of indecision. After expressing his anger to Karan Singh, General B.M. Kaul, and others when he heard of the midnight arrest, he sent his friend P. Subbaroyan to Kud. According to Abdullah, 'Subbaroyan asked me to forget the past and, once again, take up the reins of government. I told him that I had informed Panditji about this but he was deaf to my pleadings. Now he would have to stand by the consequences of his decisions. Time was the greatest arbiter and I would wait for its verdict.'[8]

One gesture shown to Abdullah was to transfer him from the Kud sub-jail to a room in Tara Nivas palace in Udhampur, but it was solitary confinement. All he had for some time was a radio for company. Later, however, Bakshi was obliged to respond to Nehru's concern by allowing a few friends and his immediate family, including Farooq, to visit him. Among those permitted to visit was the Pandit leader, Jia Lal Kilam. Rejecting his offer to secure his release, Abdullah insisted that 'time would tell who had been disloyal to India'.[9]

Sheikh Abdullah was sent back to Kud, a higher-altitude summer resort, in summer when the heat in Udhampur was oppressive. He was allowed out into the grassy meadow beside the jail. There, he raised poultry and sheep between reading and writing. Farooq, who had taken up golf, brought him a set of golf balls; the security guard mistook them for bombs and harassed him. Abdullah notes that the matter was brought to Nehru's notice and the security contingent was transferred.

With the prime minister showing so much concern for Abdullah, Bakshi was joined by Mullick in putting together a conspiracy case to ensure his continued detention. In October 1957, the Kashmir Conspiracy Case was launched; the accusations were given wide press publicity. With no hard evidence against Abdullah, his wife was accused of receiving money from Pakistan. Afzal Beg and nine others were charged with conspiring to bring about a violent revolution and overthrow the government. Later, loose charges were brought against Abdullah. Extracts from Mullick's extended account of the preparations for the case merit study:

> Upset by the Sheikh's hostile activities, Pandit Nehru made several enquiries to ascertain what progress had been made in the investgation of the conspiracy case and I assured him that it was making good progress. By the month of March, when the Sheikh's dangerous activities became only too apparent and it was clear that he was doing his best to bring about a state of anarchy in Kashmir and destroy its ties with India, Pandit Nehru became impatient with the delay in the investigation …
>
> Bakshi at this stage declared that whatever be the strength of the evidence against Begum Abdullah, he could not agree to her prosecution. Muslim opinion in Kashmir valley would not excuse him for dragging this lady, who was known as 'Madr-e-Meharban', to the courts. I argued that without her in the trial we would miss one of the main connecting links with Pakistan and this would greatly weaken our case; but on this question Bakshi would not budge; and Pandit Nehru also agreed with him ... But a greater disappointment awaited us when a couple of days later Pandit Nehru decided that Abdullah should not be prosecuted. We were in a quandary because for years we had been told that Sheikh Abdullah could not be indefinitely detained without trial and now that a proper charge-sheet had been prepared and legal opinion left no doubt about his directing hand in the conspiracy, we were told that he should not be put on trial.
>
> Of course, the reasons for this decision were political. India had built up her case about Kashmir's accession around Sheikh Abdullah; now if it were to be proved that the Sheikh was attempting to take the State to Pakistan, it might embarrass India a great deal … Ultimately, on May 21, 1958, a complaint was filed in the court of the Special Magistrate, Jammu … aganst 25 conspirators, including Mirza Afzal Beg, Pir

> Maqbool Gilani, Pir Maqbool Wilgami and others. In the charge-sheet there were also names of five Pakstanis who had assisted in this conspiracy ...
>
> When Sheikh Abdullah was brought to the court for the first time on October 24, 1958, he was in a mood of bravado and immediately assumed command over the other accused persons ... When the case opened, he would address the court in commanding tones and assumed a haughty posture and said he would expose the prosecutors. But, after the opening address and the leading in of some evidence regarding the Begam's activities, he became crestfallen and receded to the background.
>
> The leading accused like Sheikh Abdullah and Afzal Beg were enjoying all the facilities in the special jail. Their families were paid handsome allowances; all the educational expenses of their sons in colleges were met and they lived like Nawab's sons; the prisoners got special diet in jail; their rooms were fully furnished and fitted with aircoolers in summer; and there was no restriction on interviews with relatives and friends. The special consideration they got from the Government gave them an exaggerated notion of their importance. On January 25, 1962, the magistrate passed orders committing all the accused persons to the Court of Sessions.[10]

Now it was Mullick who was discovering that his plans to pillory Sheikh Abdullah and his followers were failing to find their target. His bitterness was reflected in finding that they were permitted to live in comfort. It extended to the man who he saw as letting him down at the final stage. His boss, Prime Minister Jawaharlal Nehru, had developed qualms. His version continues:

> In April 1962, when Pandit Nehru was ill, he made the first move to get the case withdrawn. At his instance, a petition was drafted by the Senior Counsel and sent to Bakshi Saheb for consideration. On coming to know of this I met the Prime Minister and protested to him against this step without

consulting me ... On seeing my strong objection to the case being withdrawn, Pandit Nehru suggested that I should visit Jammu, where the Kashmir Government was sojourning, meet Bakshi and other leaders, with whom I had a long discussion. I convinced him that it would be quite inadvisable to withdraw the case at the stage of its Session trial, because the Government would then allow itself to be subjected to the legitimate criticism that it had detained the accused persons for nothing for all these years and would come to ridicule. Moreover, the withdrawal would mean that the evidence collected over five years of hard work could not be used against the Sheikh and the other accused persons again in the future. Also, in the process of tendering evidence we had exposed some of our most secret links and all this would be futile. Bakshi agreed with me but asked me to consult others also.

I met D.P. Dhar, who had earlier rejoined the Government [Dhar was a minister in Abdullah's government], and he was also opposed to the release of the accused persons. I met the Sadar-e-Riyasat [Karan Singh], who very strongly objected to the proposal. His argument was that for years the Government had borne criticism throughout the world for detaining Sheikh Abdullah without trial and now that there was a cast-iron case against him, the validity of which had been proved in the lower court, politically it would be extremely unwise to release him without completing the case. If [after] the conviction the accused were pardoned, that would be a different matter, but by withdrawing the case at this stage the Government would unnecessarily invite a host of charges and accusations against itself to which there would be no convincing reply.

So the same night, Bakshi and I left Jammu by car, caught the train at Pathankot, and reached Delhi the next morning. We met the Prime Minister separately, giving our views in this matter and I also communicated to the Prime Minister the view expressed by D.P. Dhar, the Sadar-e-Riyasat and other persons whom I had consulted. The Prime Minister

> agreed that the proposal to withdraw the case need not be pursued.[11]

The intelligence chief combined intelligence, politics, innuendo, and character assassination in his indefatigable pursuit of Abdullah. He quoted Nehru extensively, but his memoirs were penned after the prime minister's death when they could not be contradicted.

According to him:

> To our utter surprise, Pandit Nehru started talking bitterly against Sheikh Abdullah's communalism ... He said that as a result of pressure from outside and also seeing the development of the States People's movement in the rest of India and for purely tactical reasons and probably under the advice of some of his more liberal followers, the Sheikh had converted the Muslim Conference into the Political [National] Conference to give it a non-communal appearance ... As soon as he became Prime Minister, he came out in his true colours once again and started his anti-Hindu activities. In contrast, he praised Bakshi and Sadiq and said these were really secular-minded persons. Pandit Nehru said all trouble in Kashmir was due to the Sheikh's communal outlook. The Sheikh always talked about the rights of the Muslims, forgetting that Hindus formed nearly 35 per cent of the population of the State and he never showed any consideration for them ... Therefore, he was not at all surprised that the Sheikh had conspired with Pakistan to overthrow the non-communal and secular government of Bakshi and Sadiq. What Pandit Nehru said was factually correct and was similar to what Sardar Patel had stressed to me in 1949.[12]

In fact, Nehru was finally able to get the case against Abdullah and his colleagues withdrawn, invited him home on his release, and demonstrated his confidence in him by sending him on a mission to Pakistan.

Mir Qasim, a future chief minister of the state, provides a different version of the discussions preceding Abdullah's release:

Our Government's first priority was to release Sheikh Abdullah and withdraw the conspiracy case against him. This had been Mr Nehru's long-cherished desire and we wanted to fulfil it before the approaching Id-ul-Zuha ... In Delhi it was the time before the receding winter and approaching summer. Blooming flowers and their fragrance added to the charm of the city. Mr Nehru, a lover of nature, was sitting under a tree in his Teen Murti House looking at the swaying flowers. I walked up to him and inquired after his health which had declined very much in recent months due to illness. Soon we were talking of Kashmir. I talked about the possible positive results Sheikh Abdullah's release and the withdrawal of cases against him would yield. Mr Nehru looked happy. But then, I feared, the release of Sheikh Abdullah could also have a negative aspect. Even as I expressed my fears, the colour of Mr Nehru's face changed: "You talk of fears," he roared. I explained I was putting before him both positive and negative of Sheikh Abdullah's release and that I had come to say that the sooner he was released the better—even before the coming Id.

Mr Nehru suggested we should wait for some time as this matter was under debate at the UNO. I countered by pointing out that Sheikh Abdullah had already written a letter to the UNO against his incarceration, the plight of the Kashmiris and our Government. If he repeated the same complaints after his release, we could say a free Indian was talking; but his writing a letter as a prisoner would be a much greater negative publicity for India. Mr Nehru smiled and said: "Looks [as if] you have acquired a lot of brain ... All right, fix a date for Sheikh Saheb's release".[13]

---

1 Mullick, *My Years With Nehru, Kashmir,* p. 46.

2 *Flames,* pp. 127–28.

3 Mullick, op. cit., p. 53.

4 Ibid., pp. 46–47.

5 Ibid., p. 53.

6 Ibid., p. 68.

7 Mir Qasim, *My Life and Times,* pp. 69–70.

8 *Flames,* p. 129.

9 Ibid., p. 130.

10 Mullick, op. cit., pp 86–94.

11 Ibid., pp. 97–98.

12 Ibid., pp. 101–03.

13 Mir Qasim, op. cit., pp. 100–01.

NEHRU'S SPLIT PERSONALITY

My comrades felt that we could not continue to hitch our wagon to a country in which we were treated so badly. I told them that we were wedded to certain ideals; so long as India propagated those we could not snap our ties. The ideals of socialism, secularism and democracy have no place in Pakistan. We must stay with India and continuously work towards our goals.

– Sheikh Abdullah

Differences between the Ministry of External Affairs and the Home Ministry of the Government of India over the credibility of Sheikh Abdullah's commitment to secularism and to the Indian Union came to a head while he was under detention after being divested of the office of prime minister of Jammu & Kashmir. The clash began when Sardar Vallabhbhai Patel was minister for home affairs and Jawaharlal Nehru prime minister. The department that spearheaded the campaign against Abdullah was the Central Intelligence Bureau led by its director, B.N. Mullick. As Jawaharlal Nehru was minister for external affairs as well as prime minister, officials of the ministry became aware of the Intelligence Bureau's role. The then commonwealth, and later foreign secretary, Y.D. Gundevia, ICS, provided an insider's account of Nehru's association with Mullick, among other recollections, in his *Outside the Archives*, published in 1984.

India and Nehru had earned a bad name at the UN after

Abdullah's detention. Pakistan made much of the fact that it was Abdullah who had endorsed the link between the state of Jammu & Kashmir and the Indian Union, and had represented India at the Security Council; but this was evidence that Muslim Kashmiris did not favour the link. India's tactics over the plebiscite issue indicated the same lack of confidence in Kashmiris. Nehru now argued that elections to the state constituent assembly would be an adequate occasion for the people to express their views. Under attack, India informed the Security Council that criminal proceedings would be initiated against Abdullah to establish the charges against him. This provided an opportunity to Mullick's Intelligence Bureau to give the conspiracy case top priority and create or distort the necessary evidence.

According to Abdullah, Nehru as well as the president, Rajendra Prasad, wanted to see him in Kud, but he refused to meet them while under detention. While admiring Nehru, he sees him as having a split personality: one side concerned with the moral aspects of policy, the other with the realpolitik of getting unpleasant, if politically necessary, things done.[1] Men like Mullick were retained even after there was reason to distrust them.

KARAN SINGH'S LETTER

The text of the letters exchanged between Karan Singh and Nehru provides an insight into Nehru's 'split personality'.[2] On 11 January 1956, Karan Singh wrote that Bakshi had informed him of the Government of India's advice to release Abdullah by the end of the month. He proceeded to provide a comprehensive case against the release. The language of the letter reflected a degree of political experience and awareness of Nehru's sensitivities that was remarkable for the twenty-one year-old *sadar-e-riyasat,* and more attuned to the views of the director of the Intelligence Bureau. Here are extracts:

> There is little doubt that upon his [Abdullah's] emergence from detention, he will immediately become the rallying point for all the disruptionist forces and disgruntled factions. There emerges the distinct possibility of widespread lawlessness and violent

clashes between the various parties, to cope with it, it may well be necessary to use forcible means ... There is no lack of those who are only too eager to exploit anything that might discredit the Government of India and the State Government, and this would be for them a heaven-sent opportunity ...

Apart from the grave danger to law and order, there are three other distinct possibilities that cannot be ruled out. First there is the danger that Sheikh Abdullah might be able to browbeat enough MLAs to gain a majority in the Assembly, of which he continues to be a member ... Though Bakshi Sahib denies the possibility of any considerable defection from his ranks, I find myself, in the event of stress of those particular circumstances, unable to share his optimism. Secondly, there is a section among members of the administrative services whose political bias may, in an atmosphere of communal excitement, cause large-scale desertion or even sabotage, which can render any administration virtually powerless. Thirdly, there is the danger of serious differences emerging within the ruling party itself as a result of severe stain.

One thing at least is almost certain. The atmosphere and stability that has been steadily built up will suffer a severe shock and the whole issue will, in the minds of the people of the state, be thrown into the melting pot. This may lead many who support the present situation to reconsider their position. Fresh life will be infused into the communal movement, the immediate and cumulative impact of which can hardly fail to have serious repercussions.

It is, of course, to be considered how long can he be kept in detention. I support the widely-held view that the proper time to release him, keeping in view the security of the State, which is our primary responsibility, would be only faster if it is found possible to declare that the Kashmir dispute is closed, or at least that the State Constitution has been finally enacted and the Constituent Assembly dissolved, after which the situation can be reviewed. Until that time, I venture to submit, releasing him would be [a] formidable risk ... Finally, I may submit that we cannot ignore the existence of powerful

> forces who would be eager to support financially and otherwise any disruptive movement within the State which would shatter its present stable and progressive association as an integral part of India.[3]

Nehru replied that very day, indicating the urgency with which he viewed the subject. While still addressing Karan Singh by his nickname of 'Tiger', he firmly rebutted his arguments. While seeming desirous not to intrude upon the powers of state governments, he passed on the responsibility for unethical but politically necessary actions on others; in this case Kashmir Chief Minister Bakshi and Mullick. This fitted Abdullah's analysis of split personality. Extracts from the letter:

> During the last year or more, the question of Sheikh Abdullah's release has often been discussed. Obviously, it is a difficult question and one has to balance various factors. So far as I am concerned, my whole mind rebels against the long detention of any person without trial ... But I realize that sometimes circumstances compel one to take action which is normally undesirable. In the balance, therefore, I left it to the judgement of the Jammu and Kashmir Government to decide what they should do in the matter.
>
> In every case the advantage that one gains by the action taken gradually diminishes and the disadvantage increases. It has seemed to me that this stage was passed some time ago. It may thus become progressively more risky to release Sheikh Abdullah. Sometime or other that risk has to be taken and it is impossible to keep any person indefinitely in detention. That every detention will become an increasing factor for instability and for reactions against us in India and abroad, apart from the effect in Kashmir itself.
>
> You say that it would be desirable to keep him in detention till it is found possible to declare that the Kashmir dispute is finally closed. That, I think, is not feasible. In fact, so long as Sheikh Abdullah is in prison, the dispute will not be finally closed. It is only when he has been released and we have faced the consequences of his release and survived them

> that it will be possible for the situation to develop towards a final end.
>
> There are the risks which you have mentioned. The question is whether the risks grow less or more by delay. The question also is as to whether internal stability in people's minds and administration will become more favourable later … I am inclined to think, that there will be no marked change for the better within some months or so and the change might be the other way ... .
>
> This is my broad way of thinking. But as I have said above, I have avoided imposing my wishes on Bakshi Ghulam Mohammad or his government. If he has come to the conclusion that this is suitable, I would abide by his decision and certainly not come in his way. I have no doubt that internationally speaking, the release would have powerful effect in our favour … I have a very uncomfortable feeling that our position is constantly undermined by Sheikh Abdullah's detention, both internally and abroad.
>
> I fully realize the risks involved. But one does not solve a problem or really avoid risks by running away from them. Therefore, after giving a good deal of thought to this matter, I have felt that Bakshi Ghulam Mohammad should take the action he has decided upon. This is as favourable an opportunity as is likely to occur. Of course we should be fully prepared. Having got over this problem, the future of the Kashmir problem will be very much simpler.[4]

In his own diplomatic way, Nehru chose to give Bakshi the benefit of having decided upon Abdullah's release, for which there was no evidence. The mere signal, however, was sufficient and Abdullah was briefly freed.

TRIUMPHAL RETURN

After Abdullah's release from Kud he drove to Srinagar. The crowds greeting him contradicted reports that he was losing popularity. He held a mammoth public meeting in Srinagar's Lal Chowk, while Bakshi staged a rival meeting by trucking in people from nearby villages. Thereafter, Abdullah avoided violating the order banning meetings and processions, and supervised the construction of a mosque in Saura. He complained to Nehru that Bakshi was conducting a vilification campaign against him. He wrote, 'in 1953 he misled you, which resulted in the traumatic episode of 9 August. Then, too, I was accused of plotting with a foreign power to make the State independent but the charge could not be substantiated.'

The death of a National Conference worker, Bandey, in a staged riot provided an excuse to rearrest Abdullah on 29 April 1958. According to Mir Qasim, 'We learnt that the riots were engineered by Bakshi Sahib's supporters to provide justification for the rearrest of Sheikh Sahib'. Mir Qasim flew to Delhi to convey his suspicions to the prime minister. Nehru was unhappy, but had been fed with false information by B.N. Mullick about Abdullah's plotting to merge Kashmir with Pakistan.[5] Bakshi went ahead and framed the conspiracy case charges without adequate evidence.

Abdullah recalls that the conspiracy case trial was held in Jammu after it had been examined by the then union home minister, Pandit Govind Ballabh Pant. Mirza Afzal Beg and twenty-five others were the principal accused. An additional charge-sheet was filed against him. Senior Indian lawyers refused to take the case and Dinglefoot, a well-known London barrister, was engaged. Abdullah recalled:

> The prosecution levelled various charges, such as, that we established contact with Pakistan to procure money, arms and bombs and this was done to start a bloody revolution in Kashmir. Fictitious documents were presented and large sums were paid to individuals who came forward to give false evidence ... As we opened our defence, the political events in India took a sharp turn. The Chinese invasion of 1962 caused heavy casualties ... When news of the Chinese aggression was received in Kud prison, I addressed a letter to Jawaharlal, saying that this sudden aggression on our northern borders had created a critical situation. To meet the challenge, we must be prepared

> for hardships and sacrifices. Freedom is indivisible, and must be preserved for the entire subcontinent. India must win the confidence of her neighbouring countries ...
>
> My comrades felt that we could not continue to hitch our wagon to a country in which we were treated so badly. I told them that we were wedded to certain ideals, so long as India propagated those we could not snap our ties. The ideals of socialism, secularism and democracy have no place in Pakistan. We must stay with India and continuously work towards our goals ...
>
> To produce the drama of the conspiracy case on the Kashmir stage, the two players "Bakshi" and "Delhi" displayed their best talent. It took five years and cost two and a half crore [25 million] rupees. But falsehood has a rotten core. Their vile accusations were fully exposed before the public, and the case became a joke. The global mood was displayed in the following headline in the *Observer* (published from London) dated 16 December 1963: "Sheikh Abdullah on Trial, But India in the Dock".[6]

Abdullah continued to stress his faith in Nehru: 'He was unhappy with the way things were and wanted the conspiracy case to be dropped. In July, during his Kashmir visit, he made his views known to the concerned people. Bakshi's fraud and deceit, however, outwitted Jawaharlal's aspirations.'[7]

After taking over as chief minister, Bakshi Ghulam Mohammad took steps to minimize the special status for Jammu & Kashmir won by Abdullah and strengthen New Delhi's powers over the state. The provision that the head of state would be elected by the state assembly was eroded. He would, like the governors appointed by the president in other states, be a servant of the Central government. The change had far-reaching effects because the governor was empowered to declare president's rule, a device used by New Delhi to topple inconvenient state governments. The title of prime minister which Abdullah enjoyed to indicate the special status of the state was modified to 'chief minister' to indicate equality with other states. The erosion of Kashmir's special status was responsible for increasing Bakshi's unpopularity.

A series of international events and his own failing health diverted the prime minister's attention from Kashmir. The takeover of Goa in 1961 diminished his stature in the West. However, the biggest blow was the war in the Himalaya lost with the Chinese in 1962, which coincided with the Cuban missile crisis. Nehru was virtually crippled; his vision of *Hindi–Chini bhai bhai* reduced to a nightmare. Pakistan was emerging as a stronger player than before in the region with its Western allies, and Nehru was obliged to consider plans to cede some territory in the Valley. However, when Pakistan's choleric foreign minister, Zulfiqar Ali Bhutto, demanded the entire Valley, Nehru resisted. At the same time, he began to consider conciliatory moves towards Pakistan president, General Ayub Khan, including a vague proposal for a confederation between the two countries.

Meanwhile, the ruling Congress high command evolved a procedure for changing chief ministers and other key officials to deal with serious complaints of maladministration from various parts of India, including Kashmir. A brainchild of a shrewd Congress leader from Tamil Nadu, after whom it was named, the Kamaraj Plan invited senior Congress leaders to resign their office, take up party work, and strengthen Nehru's hands. Among those who responded was Bakshi Ghulam Mohammad against whom charges of corruption and organizing a so-called 'Peace Brigade' to eliminate political opposition were multiplying. Before stepping down, he installed Shamsuddin, a relatively unknown worker, as chief minister.

MULLICK AND THE SACRED RELIC

The absence of a leader of Sheikh Abdullah's stature in Kashmir was felt on 27 December 1963, a date of remembrance in the Valley which was blanketed in snow. Reports that the revered 'Moe-e-Muqaddas' (Hair of the Prophet) had been stolen from the Hazratbal Mosque spread like wildfire from early morning. The crowds became unruly; they were leaderless without their Sheikh, who had been imprisoned since 1953, apart from the brief respite secured by the prime minister. They believed that Bakshi Ghulam Mohammad was behind the theft and attacked his property, including a cinema hall in the heart of Srinagar. The police fired, killing many. Bakshi's opponents then formed the 'Awami Action Committee', a political grouping that focused on the erosion of Kashmir's autonomy under Bakshi. This brought Mirwaiz Maulvi Farooq into prominence. Maulvi Farooq was assassinated in 1990. His son, Mohammad Omar, is now leading the Hurriyat movement for self-determination.

Jawaharlal Nehru felt the situation slipping out of control. He sent a Home Ministry team comprising the home secretary, Viswanathan, and intelligence chief, B.N. Mullick, to Srinagar. On 4 January, Mullick announced that the relic had been found, but he was not believed in the Valley and Nehru sent his trusted aide (future prime minister) Lal Bahadur Shastri, to the scene, preferring a political to an administrative approach. Against Home Ministry advice, Shastri endorsed the popular demand for a special *deedar* (inspection) by a team of clerics acceptable to the people. When they confirmed the relic as genuine, public anger faded.

Mullick's projects himself as the hero of the episode in his *My Years With Nehru: Kashmir,* though the line he advocated differed from Nehru's and Shastri's. The many pages he devotes to the 'Moe-e-Muqaddas' provide a picture at variance with the facts as they were described by future chief minister Mir Qasim and eyewitnesses. The impression he gives is that the disturbances were engineered by Abdullah and his pro-Pakistan supporters. Pran Nath Jalali, who was present, suggests that Bakshi was responsible for the mysterious disappearance.

Jalali's version of the scene at Hazratbal Mosque when the holy relic was displayed to the public contradicts Mullick's. According to Mullick, he was greeted as a hero by the crowd of onlookers who had gathered at the mosque, and a *saropa* placed on his head in recognition of his contribution to the restoration of the relic. He informed the prime minister and asked Srinagar radio to broadcast his version of the event, which was picked up by All India Radio. According to Jalali, he was not present at the scene. Mullick went on to describe a meeting with Nehru. According to him, 'Nehru held my hand in great love and told me that I had done miracles'. He went on to call on President Radhakrishnan 'who got up from his bed to show special consideration for me'. He cites the president telling him that the prime minister was in a state of depression and mental agony until he heard of Mullick's feat in restoring the relic.[8] No third person was present at these meetings to corroborate these self-congratulatory exchanges with statesmen who were dead when Mullick's book appeared. The sentiments attributed to Nehru were totally different from those that Mir Qasim and others recalled.

In fact, the holy relic episode revived Nehru's conviction that without Abdullah Kashmir could not settle down. He insisted that he be freed, though Mullik insisted that there was no sign of Abdullah changing his anti-national stance and that 'we [the Intelligence Bureau] had proceeded on the basis that Kashmir was an integral part of India and anyone who talked of secession was guilty of treason. We had an iron case against Sheikh Abdullah . . .' Nehru had however had enough. Foreign Secretary Y.D. Gundevia reports him as banging the table and exploding: 'If a damned thing can't be proved in four years and in six years, there's obviously nothing to be proved.'[9]

1 *Flames*, p. 135.

2 *Jammu & Kashmir 1949–64; Select Correspondence between Jawaharlal Nehru and Karan Singh*, ed. Jawaid Alam, Viking, 2006, pp. 184–88.

3 Ibid., pp. 185–86

4 Ibid., pp. 187–88.

5 Mir Qasim, op. cit.

6 *Flames*, pp. 136–44.

7 Ibid., p. 144.

8 B.N. Mullick, *My Years With Nehru: Kashmir*, pp. 141–44.

9 Y.D. Gundevia, monograph included in *Testament of Sheikh Abdullah*, p. 121.

MISSION TO PAKISTAN

Panditji expressed his deep anguish and sorrow at the past incidents. I also became very emotional and told him that I was glad to have convinced him that I was not disloyal to him personally or to India.

– Abdullah on his last meeting with Nehru

Photographs of Jawaharlal Nehru in early 1965 show an ailing leader conscious that his time had come. Speculation about who could possibly succeed him was rife even outside India. An American journalist, Welles Hangan, wrote a bestseller on the subject, *After Nehru Who?* The ruling Congress party began to clear the decks for the post-Nehru period with a plan devised by K. Kamraj, known after him as the Kamraj Plan, which, inter-alia, included easing Bakshi Ghulam Mohammad out of office.

The unfinished business of Kashmir was very much on Nehru's mind. His inability to prevent the prolonged detention of his old friend and comrade, Sheikh Abdullah, symbolized the failure of his Kashmir policy. The Home Ministry's colonial approach had been successful. Before he died he wanted to demonstrate his confidence in Abdullah in a manner that could wipe away the bitterness left by years of imprisonment. As for Abdullah, while his confidence in Nehru's ability to implement his promises had been eroded, in public he continued to express faith in his sincerity.

After ordering Abdullah's release, Nehru ignored Bakshi and

Mullick's advice to avoid the popular reception he was bound to receive in the Valley by keeping them out of it. Another sign of confidence was to invite the Sheikh to stay with him at the prime minister's residence and send him on a mission to Pakistan. Diplomatic messages from Pakistan indicated that President Ayub would meet him. Abdullah was keen to discuss various peace proposals with Ayub, including that of a confederation between India, Pakistan, and Kashmir.

The reception Abdullah received in Srinagar was described by Prem Bhatia, a percipient observer of the Kashmir scene, in a despatch to the *Guardian* of London dated 24 April 1964:

> While he waits for his meeting with Mr Nehru and other Indian leaders, Sheikh Abdullah holds the valley of Kashmir in an unprecedented grip of emotion. Thousands attend meetings addressed by him, and hundreds follow wherever he goes. His visit to a local hospital for a medical check-up two days ago nearly caused a riot. Patients left their sickbeds and surgeons abandoned operation. Window panes were broken in the stampede. Srinagar seems to be in the midst of an "Abdullah festival" in which slogans for a plebiscite are merged in shouts of loyalty to the "Lion of Kashmir".

Abdullah did not engage in raising passions, which he could so easily have done. Instead, he struck a note of caution against possible communal repercussions in the subcontinent by promoting rash solutions. The possible consequences on fifty million Muslims in India and ten million Hindus in East Pakistan should be borne in mind. He urged Kashmiris to maintain communal peace and set an example to India and Pakistan. No Muslim in Kashmir should raise his hand against the minorities.

From Srinagar, Abdullah flew to New Delhi, his first visit to the national capital in eleven years. Waving communal flags and shouting anti-Nehru slogans, Hindu Mahasabha volunteers staged a demonstration at the airport to protest against his demand for self-determination. However, under the prime minister's instructions, the official line was sympathetic. He laid a wreath at Gandhi's memorial at Rajghat and addressed a Friday congregration at Jama Masjid.

THE RAJAJI FORMULA

A packed programme of meetings with a wide range of Indian leaders was awaiting him. He flew to Madras to meet C. Rajagopalachari, who had advocated full autonomy for Kashmir and an understanding with Jinnah; and to Poona to meet Acharya Vinoba Bhave at his ashram. In Delhi, he consulted President Radhakrishnan, Vice-President Zakir Husain, and Jayaprakash Narayan who had campaigned for him. He did not allow representatives of Kashmir political parties campaigning for accession to Pakistan while he was in jail to join his entourage.

Before leaving Srinagar, the Sheikh had told his colleagues that he hoped for a series of meetings with Nehru. Apart from renewing their friendship, his object was to ensure that the Central government abided by its commitment to respect Jammu & Kashmir's special status. Kashmir was being debated at the United Nations at the time with plebiscite still on the agenda. Nehru was ready to meet him half way, but continued to insist that nothing would be conceded that would come in the way of accession being finalized. As Prem Bhatia reported: 'Sheikh Abdullah and Nehru will, therefore, try to win over each other.'

According to Abdullah, the reunion was emotional: 'Panditji expressed his deep anguish and sorrow at the past incidents. I also became very emotional and told him that I was glad to have convinced him that I was not disloyal to him personally or to India.' They met every day for five days; Abdullah also conferred with Foreign Secretary Y.D. Gundevia and Indian High Commissioner to Pakistan G. Parthasarathi. They are reported to have discussed a plan for a confederation between India and Pakistan, with Kashmir as an autonomous enclave between them, on the model of Andorra, between France and Spain. Recovering from a stroke suffered in Bhubaneswar,

Nehru needed rest and was taken to Dehra Dun. Abdullah saw him off before leaving the following day for Rawalpindi.[1] He was not destined to meet his old friend again.

Abdullah's entourage included his son Farooq, Mirza Mohammmad Afzal Beg, who had been imprisoned with him, and other colleagues. A group of journalists were given special visas to accompany him. Among them were Prem Bhatia and Inder Malhotra. The Sheikh issued a statement to the press drafted with great care on what he hoped to achieve in Pakistan:

> Deterioration in the relations between both countries has resulted in permanent tension which at times has assumed the proportions of a collision course and fratricidal conflict. The minorities of both countries are the worst sufferers. India and Pakistan are rapidly distancing themselves from each other. If this trend is not arrested, it will upset the balance of power in Asia and the whole of the subcontinent will be engulfed in flames. We are faced with an alarming situation. If we fail to remedy it our future generations will never pardon us …
>
> In this context, the Kashmir problem is a long-standing bone of contention. We must endeavour to defuse the situation and find a mutually acceptable solution to this problem. It goes without saying that the solution should be such that neither country should have the feeling of being outmatched nor should it weaken the foundations of Indian secularism. Further, it should bring about complete freedom to the people of the State and grant them a respectable status ...

Ayub sent his foreign minister, Zulfiqar Ali Bhutto, to welcome Abdullah at Rawalpindi airport. Prominent Kashmiri leaders who had fled to Pakistan also greeted him, among them Chaudhry Ghulam Abbas and Mirwaiz Yusuf Khan. Abdullah noted that the roads were lined with cheering crowds (he had been reviled in Pakistan when representing India at the UN). When calling on Ayub, he presented him a *santoor,* the traditional Kashmiri musical instrument.

Abdullah records that Ayub rejected the confederation proposal as a move devised by Nehru to extend Indian hegemony. When he reiterated this in his autobiography, *Friends Not Masters,*[2] Abdullah contradicted him in a letter he wrote to Ayub dated 1 September 1967: 'We had not taken with us any cut and dried proposal concerning Kashmir and, as a matter of fact, Jawaharlal Nehru had not asked us to put across any particular proposal. We are not made that way.' Critics had used the confederation proposal to embarrass Nehru, but Ayub did accept Abdullah's proposal for a summit meeting between him and Nehru in June which Abdullah announced to the press the following day.

From Rawalpindi, Abdullah left for Muzaffarabad in Pakistan-held Kashmir on 27 May, with the Indian journalists accompanying him permitted to enter 'Azad' Kashmir for the first time. It was the headquarters of Kashmiri refugees from Indian-held Kashmir. It was there that he was devastated by news of Nehru's death, and wept bitterly in the presence of journalists. The president of Pakistan sent a plane to take him back to New Delhi accompanied by Bhutto as his representative. Abdullah had a good opinion of Bhutto, noting in *Flames*: 'I felt that he was destined to lead Pakistan out of turmoil, but with the passage of time he became surrounded by sycophants who distanced him from the common man. This led to his downfall and the fragmentation of Pakistan.'

On arrival at Teen Murti House (the prime minister's residence) from Palam airport, Abdullah recalled:

> The place was full of mourners. I went to the room in which the mortal remains of Jawaharlal Nehru were wrapped in the Tricolour—I broke down. With his death a glorious chapter in Indian history came to an end. I was present at Shantivan where his last rites were performed. Britain was represented by Lord Mountbatten and the Soviet Union by Alexei Kosygin. Bakshi and Sadiq [then chief minister] had come from Srinagar. Many other world dignitaries including American Secretary of State Dean Rusk were there.

As desired by Nehru on the eve of his death, Abdullah carried some of the ashes back to Srinagar and immersed them at the confluence of the Indus and the Jhelum, addressing a condolence meeting there.

PERCEPTIVE PORTRAIT

Abdullah's portrait of his friend in *Flames of the Chinar* reflects the affection and admiration he had for him, without overlooking the hurt and problems he caused. Some extracts:

> Jawaharlal was one of the most illustrious leaders of this era. Being as enigmatic as most geniuses, he was a mixture of strengths and weaknesses. His Kashmiri ancestry was reflected in his handsome features, his apple-red cheeks! His broadmindedness and moral strength stemmed from his affluent family background. Educated along with the cream of the English society, he was part of the English liberalism, influenced by the British social tradition of the nineteenth century as well as the Fabian Society. His liberalism had a militant dimension, as evidenced by his admiration for Karl Marx. Neither a total liberal nor a staunch socialist, like Hamlet he was suspended between the two ideologies.
>
> Although he claimed to be an agnostic, he wrote in praise of India's past, which was fraught with Hindu revivalism. His *Discovery of India* often comes close to the perception of revivalist Hindus such as K.M. Munshi and Dayanand Saraswati. He regarded himself as an instrument to establish once again that old dispensation. His idealism was tainted with politicking and conjurations of Machiavelli. He was an admirer of that ancient political thinker Chanakya and kept the Arthashastra by his bedside.
>
> Nehru was influenced by Machiavelli's doctrines and practised them with us in Kashmir. He was a product of the confluence of British elegance, Hindu refinement and Muslim civility. Thus his personality was extremely attractive. He was loyal to his friends and sought to do all he could for them so long as they did not impede his country's interests or his own.

When he felt danger his attitude dramatically changed, for example his decision to throw me in prison. At his behest, Bakshi Ghulam Mohammad betrayed his benefactor and his motherland. But Nehru mercilessly put him aside when he was of no use.

Nehru had a soft spot for the gentle sex. Often he was distracted from important meetings by the arrival of a lady friend. His ladies, however, were no brainless mannequins. They were the brightest women, such as Sarojini Naidu, Padmaja Naidu, Mridula Sarabhai and Edwina Mountbatten.

Jawaharlal Nehru always maintained a strong affinity for Kashmir, the land of his ancestors. He once explained to Lord Louis Mountbatten that just before her execution, Mary Queen of Scots had claimed that if her heart was opened "Calais" would be imprinted on it. Kashmir was engraved upon his own heart. It would not be difficult to believe that when he died, like when the Emperor Jahangir passed away, Kashmir was hovering over his last few breaths. His love for Kashmir drastically shaped its fate for better or worse. Nehru's perception of Kashmir was unusual; his metaphor for its scenery was a woman of infinite grace. He called it his second Achilles heel.

It has often crossed my mind that Nehru's love of Kashmir made him jealous of my hold over its people. The resentment expressed itself in his taking action against me. Although he was essentially carefree, his last days were full of sorrow. His life was marred by the Chanakya in him. China's aggression completely broke his spirit. He claimed to be the successor of Gandhiji but doubts arose about his moral leadership during the Kashmir crisis. After the 1953 coup of Kashmir, his followers tarnished his image. During his last days, however, he tried to repair the damage done to the Valley. He removed Bakshi Ghulam Mohammad from prime ministership and, upon my release in 1964, expressed his personal regrets for what had happened. He was trying to set things right with my help when he was suddenly called back to his creator. His plans for Kashmir remained unfulfilled.[3]

---

1 Ayub Khan, Mohammad, *Friends Not Masters*, Oxford University Press, London, 1965.

2 *Flames*, pp. 152–57.

3 Ibid., pp. 74–76.

CORROSIVE COMPROMISE

Forgetting my past experiences, I agreed to compromise with the Congress but soon had to regret my decision.

– Sheikh Abdullah
on his agreement with Indira Gandhi

Sheikh Abdullah did not enjoy a long spell of freedom after Jawaharlal Nehru's death. He found the new prime minister, Lal Bahadur Shastri, cordial and 'keen to complete the work initiated by Jawaharlal Nehru'. He, however, lacked Nehru's popular appeal and did not have the 'strength to rally his colleagues around to his viewpoint.'[1] Shastri had manifested his interest in Kashmir when he was sent there by Nehru to resolve the Sacred Relic crisis, but as Abdullah noted, found it difficult to stand up to the hardline members of his cabinet. The Union Home Minister, Gulzari Lal Nanda, used his office to further the pace of integration.

Soon after assuming office, the new prime minister was faced with a major crisis. In August 1965 Pakistan inducted a new wave of infiltrators across the ceasefire line and, as in 1947, advance elements reached the outskirts of Srinagar before they were stopped. The Kashmiris however, contrary to Pakistan's expectations, failed to rise. The Indian authorities were informed by the local inhabitants that armed outsiders were crossing the line, enabling the Indian Army to push them out of the Valley. Frustrated there, Pakistan turned towards Jammu, and launched an armoured division in a surprise attack to cut the vital road from the railhead to Srinagar. This part of the front was thinly held by Indian Army units.

Even so, Prime Minister Shastri was reluctant to act. He had accepted British Prime Minister Wilson's assurance that Pakistan would not interfere in India-held Kashmir after the two countries had signed the Rann of Kutch agreement earlier that year. However, when informed by his military advisers that attacking Pakistan directly was the only way to save Kashmir, he did not hesitate. Indian troops crossed the international border in strength. The first direct Indo–Pakistan war erupted causing much bloodshed and damage to both sides. As in 1948, the United Nations imposed a ceasefire following a stormy debate. In January 1966, Shastri and President Ayub Khan of Pakistan reached an agreement in Tashkent, meeting there under Soviet auspices. Shastri was persuaded to agree to withdraw Indian troops from areas they had captured, including Haji Pir that dominated the ceasefire line in Kashmir. He did not survive the criticism that followed.

MIDDLE EAST VISIT

Meanwhile, Abdullah was permitted by the government to tour Islamic countries in the Middle East. He met President Gamal Abdel Nasser of Egypt and Anwar Sadat, then speaker of the Assembly, King Faisal of Saudi Arabia, President Ben Bella of Morocco, and other dignitaries. He was invited to attend the Islamic International Conference in Morocco. There he found much sympathy for Kashmir, but intervened during the proceedings to reiterate his commitment to secularism and to present India's viewpoint:

> When the problems of the Indian Muslims were discussed, I intervened and asserted that the Indian Muslims wanted their complete involvement in the affairs of their country and had consistently supported secularism. Although it was resented by representatives of certain countries, the conference accepted my suggestion that no reference regarding Indian Muslims be made.[2]

Chou En-lai, premier of Communist China, who was also visiting Morocco, invited him to dinner. Abdullah accepted. According to him, they discussed the future of the slice of Kashmir territory beyond Gilgit that Pakistan had ceded to China. Chou told him that the agreement would be modified if India or any other country got control of the territory. He was very critical of Jawaharlal Nehru and suggested that he wanted to revive Hindu imperial ambitions in Java and Sumatra.[3]

Press reports of his meeting a leader still regarded as a near-enemy after the 1962 war aroused widespread concern in India. When Chou invited him to visit China, there was uproar in parliament and the Shastri government was criticized for allowing him to go abroad. When he reached London, the Indian high commissioner told him to return to India immediately or his passport would be withdrawn. Abdullah and his wife took the next flight back, though they would have gladly been given official refuge in many countries, including Pakistan.

DETAINED AGAIN

On his return, Abdullah was detained at Palam airport by a posse of officials. He was flown to Madras, then on to the southern hill resort of Ootacamund. Security arrangements at the local prison were found inadequate and he was taken to Kodaikanal, an attractive but remoter hill station. No charges could be held against him (Shastri had allowed B.N. Mullick to retire after his mishandling of the Moe-e-Muqaddas crisis in Kashmir). Begum Abdullah was permitted to join him in Kodaikanal and his sons to visit him. After the manner in which he had returned to India on being instructed to do so, it was obvious that he would not try to escape.

A new chapter in Kashmir's eventful history opened after Indira Gandhi succeeded Shastri as prime minister. She was confident that in poor health after his long incarceration, Abdullah would be receptive to fresh moves for a settlement with New Delhi. She therefore arranged for him to be moved to a bungalow in New Delhi, where he could meet friends, though still under detention. He was finally released on 2 January 1968, fifteen years after he and Begum Abdullah were arrested in Gulmarg. He did not, however, express any bitterness at a press conference two days later, stressing the need for mutual accommodation. Indira Gandhi responded by inviting him to see her. Abdullah was impressed by her personality, if not her policies, and writes in his memoirs: 'Within two years, she had created an impact on the nation. She had an independent temperament, excellent administrative ability and political sagacity. I had a detailed discussion with her about my view of the Kashmir problem. I was prepared to take up where Nehru had left off. But the Government of India did not seem interested.'[4]

Abdullah was allowed to return to Srinagar where he received the welcome accorded to a returning hero. He was presented a substantial purse collected by public donation. Much of it was spent on developing Saura, the village in which he was born and brought up, which was now a suburb of Srinagar. Work began on the magnificent medical institute that has been set up there. Money was also spent on reconstructing Hazratbal Mosque and on other charitable projects.

With his popularity re-established, Abdullah began reviewing his stand on relations with New Delhi. A people's convention with delegates from throughout the state was organized in Srinagar. His friend and popular advocate, Jayaprakash Narayan (popularly known as JP) was invited to inaugurate it. The convention did not prove to be quite what Abdullah had planned. While reiterating support for the state's special status, JP stated that after the 1965 war the time had come to finalize ties with India. Abdullah was disappointed; he was still publicly committed to self-determination. With the National Conference now associated with the Congress, the Plebiscite Front, which reflected his stand, became the most popular party in the Valley.

At the same time there were disturbing signs that the youth were becoming impatient. Some incidents of violence and sabotage were reported. More serious was the hijacking of an Indian Airlines plane from Srinagar to Lahore in January 1971 by two young Kashmiri men. A group known as Al Fatah was the first to endorse violence in Kashmir.

When Indira Gandhi called for mid-term elections in March

1971, Abdullah advised the Front to contest. New Delhi's response was however firm. Abdullah and Plebiscite Front President Afzal Beg were deplaned from a flight from New Delhi to Srinagar, on the plea that a bomb had been found on the plane, and then served orders prohibiting them from entering Jammu & Kashmir. The Front was declared unlawful and the state assembly passed a law prohibiting its members from standing for elections. The Government of India made it plain that it would not tolerate any questioning of the finality of accession.

AGONIZING CHOICE

Abdullah was faced by an agonizing choice after the Indo–Pakistan war of 1971. For forty years he had been the symbol of the Kashmiri dream of self-determination. Even so, the possibility of plebiscite, as originally proposed by the United Nations, receded into history after the defeat of Pakistan and emergence of Bangladesh. The two-nation theory used by Pakistan to justify religion as a national link lay in shambles. There seemed to be no future in continuing to lead a struggle for self-determination that New Delhi had shown it would never consider. His poor health and hopes of reviviving a sense of identity and purpose in Kashmir while he was still active were other considerations.

He belatedly accepted Jayaprakash Narayan's advice and dropped his insistence on accession being temporary in return for the assurance that Article 370 of the Indian Constitution, which provided a special status for Jammu & Kashmir, would be permanently retained. The Plebiscite Front was wound up and the National Conference revived. Negotiations with New Delhi were described as being over the quantum of accession, not accession itself. In March 1972, Abdullah was quoted in the *Times* (London) as stating in an interview: 'There is no quarrel with the Government of India over accession; it is over the structure of internal autonomy.'

The Sheikh recalls in *Flames of the Chinar:*

> I assured the Centre that we had no differences with them regarding accession. We only wanted Article 370 [of the Constitution guaranteeing autonomy to Jammu & Kashmir

> state] to be maintained in its original form. Her Principal Secretary, P.N. Haksar, came to see me and fixed a date for our meeting. Our talks proved most useful. Restrictions were removed from the Plebiscite Front and my wife and Mirza Mohammad Afzal Beg were allowed to enter Kashmir. On June 5, 1972, I was released from prison. Several meetings were held between Indira Gandhi and myself. Arriving in Srinagar on June 19, I addressed a public meeting at Hazoori Bagh at which I informed the people of my talks with Indira Gandhi. The meeting nominated Mirza Mohammad Afzal Beg for further negotiations with the Prime Minister's representative, G. Parthasarathi.
>
> Our readiness to come to the negotiating table did not represent a change in our objectives but a change in our strategy ... It pained me that the Prime Minister was not prepared to dissolve the State Assembly and hold fresh elections. Our talks ended on February 24, 1975, with both representatives reporting back to their principals. After that I had another meeting with Indira Gandhi and signed the "Kashmir Accord"... During negotiations for the Kashmir Accord I had made it clear to Prime Minister Indira Gandhi that our new political phase demanded free and fair elections. She was unwilling to give her consent and, for the time being, only wanted the Congress Parliamentary Party [in the state assembly] to elect me as its leader. I agreed to cooperate with the Congress, but soon had to regret my decision.[5]

Indira Gandhi refused to consider Abdullah's attempts to secure a return to the limited relationship between the Centre and Kashmir prior to his arrest in 1953. The clock can't be turned back was her repeated response. The accord was one-sided, not going beyond providing assurances that proposals to repeal changes in the constitution affecting the state would be 'considered on merits [by the Centre]'. The Centre's powers to take over governance of the state under Article 356 of the constitution and to appoint governors remained. Other measures extending Central control were also unaffected.

One paragraph of the accord cemented the link between Jammu & Kashmir and the Centre in unmistakeable terms:

> Parliament will continue to have power to make laws relating to the prevention of activities directed towards disclaiming, questioning or disrupting the sovereignty and territorial integrity of India or bringing about cession of a part of the territory of India or secession of part of the territory of India from the Union or causing insult to the Indian National Flag, the Indian Anthem and the Constitution.

An assurance that did not figure in the agreement, but contributed to its acceptance, was that Abdullah would return to Kashmir as chief minister. As noted in his memoirs, he was elected by the Congress Legislature Party in the state assembly, an attempt to tie him closely to the Congress. The prime minister rubbed salt into the wound with a statement broadcast by All India Radio that relations between the state and the Centre would continue as before. When he heard it, Abdullah was described as livid with rage by Mir Qasim, who had resigned as chief minister to make way for him. According to Mir Qasim, he said: 'You have made a statement as if I have sold out Kashmir for the chair of Chief Minister … I pleaded that he should not be influenced by the radio version of the statement [by Mrs Gandhi].'[6]

---

1 *Flames*, p. 157.
2 Ibid., p. 159.
3 Ibid., pp. 159–60.
4 Ibid., pp. 161–62.
5 Ibid., p. 164.
6 Mir Qasim, *My Life and Times*, pp. 142–43, Allied, New Delhi, 1992.

END OF AN ERA

I hold that sovereignty resides in the people, all relationships, political, social and economic, derive authority from the collective will of the people.

– Plaque on Abdullah's memorial

Notwithtanding its optimistic title, the Kashmir Accord led to a steady downward spiral in relations between Indira Gandhi and Sheikh Abdullah, and both were disappointed with the outcome. The prime minister had presented it to parliament as a victory for the Congress in securing his assent to accession without conceding any of the demands for a return to the special status enjoyed in 1953. Her strategy was to reduce him to the status of a Congress chief minister dependent on her support and miscalculated his reaction.

Abdullah was sworn in as chief minister on 25 February 1975 with fewer powers than he had enjoyed as prime minister of the state in 1953. Even so, it was a dramatic turnaround in history. Nearly twenty-two years had passed since he was evicted from office and arrested on charges of anti-national activity. His return to office was greeted by cheering crowds lining the road to Srinagar as he entered the Valley by road after being sworn in at Jammu, the winter capital. Although now reluctantly accepting the finality of accession to the Indian Union, he was not prepared to forget his commitment to preserving the separate identity of the people of Kashmir. The charge that he had sold out for the sake of office provoked him to distance himself from the Centre. The first measure he took after assuming office was designed to demonstrate that Kashmiris could resist New Delhi's bribes. He ordered an end to the subsidy on rice provided by the Centre since his arrest. In consequence, the price of rice, the staple diet of Kashmiris, rose, but describing the subsidy as 'amoral and apolitical,'[1] he asked his people to bear it although local Congressmen used it against him.

Of greater concern to the Centre was the Resettlement Bill that he pushed through the state assembly. It was designed to give anyone outside the state who could establish that he was a subject of Jammu & Kashmir between 1947 and 1954, or a descendant, the right of return provided the person swore allegiance to the Constitution of India and the state. If it became law, thousands who had fled Maharaja Hari Singh's oppression would be able to return and reclaim their property. The maltreatment and expulsion of Muslims in Jammu during and after Hari Singh's reluctant accession to India had been Abdullah's gravest charge against the maharaja. The Bill evoked much popular support as an attempt to undo the wrong and reunite disrupted families. New Delhi, however, saw the prospect of unchecked entry into India from Pakistan and Pakistan-held Kashmir as an unacceptable security threat. Hindutva parties revived their campaign against Abdullah as communal and anti-national. The communal ratio had changed in Jammu, and those who had occupied evacuee property feared it would be reclaimed. Governor B.K. Nehru delayed assent to the Bill in view of its sensitive nature. There were doubts whether it exceeded the powers of a state legislature. (The Bill continued to strain relations between Srinagar and New Delhi after Abdullah's death.)

The gap between Abdullah and Indira Gandhi widened further as his moves to revive the National Conference gathered momentum at the cost of the Congress. Local Congress leaders refused to join Abdullah's cabinet, though it was meant to be a coalition government. He was unhappy when she imposed the Emergency of 1975 and criticized the harsh measures adopted in Delhi.[2] Abdullah did not, however, abandon efforts at reconciliation and gave the prime minister a traditional river-boat welcome when she visited Srinagar.

MOMENTOUS ELECTIONS

Abdullah had thus far been the subject of Indira Gandhi's skill in exploiting his weaknesses but there was an unexpected change in his fortunes when she was obliged to resign as prime minister after the massive Congress defeat in the March 1977 parliamentary elections. Her successor, Morarji Desai, was more responsive to his plea for fresh elections to be held in Jammu & Kashmir, and under his supervision they were the fairest the state had known. This did not prevent the new prime minister and other ministers of the fledgling Janata Party that had assumed power in New Delhi from entering the fray. Among them were the then foreign minister (and later prime minister) Atal Behari Vajpayee and elements of the Hindutva Jana Sangh parties. They revived the issue of closer integration with the Indian Union, while Home Minister Charan Singh even favoured abrogation of Article 370[3] (which had been reinforced by the Kashmir Accord).

Abdullah, who had not been keeping very well, suffered a heart attack before polling day but the issue could not be ignored. Cassettes of his taped speeches demanding the restoration of the special status that Kashmir had enjoyed were widely distributed. They described the elections as an opportunity to show that Kashmiris could decide their own future. Advised against speaking, he greeted the crowds that came to see him by raising his hand from his sickbed.

The results announced on 5 July 1977 amounted to a virtual referendum. The National Conference won 46 of the 75 seats in the assembly. It swept the Valley winning 42 seats, yielding only two to the Janata Party and none to the Congress. The Jamaat-i-Islami, which was known to favour Pakistan, was also cut to size, losing four of its five seats. Popular support for restoration of the autonomy the state had enjoyed was confirmed.

This was the high point of the last phase of Abdullah's eventful career. He returned to the chief minister's office in July victorious but ill. His last years were unhappy. Far from considering the demand for enhanced autonomy reflected by the elections, the Centre was hostile. A revengeful Indira Gandhi was back as prime minister in 1980. During a tour of the state, she attacked Abdullah by name and declared that without the Centre's help, his government could not last half an hour. Income-tax raids were organized against businessmen close to him. Abdullah complained: 'The victim was myself.'[4]

LAST SPEECH

Sheikh Abdullah responded in his last speech in the state assembly. Returning to the emotive subject of maintaining Kashmir's national honour and dignity, he justified over-dependence on the Centre:

> I have made it clear that I do not believe that the people of this State, or of this great country, should be made to live on doles and charity. I want a place of honour and dignity for them, the poorest and humblest of our citizens. I want the peasant, the factory worker, the low paid employee—all who earn their bread by the sweat of their brow—to feed themselves, and their children and their families, on their own steam, unaided by crutches such as food subsidy.[5]

Contrary to allegations that had contributed to his dismissal, Abdullah showed a lasting concern for secularism. The threat from the inflow of large sums of money from orthodox oil-rich Gulf countries, especially Saudi Arabia, to Muslim communal organizations became a source of concern in the 1970s. The principal beneficiary of these funds in Kashmir was the Jamaat-i-Islami which campaigned to become an Islamic state associated with Pakistan. It created a network of schools which propagated a narrow, fundamentalist version of Islam, as opposed to the tolerant, eclectic traditions of the Valley inherited from the Sufis and the wandering mystics. In 1975, Abdullah ordered the closure of such schools, describing them as 'centres for spreading communal poison'. When the Jamaat set up a youth organization, the Jamaat-i-

Tulba, for continued indoctrination, he banned it from holding a convention in Srinagar.

Abdullah's last days were troubled. His weakening hold over the party and the state administration led to increased corruption and intrigue. Fingers were pointed at his wife and family. The principal rivals for the succession were his son Farooq and son-in-law Ghulam Mohammad (Gul) Shah. Farooq was pleasant and well-liked but lacked political experience and showed little taste for politics. Gul Shah was the opposite; he had secured a following in the National Conference through intrigue and corruption, and was known to be planning to take over as chief minister. According to B.K. Nehru, who was governor of the state, Abdullah feared that Farooq was too easygoing to be given the responsibility of governance and was reluctant to name him as his successor until near the end.[6] He, however, increasingly involved him more closely in party politics by appointing him his successor as president of the National Conference on 21 August 1975.

Bilqees Taseer, a friend of the Abdullahs, arrived in Srinagar on 26 June 1982. The patriarch had suffered a serious heart attack. She was close to Begum Abdullah and describes her devoted service to her husband in the last days:

> Supervising the treatment of her husband's illness, showing diplomacy in receiving all kinds of guests and visitors, deciding who was to see Shaikh sahib for a few minutes, those with whom she must sit and chat for a while, the supervision of the domestic arrangements, no light task when visitors were pouring in all day … Always she had to show patience, good temper, tact. Her tirelessness was amazing, for after all she is now not a young woman. So many political problems also had to be dealt with, Sheikh sahib conscious of each and every battle that had to be fought …[7]

His compromise with Indira Gandhi, of accepting Jammu & Kashmir's accession to India without the Centre honouring its promise to revive the state's special status, dented Abdullah's reputation. When however his death was announced on September 1982, the crowds remembered him as the Sher-e-Kashmir who had given a voice and identity to Kashmiris. Mourners thronged the polo ground where the body was laid out in state. Weeping and chanting dirges, they lined the entire route to the site adjoining Hazratbal Mosque where he was buried. Farooq, who had been sworn in as acting chief minister, led the funeral procession.

Abdullah's national status was recognized by the presence of the president and prime minister at the funeral. New Delhi had, however, miscalculated if it believed that the desire for *azaadi* had died with him. Instead of the continuing democratic campaign for self-determination he had waged, it was replaced by increasing violence and communalism, by terror and state counter-terror. Abdullah himself became a victim of militancy, with many of his followers distancing themselves from his compromise with Indira Gandhi.

DESERTED MEMORIALS

The site selected for Abdullah's memorial is one of the loveliest in Srinagar. Its cupola reflects the shimmering waters of the Nagin, the most picturesque of the Valley's lakes. The sloping terraces of Nishat Bagh, laid down by Mughal Emperor Jahangir 400 years ago, are glimpsed on the distant bank, as are the towering *chinars* of the Shalimar. *Shikaras* shuttle between the banks. Adjacent is the marble dome of Hazratbal Mosque; behind the forested campus of Kashmir University.

The steps leading down to the marble grave are flanked by platforms meant for visitors. Beside the grave, another cupola marks the resting place of his begam, Akbar Jahan. On one wall of the steps a marble plaque recalls an extract from Abdullah's eloquent defence against the charges brought against him in the Quit Kashmir trial of May 1946. It testifies to the vision of the man who awakened his people to *azaadi* when Kashmir was under the rule of the Dogra maharajas and India still part of the British Empire:

> Where law is not based on the will of the people, it can lead to the suppression of their aspirations. Such law has no moral validity even though it may be enforced for a while. There is law higher than that, the law that represents the people's will and

> secures their well being; and there is the tribute of the human conscience, which judges the ruler and the ruled alike by standards that do not change by the arbitrary will of the most powerful. To this law I gladly submit and that tribunal I shall face with confidence and without fear, leaving it to history and posterity to pronounce their verdict on the claims that I and my colleagues have made not merely on behalf of the four million people of Jammu and Kashmir but also of the ninety-three million people of all the States of India [under princely rule].
>
> This claim has not been confined to a particular race or religion or colour. It applies to all, for I hold that humanity as a whole is indivisible by such barriers and human rights must always prevail. The fundamental rights of all men and women to live and act as free beings, to make laws and fashion their political, economic and social fabric, so that they may advance the cause of human freedom and progress, are inherent and cannot be denied though they may be suppressed for a while. I hold that sovereignty resides in the people, all relationships political, social and economic, derive authority from the collective will of the people.

When I visited the memorial and its environs in April 2007 it was deserted, barring two police guards lazing on the steps. Isolated, empty; no-one there to read the moving plaque on the steps. A visit to Saura evoked the same feeling. The house where he was born and from where he trudged to school has disappeared. He himself did not forget it. He rebuilt an attractive, large, double-storeyed mansion there for his begum and growing family. She had inherited a taste for European-style architecture from her father, the Swiss hotelier who built the first hotels in Lahore, Rawalpindi, and Srinagar. The Abdullahs were unable to stay long in the house, for during that period the Sheikh was in and out of jail.

Today the house is approached through a narrow lane in bustling Saura. Visitors must ask their way. The iron entrance gate is guarded. Inside they see a structure that resembles the remnants of the set of a horror film. The well-proportioned frontage of a two-storeyed mansion with octagonal walls confronts them. Wide steps invite you within. On either side are high Italian-style windows framed by remnants of stone tracery, but the glass is shattered. The structure has no roof, no ceiling; the walls are black with smoke; the remaining chimneys askew. The house, furniture, and library were destroyed during the wave of militancy in 1989. No attempt has been made to repair them. No visitors here too; even the family had distanced itself from the patriarch.

---

1 *Flames*, p. 165.

2 Ibid., pp. 166–67.

3 Akbar, op. cit., p. 191.

4 *India Today*, 16 May 1981.

5 Gul Wani, op. cit., p. 87.

6 B.K. Nehru, op. cit., *Nice Guys Finish Second*, Viking, 1997, pp. 599–603.

7 C. Bilqees Taseer, op. cit., p. 89.

APPENDIX ONE

INSTRUMENT OF ACCESSION OF JAMMU & KASHMIR STATE

The following is the complete text of the Instrument of Accession executed by the Ruler of Jammu & Kashmir state on 26 October 1947:

Whereas, the Indian Independence Act, 1947, provides that as from the fifteenth day of August 1947, there shall be set up an independent Dominion known as India, and that the Government of India Act, 1935, shall with such omissions, additions, adaptations and modifications as the Governor-General may by order specify, be applicable to the Dominion of India;

And whereas the Government of India Act, 1935, as so adapted by the Governor-General provides that an Indian State may accede to the Dominion of India by an Instrument of Accession executed by the Ruler thereof:

Now, therefore, I Shriman Indar Mahandar Rajrajeshwar Maharajadhiraj Shri Hari Singhji, Jammu Kashmir Naresh Tatha Tibbet adi Deshadhipathi, Ruler of Jammu and Kashmir State, in the exercise of my sovereignty in and over my said State do hereby execute this my Instrument of Accession and

1. I hereby declare that I accede to the Dominion of India with the intent that the Governor-General of India, the Dominion

Legislature, the Federal Court and any other Dominion authority established for the purposes of the Dominion shall, by virtue of this my Instrument of Accession but subject always to the terms thereof, and for the purposes only of the Dominion, exercise in relation to the State of Jammu and Kashmir (hereinafter referred to as 'this State') such functions as may be vested in them by or under the Government of India Act, 1935, as in force in the Dominion of India, on the 15th day of August 1947 (which Act as so in force is hereafter referred to as 'the Act').

2. I hereby assume the obligation of ensuring that due effect is given to the provisions of the Act within this State so far as they are applicable therein by virtue of this my Instrument of Accession.

3. I accept the matters specified in the Schedule hereto as the matters with respect to which the Dominion Legislature may make laws for this State.

4. I hereby declare that I accede to the Dominion of India on the assurance that if an agreement is made between the Governor-General and the Ruler of this State of any functions in relations to the administration in this State of any law of the Dominion Legislature shall be exercised by the Ruler of this State, then any such agreement shall be deemed to form part of this Instrument and shall be construed and have effect accordingly.

5. The terms of this my Instrument of Accession shall not be varied by any amendment of the Act or of the Indian Independence Act, 1947, unless such amendment is accepted by me by an Instrument supplementary of this instrument.

6. Nothing in this Instrument shall empower the Dominion Legislature to make any law for this State authorizing the compulsory acquisition of land for any purpose, but I hereby undertake that should the Dominion for the purposes of a Dominion law which applies in this State deem it necessary to acquire any land, I will at their request acquire the land at their expense or if the land belongs to me transfer it to them on such terms as may be agreed, or, in default of agreement, determined by an arbitrator to be appointed by the Chief Justice of India.

7. Nothing in this Instrument shall be deemed to commit me in any way to acceptance of any future constitution of India or to fetter my discretion to enter into arrangements with the Government of India

under any such future constitution.

8. Nothing in this Instrument affects the continuance of my sovereignty in and over this state, or, save as provided by or under this Instrument, the exercise of any powers, authority and rights now enjoyed by me as Ruler of this State or the validity of any law at present in force in this State.

9. I hereby declare that I execute this Instrument on behalf of this State and that any reference in this Instrument to me or to the Ruler of the State is to be construed as including a reference to my heirs and successors.

Given under my hand this 26th day of October, nineteen hundred and forty-seven.

(Sd.) HARI SINGH
Maharajadhiraj of Jammu and Kashmir State

Acceptance of Instrument of Accession of Jammu and Kashmir State by the Governor-General of India

I do hereby accept this Instrument of Accession.

Dated this twenty-seventh day of October, nineteen hundred and forty-seven.

(Sd) Mountbatten of Burma
Governor-General of India

SCHEDULE

The matters with respect to which the Dominion Legislature may make laws for this State.

Defence

1. The naval, military and air forces of the Dominion and any other armed forces raised or maintained by the Dominion; any armed forces, including forces raised or maintained by an acceding State, which are attached to, or operating with, any of the armed forces of the Dominion.

2. Naval, military and air force works, administration of cantonment areas.

3. Arm, fire-arms, ammunition.

4. Explosives

EXTERNAL AFFAIRS

1. External affairs; the implementing of treaties and agreements with other countries; extradition, including the surrender of criminals and accused persons to parts of His majesty's dominions outside India.

2. Admission into, and emigration and expulsion from, India including in relation thereto the regulation of the movements in India of persons who are not British subjects domiciled in India or subjects of any acceding State, pilgrimages to places beyond India.

3. Naturalization.

COMMUNICATIONS

1. Posts and telegraphs, including telephone, wireless, broadcasting, and other like forms of communication.

2. Federal railways; the regulation of all railways other than minor railways in respect of safety, maximum and minimum rates and fare, station and services terminal charges, interchange of traffic and the responsibility of railway administrations as carriers of goods and passengers; the regulation of minor railways in respect of safety and the responsibility of the administration of such railways as carriers of goods and passengers.

3. Maritime shipping and navigation, including shipping and navigation on tidal waters; Admiralty jurisdiction.

4. Port quarantine.

5. Major ports, that is to say, the declaration and delimitation of such ports and the constitution and powers of Port Authorities therein.

6. Aircraft and air navigation; the provision and aerodromes; regulation and organization of air traffic and of aerodromes.

7. Lighthouses, including lightships, beacons and other provisions for the safety of shipping and aircraft.

8. Carriage of passengers and goods by sea or by air.

Extension of the powers and jurisdiction of members of the police force belonging to any unit to railway area outside that unit.

ANCILLARY

1. Elections to the Dominion Legislature, subject to the provisions of the Act and of any Order made thereunder.

2. Offences against laws with respect to any of the aforesaid matters.

3. Inquiries and statistics for the purposes of any of the aforesaid matters.

4. Jurisdiction and powers of all courts with respect to any of the aforesaid matters but, except with the consent of the Ruler of the Acceding State, not so as to confer any jurisdiction or powers upon any courts other than ordinarily exercising jurisdiction in or in relation to that State.

APPENDIX TWO

SPEECH OF SHEIKH ABDULLAH IN THE CONSTITUENT ASSEMBLY

We must remember that our struggle for power has now reached its successful climax in convening of this Constituent Assembly. It is for you to translate the vision of New Kashmir into a reality, and I would remind you of its opening words, which will inspire our labours:

> We the people of Jammu & Kashmir, Ladakh and the Frontier regions, including Poonch and Chenani Illaqas commonly known as Jammu and Kashmir State in order to perfect our union in the fullest equality and self-determination to raise ourselves and our children forever from the abyss of oppression and poverty, degradation and superstition, from medieval darkness and ignorance, into the sunlit valleys of plenty, ruled by freedom, science and honest toil, in worthy participation of the historic resurgence of the peoples of the East, and the working masses of the world, and in determination to make this our country a dazzling gem on the snowy bosom of Asia, to propose and propound the following constitution of our State.

This was passed at the 1944 session of the National Conference in Srinagar. Today, in 1951, embodying aspirations, men and women from the four corners of the state in this Constituent Assembly have become the repository of its sovereign authority. This Assembly, invested with the authority of a constituent body, will be the fountain-head of basic laws laying the foundation of a just social order and safeguarding the democratic rights of all the citizens of the State.

You are the sovereign authority in this State of Jammu and Kashmir; what you decide has the irrevocable force of law. The basic democratic principle of sovereignty of the nation embodied ably in the American and French Constitutions, is once again given shape in our midst. I shall quote the famous words of Article 3 of the French Constitution of 1791:

> The source of all sovereignty resides fundamentally in the nation ... Sovereignty is one and indivisible, inalienable and imprescriptable. It belongs to the nation.

We should be clear about the responsibilities that this power invests us with. In front of us lie decisions of the highest national importance which we shall be called upon to take. Upon the correctness of our decisions depends not only the happiness of our land and people now, but the fate as well of generations to come.

What then are the main functions that this Assembly will be called upon to perform?

One great task before this Assembly will be to devise a Constitution for the future governance of the country. Constitution-making is a difficult and detailed matter. I shall only refer to some of the broad aspects of the Constitution, which should be the product of the labowrs of this Assembly.

Another issue of vital import to the nation involves the future of the Royal Dynasty. Our decision will have to be taken both with urgency and wisdom, for on that decision rests the future form and character of the State.

The Third major issue awaiting your deliberations arises out of the Land Reforms which the Government carried out with vigour and determination. Our 'Land to the tiller' policy brought light into the dark homes of the peasantry; but, side by side, it has given rise to the problem of the landowners demand for compensation. The nation being the ultimate custodian of all wealth and resources, the representatives of the nation are truly the best jury for giving a just and final verdict on such claims. So in your hands lies the power of this decision.

Finally, this Assembly will after full consideration of the three alternatives that I shall state later, declare its reasoned conclusion regarding accession. This will help us to chanalize our energies resolutely and with greater zeal in directions in which we have already started moving for the social and economic advancement of our country.

To take our first task, that of Constitution-making, we shall naturally be guided by the highest principles of the democratic constitutions of the world. We shall base our work on the principles of equality, liberty and social justice which are an integral feature of all progressive constitutions. The rule of law as understood in the democratic countries of the world should be the cornerstone of our political structure. Equality before the law and the independence of the judiciary from the influence of the Executive are vital to us. The freedom of the individual in the matter of speech, movement and association should be guaranteed: freedom of the press and of opinion should also be features of our Constitution. I need not refer in great detail to all those rights and obligations, already embodied in New Kashmir, which are Integral parts of democracy which has been defined as 'an apparatus of social organization wherein people govern through their chosen representatives and are themselves guaranteed political and civil liberties'.

You are no doubt aware of the scope of our present constitutional ties with India. We are proud to have our bonds with India, the goodwill of those people and government is available to us in unstinted and abundant measure. The Constitution of India has provided for a federal union and in the distribution of sovereign powers has treated us differently from other constituent units. With the exception of the items grouped under Defence, Foreign Affairs and Communications in the instrument of Accession, we have complete freedom to frame our Constitution in the manner we like. In order to live and prosper as good partners in a common endeavour for the advancement of our peoples, I would advise that, while safeguarding our autonomy to the fullest extent so as to enable us to have the liberty to build our country according to the best traditions and genius of our people, we may also by suitable constitutional arrangements with the Union establish our right to seek and compel Federal cooperation and assistance in this great task, as well as offer our fullest cooperation and assistance to the Union.

Whereas it would be easy for you to devise a document calculated to create a framework of law and order, as also a survey of the duties and rights of citizens. It will need more arduous labour to take concrete decisions with regard to the manner in which we propose to bring about the rapid economic development of the State and more equitable distribution of our national income among the people to which we are pledged. Our National Conference avows its faith in the principal that there is one thing common to men of all castes and creeds, and that is their humanity. That being so, the one ailment which is ruthlessly sapping the vitality of human beings in Jammu & Kashmir is their appalling poverty, and if we merely safeguard their political freedom in solemn terms, it will not affect their lives materially unless it guarantees them economic and social justice. New Kashmir contains a statement of the objectives of our social policy. It gives broadly a picture of the kind of life that we hope to make possible for the people of Jammu & Kashmir and the manner in which the economic organization of the country will be geared to that purpose. These ideals you will have to integrate with the political structure which you will devise.

The future political set-up which you decide upon for Jammu & Kashmir must also take into consideration the existance of various sub-national groups in our State. Although culturally diverse history has forged an uncommon unity between them, they all are pulsating with the same hopes and aspirations, sharing in each others joys and sorrows. While guaranteeing this basic unity of the State, our constitution must not permit the concentration of power and privilege in the hands of any particular group or territorial region. It must afford the fullest possibilities to each of these groups to grow and flourish in conformity with their cultural characteristics without detriment to the integral unity of the State or the requirements of our social and economic policies.

Now let us take up an issue of basic importance which involves the fundamental character of the State itself. As an instrument of the will of a self-determining people who now become sovereign in their own right, the Constituent Assembly will now re-examine and decide upon the future of the present ruling dynasty, in respect of its authority.

* * *

It is clear that this dynasty can no longer exercise authority on the basis of an old discredited Treaty. During my trial for sedition in the 'Quit Kashmir', movement, I had clarified the attitude of my party when I said:

> The future constitutional set-up in the State of Jammu & Kashmir cannot derive authority from the old source of relationship which was expiring and was bound to end soon. The set-up could only rest on the active will of the people of the State, conferring on the head of the State the title and authority drawn from the true and abiding source of sovereignty, that is the people.

On this occasion, in 1946, I had also indicated the basis on which an individual could be entrusted by the people with the symbolic authority of a Constitutional Head:

> The State and its Head represent the constitutional circumference and the centre of this sovereignty respectively, the Head of the State being the symbol of the authority with which the people may invest him [sic] for the realization of their aspirations and the maintenance of their rights.

In consonance with these principles, and in supreme fulfillment of the people's aspirations, it follows that a Constitutional Head of the State will have to be chosen to exercise the function which this Assembly may chose to entrust to him.

So far as my Party is concerned, we are convinced that the

institution of monarchy is incompatible with the spirit and needs of modern times which demand an egalitarian relationship between one citizen and another. The supreme test of a democracy is the measure of equality of opportunity that it affords to its citizens to rise to the highest point of authority and position. In consequence monarchies are fast disappearing from the world picture, as something in the nature of feudal anachronisms. In India, too, where before the partition, six hundred odd Princes exercised rights and privileges of rulership, the process of democratization has been taken up and at present hardly ten of them exercise the limited authority of constitutional heads of States.

After the attainment of complete power by the people, it would have been an appropriate gesture of goodwill to recognize Maharaja Hari Singh as the first constitutional Head of the State. But I must say with regret that he has completely forfeited the confidence of every section of the people. His incapacity to adjust himself to changed conditions and his antiquated views on vital problems constitute positive disqualifications for him to hold the high office of a democratic Head of the State. Moreover, his past actions as a ruler have proved that he is not capable of conducting himself with dignity, responsibility and impartiality. The people still remember with pain and regret his failure to stand by them in times of crisis, and his incapacity to afford protection to a section of his people in Jammu.

* * *

Finally we come to the issue which has made Kashmir an object of world interest, and has brought her before the forum of the United Nations. This simple issue has become so involved that people have begun to ask themselves after three and a half years of tense expectancy. 'Is there any solution?' Our answer is in the affirmative. Everything hinges round the genuineness of the will to find a solution. If we face the issue straight, the solution is simple.

The problem may be posed in this way. Firstly, was Pakistan's action in invading Kashmirin 1947 morally and legally correct, judged by any norm of international behaviour? Sir Owen Dixon's verdict on this issue is perfectly plain. In unambiguous terms he declared Pakistan an aggressor. Secondly, was the Maharajah's accession to India legally valid or not? The legality of the accession has not been seriously questioned by any responsible or independent person or authority.

These two answers are obviously correct. Then where is the justification of treating India and Pakistan at as par in matters pertaining to Kashmir? In fact, the force of logic dictates the conclusion that the aggressor should withdraw his armed forces, and the United Nations should see that Pakistan gets out of the State.

In that event, India herself, anxious to give the people of the State a chance to express their will freely, would willingly cooperate with any sound plan of demilitarization. They would withdraw their forces, only garrisoning enough posts to ensure against any repetition of that earlier treacherous attack from Pakistan.

These two steps would have gone a long way to bring about a new atmosphere in the State. The rehabilitation of displaced people, and the restoration of stable civic conditions would have allowed people to express their will and take the ultimate decision.

We as a Government are keen to let our people decide the future of our land in accordance with their own wishes. If these three preliminary processes were accomplished, we should be happy to have the assistance of international observers to ensure fair play and the requisite conditions for a free choice by the people.

Instead, invader and defender have been put on the same plane. Under various garbs, attempts have been made to sidetrack the main issue. Sometimes, against all our ideals of life and way of living, attempts to divide our territories have been made in the form of separation of our state religionwise, with ultimate plans of further disrupting territorial integrity. Once an offer was made to police our country with Commonwealth forces, which threatens to bring in Imperial control by the back door. Besides the repugnance which our people have, however, to the idea of bringing foreign troops on their soil, the very presence of Commonwealth troops could have created suspicions among our neighbours that we were allowing ourselves to be used as a base of possible future aggression against them. This could easily have made us into a second Korea.

The Cabinet Mission Plan has provided for three courses which may be followed by the Indian States when determining future affiliations. A State can either accede to India or accede to Pakistan, but failing to do either, it still can claim the right to remain independent. These three alternatives are naturally open to our State. While the intention of the British Government was to secure the privileges of the Princes, the representatives of the people must have the primary consideration of promoting the greatest good of the common people. Whatever steps they take must contribute to the growth of a democratic social order wherein all invidious distinctions between groups and creeds are absent. Judged by this supreme consideration, what are the advantages and disadvantages of our State's accession to either India or Pakistan or of having an independent Status.

As a realist I am conscious that nothing is all black or all white, and there are many facts to each of the propositions before us. I shall first speak on the merits and demerits of the State's accession to India. In the final analysis, as I understand it, it is the kinship of ideals which determines the strength of ties between two States. The Indian National Congress has consistently supported the cause of the State's peoples' freedom. The autocratic rule of the Princes has been done away with and representative government have been entrusted with the administration. Steps towards democratization have been taken and these have raised the people's standard of living, brought about much-needed social reconstruction, and above all built up their very independence of spirit. Naturally, if we accede to India there is no danger of a revival of feudalism and autocracy. Moreover, during the last four years the Government of India has never tried to interfere in our internal autonomy; this experience has strengthened our confidence in them as a democratic state.

The real character of a State is revealed in its Constitution. The Indian Constitution has set before the country the goal of secular democracy based upon justice, freedom and equality for all without distinction. This is the bedrock of modern democracy. This should meet the argument that the Muslims of Kashmir cannot have security in India, where the large majority of the population are Hindus. Any unnatural cleavage between religious groups is the legacy of Imperialism, and no modern State can afford to encourage artificial division if it is to achieve progress and prosperity. The Indian Constitution has amply and finally repudiated the concept of a religious State, which is a throwback to medievalism, by guaranteeing the equality of rights of all citizens irrespective of their religion, colour, caste and class.

The national movement in our State naturally gravitates towards these principles of secular democracy. The people here will never accept a principle which seeks to favour the interests of one religion or social group against another. This affinity in political principles, as well as in past association, and our common path of suffering in the cause of freedom, must be weighed properly while deciding the future of the State.

We are also intimately concerned with the economic well-being of the people of this State. As I said before while referring to constitution-building, political ideals are often meaningless unless linked with economic plans. As a State, we are concerned mainly with agriculture and trade. As you know, and I have detailed before, we have been able to put through our 'land to the tiller' legislation and make of it a practical success. Land and all it means is an inestimable blessing to our peasants who have dragged along in servitude to the landlord and his allies for centuries without number. We have been able under present conditions to carry these reforms through, are we sure that in alliance with landlord-ridden Pakistan, with so many feudal privileges intact, that the economic reforms of ours will be tolerated. We have already heard that news of our Land Reforms has travelled to the peasants of the enemy-occupied area of our State, who vainly desire like status, and like benefits. In the second place, our economic welfare is bound up with our arts and crafts. The traditional markets for these precious goods for which we are justly known all over the world, have been centred in India. The volume of our trade, in spite of the dislocation of the last few years, shows this. Industry is also highly important to us. Potentially we are rich in minerals, and in the raw materials of industry; we need help to develop our resources. India, being more highly industrialized than Pakistan, can give us equipment, technical services and materials. She can help us too in marketing. Many goods also which it would not be practical for us to produce here, for instance sugar, cotton, cloth, and other essential commodities, can be got by us in large quantities from India. It is around the efficient supply of such basic necessities that the standard of the man in-the-street depends.

I shall refer now to the alleged disadvantages of accession to India.

To begin with, although the land frontiers of India and Kashmir are contiguous, an all-weather road-link as dependable as the one we have with Pakistan does not exist. This must necessarily hamper trade and commerce to some extent, particularly during the snowy winter months. But we have studied this question, and, with improvements in modern engineering, if the State wishes to remain with India the establishment of an all-weather stable system of communication is both feasible and easy. Similarly, the use of the State rivers as a means of timber transport is impossible if we turn to India, except in Jammu where the river Chenab still carries logs to the plains. In reply to this argument, it may be pointed out that accession to India will open up possibilities of utilizing our forest wealth for industrial purposes, and that, instead of lumber, finished goods, which will provide work for our carpenters and labourers, can be exported to India where there is a ready market for them. Indeed, in the presence of our fleets of timber carrying trucks, river-transport is a crude system which inflicts a loss of some 20 per cent to 35 per cent, in transit.

Still another factor has to be taken into consideration. Certain tendencies have been asserting themselves in India which may in the future convert it into a religious State wherein the interests of Muslims will be jeopardized. This would happen if a communal organization had a dominant hand in the Government, and Congress ideals of the equality of all communities were made to give way to religious intolerance. The continued accession of Kashmir to India should, however, help in defeating this tendency. From my experience of the last four years, it is my considered judgment that the presence of Kashmir in the Union of India has been the major factor in establishing relations between the Hindus and Muslims of India. Gandhiji was not wrong when he uttered words before his death which paraphrase, I lift up mine eyes into the hills, from whence cometh my help.

As I have said before, we must consider the question of accession with an open mind, and not let our personal prejudices stand in the way of a balanced judgement. I will now invite you to evaluate the alternative of accession to Pakistan.

The most powerful argument which can be advanced in her favour is that Pakistan is a Muslim State, and, big majority of our people being Muslims the State must accede to Pakistan. This claim of being a Muslim State is of course only a camouflage. It is a screen to dupe the common man, so that he may not see clearly that Pakistan is a feudal State in which a clique is trying by these methods to maintain itself in power. In addition to this, the appeal to religion constitutes a sentimental and a wrong approach to the question. Sentiment has its own place in life but often it leads to irrational action. Some argue, as a supposedly natural corollary to this, that on our acceding to Pakistan our annihilation or survival depends. Facts have disproved this; right-thinking men would point out that Pakistan is not an organic unity of all the Muslims in this subcontinent. It has on the contrary, caused the dispersion of the Indian Muslims for whose benefit it was claimed to have been created. There are two Pakistans at least a thousand miles apart from each other. The total population of Western Pakistan, which is contiguous to our State, is hardly 15 million. While the total number of Muslims, resident in India is as many as 40 million. As one Muslim is as good as another, the Kashmiri Muslims, if they are worried by such considerations, should choose the forty millions living in India.

Looking at the matter too from a more modern political angle, religious affinities alone do not and should not normally determine the political alliance of States. We do not find a Christian bloc, a Buddhist bloc, or even a Muslim bloc, about which there is so much talk nowadays in Pakistan. These days economic interests and a community of political ideals more appropriately influence the policies of States.

We have another important factor to consider. If the State decides to make this the predominant consideration, what will be the fate of the one million non-Muslims now in our State? As things stand at present, there is no place for them in Pakistan. Any solution which will result in the displacement or the total subjugation of such a large number of people will not be just or fair, and it is the responsibility of this House to ensure that the decision that it takes on accession does not militate against the interests of any religious group.

As regards the economic advantages. I have mentioned before the road and river links with Pakistan. In the last analysis, we must however remember that we are not concerned only with the movement of people but also with the movement of goods and the linking up of markets. In Pakistan there is a chronic dearth of markets for our products. Neither, for that matter, can she help us with our industrialization, being herself industrially backward.

On the debit side we have to take into account the reactionary character of her politics and State policies. In Pakistan we should remember that the lot of the State' subjects has not changed and they are still helpless and under the heel of their Rulers, who wield the same unbridled power under which we used to suffer here. This clearly runs counter to our own aspirations for freedom.

Another big obstacle to a dispassionate evaluation of her policies is the lack of a constitution in Pakistan. As it stands at present, this State enjoys the unique position of being governed by a Constitution enacted by an outside Parliament which gives no idea whatsoever of the future shape of civic and social relations. It is reasonable to argue that Pakistan cannot have the confidence of a freedom-loving and democratic people when it has failed to guarantee even the fundamental rights of its citizens. The right of self-determination for nationalities is being consistently denied, and those who fought against Imperialism for this just right are being suppressed with force. We should remember Badshah

Khan and his comrades who laid down their all for freedom, also Khan Abdus Samad Khan and other fighters, in Baluchistan. Our national movement in the State considers this right of self-determination inalienable, and no advantage, however great, will persuade our people to forego it.

The third course open to us has still to be discussed. We have to consider the alternative of making ourselves an Eastern Switzerland, of keeping aloof from both States but having friendly relations with them. This might seem attractive, in that it would appear to pave the way out of the present deadlock. To us as a tourist country it could also have certain obvious advantages, but in considering independence we must not ignore practical considerations. Firstly, it is not easy to protect sovereignty and independence in a small country which has not sufficient strength to defend itself on our long and difficult frontiers bordering so many countries. Secondly, we must have the goodwill of all our neighbours. Can we find powerful guarantors among them to pull together always in assuring us freedom from aggression? I would like to remind you that from August 15 to October 22, 1947 our State was independent and the result was that our weakness was exploited by the neighbour with invasion. What is the guarantee that in future too we may not be victims of a singular aggression.

I have now put the pros and cons of the three alternatives before you. It should not be difficult for men of discrimination and patriotism gathered in this Assembly to weigh all these in the scales of our national good and pronounce the well being of the country lies in the future.

BIBLIOGRAPHY

Abdullah, Farooq, *My Dismissal,* Vikas, New Delhi, 1985.

Abdullah, Sheikh Mohammad, *Flames of the Chinar (Aatish-e-Chinar)* (autobiography) trans. from Urdu by Khushwant Singh, Viking, New Delhi 1993.

Abdullah, Sheikh Mohammad, *Testament of Sheikh Abdullah with a Monograph by Y. D. Gundevia,* Palit & Palit, Dehra Dun, 1974.

Akbar, M.J., *Kashmir: Behind the Vale,* Viking, London, 1991.

——, *Nehru: The Making of India,* Viking, London, 1988.

——, *The Siege Within,* Viking, London, 1985.

Andersen, Walter, and Shridhar Damle, *The Brotherhood in Saffron,* Westview Press, USA, 1987.

Ayub Khan, Mohammad, *Friends Not Masters,* Oxford University Press (OUP), London, 1967.

Azad, Abul Kalam, *India Wins Freedom,* Orient Longman, New Delhi and Madras, 1967 and 1988.

Behera, Navnita Chadha, *Demystifying Kashmir,* Pearson Longman, The Brookings Institute, Washington, 2006.

——, *State Identity and Violence: Jammu, Kashmir and Ladakh,* Manohar, New Delhi 2000.

Bamzai, P.N.K., *A History of Kashmir: Political-Social-Cultural from the Earliest Times to the Present Day,* Metropolitan Book Co., Delhi, 1962.

Bamzai, Sandeep, *Bonfire of Kashmiryat: Deconstructing the Accession,* Rupa, New Delhi, 2006.

Baxter, Craig, *Jana Sangh,* Oxford University Press, London, 1971.

Bazaz, Nagin, *Ahead of his Times, Prem Nath Bazaz: His Life and Times*, Sterling Publications, New Delhi, 2006.

Bazaz, Prem Nath, *Kashmir in Crucible*, Pamposh Publications, New Delhi, 1967.

Bazaz, Prem Nath, *The History of the Struggle for Freedom in Kashmir, Cultural and Political: From the Earliest Times to the Present Day*, Pamposh Publications, New Delhi, 1954.

Beg, Mohammad Afzal, *Sheikh Abdullah Defended, Srinagar* (other details not available).

Birdwood, Lord, *Two Nations and Kashmir*, Robert Hale, London, 1956.

Bourke-White, Margaret, *Halfway to Freedom*, Simon & Schuster, New York, 1949.

Brecher, M., *Nehru: A Political Biography*, Oxford University Press, London, 1959.

Brecher, M., *The Struggle for Kashmir*, Oxford University Press, New York, 1953.

Burke, S.M., *Pakistan's Foreign Policy*, Oxford University Press, London, 1973.

Campbell-Johnson, Alan, *Mission with Mountbatten*, Robert Hale, London, 1951.

Collins, Larry, and Dominique Lapierre, *Freedom at Midnight*, Vikas, New Delhi, 1976.

Crocker, W.R., *Nehru: A Contemporary's Estimate*, George Allen & Unwin, London, 1966.

Cunningham, Joseph Davy, *A History of the Sikhs*, Oxford University Press, London, 1918.

Deora, M.S. and R. Grover, *Documents on Kashmir Problem* (15 vols), Discovery Publishing House, New Delhi, 1991.

Gagendragadkar, P.B., *Kashmir: Retrospect*, University of Bombay, Bombay, 1967.

Galbraith, J.K., *Ambassador's Journal*, Hamish Hamilton, London, 1969.

Gandhi, M.K., *Collected Works* (89 vols), Publication Division, Government of India, New Delhi.

Gandhi, Rajmohan, *Patel: A Life*, Navajivan Trust, Ahmedabad, 1990.

Gandhi, Sonia, *Two Alone: Two Together: Letters between Indira Gandhi and Jawaharlal Nehru* (1940-64), Hodder & Stoughton, London, 1992.

Gopal, S., *Jawaharlal Nehru: A Biography* (3 vols), Oxford University Press, New Delhi, London, 1979.

Gundevia, Y.D., *Outside the Archives*, Sangam Books, Hyderabad, 1984.

Gupta, Sisir, *Kashmir: A Study in India–Pakistan Relations*, Asia Publishing House, New Delhi, 1966.

Hasan, Mushirul, *Nationalism and Communal Politics in India*, Manohar Books, New Delhi, 1991.

Hodgson, H.V., *The Great Divide: Britain–India–Pakistan*, Hutchinson, London, 1969.

Jagmohan, *My Frozen Turbulence in Kashmir*, Allied Publishers, New Delhi, 1991.

Joshi, D.K., *A New Deal for Kashmir*, Ankur Publishing House, New Delhi, 1978.

Kalhana, *Rajatarangini*, trans. M.A. Stein (2 vols), Archibald Constable, London, 1900; Indian edn. Motilal Banarsidass, Delhi, 1961.

Kapur, M.L., *Studies in the History and Culture of Kashmir*, Trikuta Publisher, Jammu, 1976.

Kaul, B.M., *Confrontation with Pakistan*, Barnes & Noble, New York, 1972.

Kaul, R.N., *Sheikh Mohammad Abdullah: A Political Phoenix*, Sterling, New Delhi, 1985.

Khaitan, Rajesh, *The Kashmir Tangle*, Vision Books, New Delhi, 1992.

Khaliquzzaman, Chaudhary, *Pathways to Pakistan*, Orient Longman, Lahore, 1961.

Khan, G.H., *Freedom Movement in Kashmir 1931-40*, Light and Life Publishers, New Delhi, 1980.

Kheer, Dhananjay, *Veer Savarkar*, Popular Prakashan, Bombay, 1967.

Khosla, G.D., *Stern Reckoning*, Delhi, 1948.

Knight, E.F., *Where Three Empires Meet*, Longmans Green, London, 1893.

Korbel, Josef, *Danger in Kashmir*, Princeton University Press, Princeton, 1954.

Lakhanpal, P.L., *Essential Documents and Notes on Kashmir Dispute*, International Books, Delhi, 1965.

Lamb, Alastair, *Crisis in Kashmir: 1947-66*, Routledge & Kegan Paul, London, 1966.

—, *Kashmir: A Disputed Legacy*, Roxford Books, UK, 1991.

Lawrence, Walter, *The Valley of Kashmir*, Oxford University Press, London, 1895.

—, Walter, *The India We Served*, Houghton Mifflin, New York, 1928.

Madhok, Balraj, *Kashmir: Center of New Alignments*, Deepak Prakashan, Delhi, 1987.

—, *Rationale of Hindu State*, Indian Book Gallery, Delhi, 1982.

Mahajan, Mehr Chand, *Looking Back: An Autobiography*, Asia Publishing House, New Delhi, 1963.

Mansergh, N. (ed.), *The Transfer of Power 1942–47* (12 vols), HMSO, London.

Mazumdar, R.C., *History of the Freedom Movement in India, Vol III*, Firma KLM Ltd, Calcutta, 1963.

Menon, V.P., *The Transfer of Power in India*, Orient Longman, London, 1957.

—–, *The Story of the Integration of the Indian States,* Orient Longman, New Delhi, 1985.

Moon, Penderel, *Divide and Quit,* Chatto & Windus, London, 1964.

Moore, R.J., *Endgames of Empire,* Clarendon Press, Oxford, 1988.

—–, *Escape from Empire: The Attlee Government and the Indian Problem,* Clarendon Press, Oxford, 1983.

Moore, Thomas, *Lalla Rookh,* George C. Harrap, London, 1846.

Mosley, Leonard, *The Last Days of the British Raj,* Weidenfeld & Nicolson, London, 1962.

Mullik, B.N., *My Years with Nehru: Kashmir,* Allied Publishers, New Delhi, 1971.

Musa, Mohammad, *My Version,* Wajidalis, Lahore, 1983.

Nehru, Jawarharlal, *An Autobiography,* Bodley Head, London, 1936.

Nehru, Jawaharlal, *Selected Works,* Jawaharlal Nehru Memorial Fund, New Delhi, 1986.

Nehru, Jawaharlal, Introduction to *State versus Sheikh Abdullah; Kashmir on Trial,* The Lion Press, Lahore, 1947.

Neve, Arthur, *Thirty Years in Kashmir,* Edward Arnold, London, 1913.

Noorani, A.G., *The Kashmir Question,* P.C. Manaktalas, Bombay, 1964.

Pandey, B.N., *Nehru,* Macmillan, London, 1976.

Pandit, K.N., *Baharistan-i-Shahi: A Chronicle of Medieval Kashmir,* Firma K.L. Mukhopadhyay, Calcutta, 1991.

Patel, Vallabhbhai, *Sardar Patel's Correspndence* (10 vols), ed. Durga Das, Navajivan Trust, Ahmedabad.

Pirzada, Syed Sharifuddin, *Evolution of Pakistan,* Lahore, 1963.

Puri, Balraj, *Jammu and Kashmir: Triumph and Tragedy of Indian Federalisation,* New Delhi, 1981.

—–, *Kashmir: Towards Insurgency,* Orient Longman, New Delhi, 1993.

Pyarelal, *Mahatma Gandhi: The Last Phase,* Vol. II, Navajivan Trust. Ahmedabad, 1958.

Qasim, Mir, *My Life and Times,* Allied Publishers, New Delhi, 1992.

Quraishi, Humra, *Kashmir: The Untold Story,* Penguin, Delhi, 2004.

Rai, Mridu, *Hindu Rulers, Muslim Subjects,* Permanent Black, Delhi, 2004.

Raina, Dina Nath, *Unhappy Kashmir: The Inside Story,* Reliance Publishing House, New Delhi, 1990.

Rao, Amiya and B.G. Rao, *Six Thousand Days,* Sterling Publishers, New Delhi, 1974.

Rogers, Alexander (trans.), *Tuzuk-i-Jahangiri* (The Memoirs of Jahangir), Royal Asiatic Society, London, 1909; rpt Munshiram Manoharlal, Delhi, 1968.

Sen, L.P., *Slender Was the Thread: Kashmir Confrontation 1947–48*, Orient Longman, New Delhi, 1969.

Shankar, V.M., *My Reminiscences of Sardar Patel* (2 vols), Macmillan, New Delhi, 1974.

Shankardas, Rani Dhawan, *Vallabhbhai Patel: Power and Organisation in Indian Politics*, Orient Longman, New Delhi, 1988.

Sharma, B.L., *Kashmir Awakens*, Vikas, New Delhi, 1977.

Singh, Lt Gen. Harbaksh, *War Despatches*, Lancer International, New Delhi, 1991.

Singh, Karan, *Sadar-i-Riyasat*, Oxford University Press, New Delhi, 1985.

Singh, Karan, *Heir Apparent*, Oxford University Press, New Delhi, 1982.

Singh, Khushwant, *A History of the Sikhs*, Princeton University Press, Princeton, 1963.

Sinha, Aditya, *Farooq Abdullah: Kashmir's Prodigal Son*, UBSPD, New Delhi, 1996.

Sinha, S.K., *Operation Rescue: Military Operations in Jammu and Kashmir 1947–49*, Vision Books, New Delhi, 1977.

Stein, M.A., *Memoir on the Ancient Geography of Kashmir*, Archibald Constable, London, 1902.

Stephens, Ian, *Horned Moon*, Chatto and Windus, London, 1953.

Sufi, G.M.D., *Kashmir* (2 vols), Light & Life Publishers, New Delhi, 1974.

Taseer, C. Bilqees, *The Kashmir of Sheikh Abdullah*, Gulshan, Srinagar.

Tendulkar, D.G., *Mahatma* (8 vols), Publications Division, Government of India, New Delhi, 1954.

Teng, M.K., R.K.K. Bhatt, and Santosh Kaul, *Kashmir: Constitutional History and Documents*, Light & Life Publishers, New Delhi, 1977.

Teng, M.K. and S. Kaul, *Kashmir's Special Status*, Light & Life Publishers, New Delhi, 1975.

—, *Kashmir: Article 370*, Light & Life Publishers, New Delhi, 1990.

Thomas, Raju G.C., *Perspecitves on Kashmir: The Roots of Conflict in South Asia*, Westview, USA, 1992.

Trivedi, Vijaya R., *Facts about Kashmir*, New Delhi, 1990.

Tyndale-Biscoe, Canon, *Kashmir in Sunlight and Shade*, London, 1922.

British Government, *Transfer of Power 1942-47 Documents*, HMG, London, 1983.

United States Government, *Foreign Relations of the US, Washington DC, 1948-53.*

Vashist, S., *Sheikh Abdullah: Then and Now*, Maulik Satya Prakashan, Delhi, 1968.

Vigne, G.T., *Travels in Kashmir, Ladakh, Iskardo and the Himalayas North of Punjab* (2 vols), Henry Colburn, London, 1842.

Wakhlu, Khem Lata and O.N. Wakhlu, *Kidnapped*, Konark, Delhi, 1993.

Wani, Gul Mohammad, *Kashmir Politics: Problems and Prospects*, Ashish Publishing House, New Delhi, 1993.

Wolpert, S., *Jinnah of Pakistan*, Oxford University Press, New York, 1984.

Yasin, Mohammad, *History of the Freedom Struggle in Jammu and Kashmir*, New Delhi, 1980.

Younghusband, Sir Francis, *Kashmir*, Adam & Charles Black, London, 1909.

Zeigler, P., *Mountbatten: The Official Biography*, Collins, London, 1985.

Zutshi, Chitralekha, *Languages of Belonging: Islam, Regional Identity and the Making of Kashmir*, Permanent Black, New Delhi, 2003.

INDEX